The Cerne Giant
An antiquity on trial

*Three cases presented to an enquiry
convened to consider the origin of the Cerne Giant,
held in Cerne Abbas Village Hall, Dorset,
on 23rd March 1996*

By
Timothy Darvill, Katherine Barker,
Barbara Bender and Ronald Hutton

With contributions from
Hamish Beeston, Joseph Bettey, Martin Brown, Rodney Castleden,
Jeffrey Chartrand, Sue Clifford, David Morgan Evans,
Jan Farquharson, John Gale, Hilary Jones, William Keithley,
Rodney Legg, David Miles, Paul Newman, Martin Papworth,
Bill Putnam, Sandra Tappenden, David Thackray, James Turner,
Vivian Vale and Tom Williamson

Bournemouth University
School of Conservation Sciences
Occasional Paper 5
published by
Oxbow Books
1999

Bournemouth University School of Conservation Sciences
Occasional Paper 5

Series Editor (Archaeology): Timothy Darvill

ISSN 1362–6094

Published by Oxbow Books
Park End Place
Oxford OX1 1HN

Tel.: 01865–241249
Fax.: 01865–754449
Email: oxbow@oxbowbooks.com

ISBN 1 900188 94 5

A CIP record for this book is available from the British Library

The photograph of the Cerne Giant on the front cover and in the section headings was taken by Francesca Radcliffe in July 1997. (Copyright reserved)

Printed in Great Britain at the Short Run Press, Exeter

Contents

Preface

Long gone are the days when it was possible simply to write history, or indeed prehistory. In this post-modern age history is something dynamic and fluid; we rehearse, negotiate, challenge, and contest our history. We use history to create new histories, and we have not one but many alternative histories each made, told, and viewed from a different perspective. Debate, argument, and sometimes even a little assertion, lie at the heart of the process by which history is made, but it is the contentious and controversial nature of the interpretative process that provides both the life-blood of intellectual endeavour and the motor that drives research forward. Moreover, it is an infectious process that inspires and interests not only academics but also wider audiences too.

The idea of harnessing the energy of debate and controversy both for academic ends and as a means of taking our researches out to the general public came in a flash, as such things often do. Exactly what prompted the desire to focus on the Cerne Giant is hard to identify, although one contributory factor was undoubtedly an innocent West Dorset Tourist Authority outing in 1990 when it became clear that no-one, least of all the Guide, had any idea that the Cerne Giant was not inevitably of prehistoric or ancient origin, and that a number of respected academics had argued quite different interpretations that might all have been of interest to those on the tour.

To generations of scholars, travellers, romantics, tourists and local residents, the Cerne Giant has been an archaeological mystery waiting to be solved. It is one of the best-known but least-understood monuments in Britain, yet it has penetrated deep into public consciousness. It was Glyn Daniel (1980, 29) who noted that the Cerne Giant is probably the only pornographic material accepted by the British Post Office. And the Giant's outline is now-a-days also found on T-shirts, mugs, and fridge magnets, while his raised image graces local shortbread biscuits.

Perhaps one of the greatest marks of recognition is that the Cerne Giant's double has recently entered paperback fiction in the guise of Ian Ogilvy's 'Polkerton Giant', notionally set in neighbouring Somerset. The Polkerton Giant 'had lain, certainly dormant by the nature of its being, on the side of Giant's Hill for a very long time ... until the publicity started.' Things, we read, had come to a head in Polkerton and in the neighbouring villages regarding 'the rising tide of immorality among Polkerton youth. Two opposing elements seemed to dominate the social scene ... and it was the collision of these elements that brought the Polkerton Giant to the front pages of the tabloid press, the back pages of the family press, and into the tag stories, mostly of the humorous content of the evening television news ...' (Ogilvy 1997, 19–20).

The fictional Polkerton Giant had come to public notice through the enterprise of the local farmer who had started charging for viewing the hill-figure (sited in rather an out-of-the-way location) and for setting up a campsite. A letter to the press described the Polkerton Giant as 'an open obscenity in the West of England' whilst another noted that it represented 'Man's early struggle to understand his nature ... and those Palaeolithic peoples who created him did so with simple innocence intact ...' (Ogilvy 1997, 83–5).

The supposed age of the Polkerton hill-figure clearly far outstrips that of the Cerne hill-figure because the Polkerton Giant of fiction has clearly to be so old as to be wholly removed from any attempt at understanding it. For what Ogilvy has constructed is a contemporary story, one of stock figures of fun, local politics and media-hype, based on the timeworn – indeed rather tired – theme of the sophisticated sensibilities of modern people confronted by the perceived primeval innocence of the ancients.

By contrast, the Cerne Giant today is real, it is a major tourist attraction, and it remains the focus of much ribald interest. This hill-figure has appeared in countless advertisements and never fails to raise a chuckle when brought into conversation. The Giant's existence is legendary, his being phenomenal. But there are some people who would like to change him. For decades there have been campaigners keen to hide the Giant's phallus. In 1868 the vicar of Cerne Abbas expressed concern that the cleaning of the figure might have a corrupting effect (Castleden 1996, 25). Glyn Daniel (1976, 93–94) expresses editorial gratitude to Julian Mumby for drawing his attention to a Home Office file entitled *Obscene publications: the Cerne Giant*, described as 'a well-handled file relating to an incident in 1932' deposited with the Public Record Office in 1967. Daniel suggests the letter concerned was written in jest, but the Home Office did not take this view. 'This is a serious charge of indecency against a scheduled prehistoric national monument, made, with apparent deliberation, after a lapse of 2,000 or 3,000 years ...' says the report.

The Chief Constable of Dorset also saw the letter as serious in tone. In due course the Secretary of State replied to the complaint noting that the 'Giant of Cerne is a national monument, scheduled as such, and vested in the National Trust. In the circumstances the Secretary of State regrets that he cannot see his way to take any action in the matter.' In 1932 and again in 1938, Stuart Piggott published the view that the figure was a recognizable representation of a classical Hercules; subsequently the matter went quiet during the Second World War when the whole figure was camouflaged.

As recently as September 1994 the matter re-emerged when both *The Times* and *The Guardian* carried pieces encouraging the National Trust to instigate a cover-up. But others have been happy to seek to enhance the blatant sexuality of the figure. Devon-based artist Kenneth Evans-Loude, for example, suggested creating a partner for the Giant in the form of Marilyn Munroe etched into the facing hill-slope (*The Sunday Times* 9th March 1980). A second – albeit temporary – female figure was set out beside the Giant by Bournemouth University students as an exercise in experimental field archaeology in the summer of 1997 (Barker 1997).

What has also gone quiet until relatively recently was the question of the age of this rather extraordinary hill-figure, a question that has long been the subject of debate. He is 'that mysterious figure whose impudent anatomy rouses every sort of surmise and emotion in the archaeologist, the boor, the innocent, the nidderling of towns, the philosopher, and the moralist, each after his own kind' writes Harvey Darton (1935, 26–36) in inimitable between-the-wars style. Surely an example of that 'sentimental and formless slush' that Hoskins (1955, 13) saw as bedevilling so much of superficial writing on the landscape.

'What the Giant is or may have been I will conjecture later' continues Darton.[1] 'At that moment he mastered my imagination ... I would wish that every village had some huge memorial of time itself, fantastic enough, even gross enough, to strike the imagination always and dwarf the little cenotaphs of the latest half-hour of man's long history. ... His hard round skull holds fantastic secrets ... he is an archive ... power, ferocity, fertility, endurance, independence – these are the qualities he claims blatantly. They underlie all village life.' (1935, 36) There are echoes here of what we read, re-worked and re-phrased half a century later by Ian Ogilvy in his work of rural fiction.

'I cannot resist', says Darton (1935, 264) 'when I see the gulf between the two societies – not between town and country, but between the ideals of country life – going back to history and bringing my old myth of the Giant into what may be its proper perspective. I have said I do not believe the semi-anthropological or archaeological theories about him. He is not recorded as having been seen before 1754,[2] and the various guesses about his age then and for some time afterwards do not, when you get down to precise tradition, amount to more that saying he might have been really about a hundred years old then.' (1935, 264–265).

Even today, the countryside encourages a certain incredulity in the observer which Darton would have recognized. A mystery is always good value; an archaeological mystery not only exercises the imagination of the general public, but the intellect of those in the position to pose the questions with a view to finding out more. And this is what prompted the idea of putting of the Cerne Abbas Giant on trial.

It was decided early on that the format for the debate would not follow traditional extra-mural day-school lines with a panel of speakers each taking turns to say their piece. Rather, it would be modelled on the lines of a local public inquiry of the kind now familiar in village halls the length and breadth of the kingdom as local people, bureaucrats, developers, and government officials argue their respective cases for and against a road scheme here, a housing estate there, or a new factory down the road. The Giant would literally be on trial in the best-known intellectual tradition; an enquiry to find out what is known, how we know what we know, and what it all means. History, archaeology, landscape studies, literature, religion, geography, geophysics, soil science, mapping, antiquarianism, art history, iconography, folklore, poetry, heritage tourism – and the media – all potentially had things to contribute.

The trial was held in the Village Hall at Cerne Abbas on Saturday 23rd March, 1996. Over 120 people packed the room to capacity; many more were disappointed they could not get tickets. Three cases were presented: that the Giant is prehistoric/Romano-British in origin; that he is of medieval or post-medieval origin; and thirdly, that he is important irrespective of age, his date is of less significance than the fact of his existence. Tim Darvill, Ronald Hutton, and Barbara Bender acted as advocates, for each case respectively (Figure 1), each introducing a succession of expert witnesses to unfold their experiences and knowledge to the audience. A panel of assessors led by legal expert Colin Patrick and supported by David Morgan Evans (General Secretary of the Society of Antiquaries of London) and Ivan Smith (Regional Land Agent with the National Trust) steered the enquiry, co-ordinated cross-examination and third-party questioning of the witnesses, and ensured fair play for each case. At the end of the day the audience acted as the jury, and were invited to vote on what, in their opinion, was the most convincing case.

It is hard to capture the excitement and enthusiasm of the day's proceedings between the covers of a book, but we hope you will enjoy reading this as much as we enjoyed preparing it. The text is divided into five parts to reflect the structure of the enquiry. Part I is by way of a preliminary briefing to set the scene and to

Figure 1. *The advocates being interviewed at the Cerne Giant viewpoint. Left to right: Barbara Bender, Ronald Hutton, Timothy Darvill and TV Crew. (Photograph: by Katherine Barker for Bournemouth University Liberal Adult Education Programme, copyright reserved)*

Figure 2. The Cerne Giant in action! A still image taken from the computer-generated animation by Evangelina Sirgado da Sousa. (Image courtesy of the School of Media Arts and Communication, Bournemouth University)

help those coming fresh to the problem of the Cerne Giant. It includes three short introductory chapters summarizing a little of the background, and explaining something of the setting, context, and current management of the Giant.

Parts II, III and IV contain the three separate cases, presented here by the respective advocate who in turn introduce their witnesses and set the evidence in context. None of the advocates are legally trained, although they all bring to their case a passion for debate, structured argument, and penetrating academic analysis. As might be expected, each case was slightly differently conducted, and we have retained this diversity in the text. All the witnesses called at the trial have contributed to the printed version except Dr Keith Walker who's views on relevant Elizabethan literature have been incorporated into Ronald Hutton's presentation. Two pieces are included here that were not given at the enquiry. Joe Bettey's review of his earlier published work on the Giant has been added because it was extensively referred to at the enquiry and in part introduced by Dr Betty himself during third-party questions. David Morgan Evans' contribution on the mid eighteenth-century sources is included here in Ronald Hutton's case because much of it was introduced from the bench during the trial. References and some academic apparatus has been added to the contributions to allow readers to follow-up points raised and material referred to.

Finally, Part V provides an epilogue to the enquiry in two chapters. First is a brief commentary on the jury's decision and a note of some representations received after the trial. This is followed by an account of how the enquiry was televised and a documentary-style programme covering the enquiry put together.

One element of the day's events not covered here is a computer animation of the Giant prepared by Evangelina Sirgado da Sousa of the School of Media Arts and Communication in Bournemouth University (Figure 2). Her 5-minute long video of the animation ran during refreshment breaks at the enquiry. It brought many smiles and chuckles, as well as admiration from those watching.

The enquiry was organized and run as part of Bournemouth University's on-going Liberal Adult Education Initiative, and was held in association with the National Trust. Its presentation in Cerne Abbas was by kind invitation of the chairman and members of the Cerne Historical Society who assisted greatly in the smooth running of the event. The advocates, witnesses and assessors came from far and wide, and all deserve many thanks for agreeing to participate in what must at first have seemed a crazy scheme and for laying their ideas and researches open to debate and cross-examination. Many others helped the day run smoothly and the publication come to fruition, our thanks go to all of them but especially: Bryan Brown, Louise Pearson, Eileen Wilkes, Penny Dale, Angela Hand, Chris Parker and John Ellis (Bournemouth University), Celia Read, David Thackray and Martin Papworth (National Trust), Vivian Vale (Cerne Historical Society), and David Brown (Oxbow Books).

Notes

1. To give him his full due, Darton includes an Appendix on the Cerne Abbas Giant in which he explores some of its possible origins (1935, 319–331). He notes the Ordnance Survey's *Map of Neolithic Wessex* of 1932 marks nothing at all on Giant Hill. 'That does not preclude a conjecture that the Giant is of the Iron Age, or, as has been more insistently urged, a pre-Christian Saxon work.' But he comes to no firm conclusion.

2. Until the publication of the note by Vivian Vale in the *Times Literary Supplement* of 14th November 1992, it was thought that Francis Wise's reference to the Giant in 1742 was the earliest. That date has now become 1694, the reference in the Cerne Abbas Churchwardens' Accounts. Harvey Darton's date of 1754 is that given by Dr Richard Pococke who saw the hill-figure during his travels that year (Darton 1935, 327).

Bibliography

Barker, K, 1997, Brief Encounter: the Cerne Abbas Giantess Project, Summer 1997. *Proceedings of the Dorset Natural History and Archaeological Society*, 119, 179–182

Castleden, R, 1996, *The Cerne Giant*. Wincanton. Dorset Publishing Company

Daniel, G, 1976, Editorial. *Antiquity*, 50, 93–94

Daniel, G, 1980, [Stand-first note]. *Antiquity*, 54, 29

Darton, H F J, 1935, *English fabric: a study of village life*. London. George Newnes

Hoskins, W G, 1955, *The making of the English landscape*. London. Hodder and Stoughton

Ogilvy, I, 1997, *The Polkerton Giant*. London. Headline Book Publishing

Piggott, S, 1932, The Name of the Giant of Cerne. *Antiquity*, 6, 214–216

Piggott, S, 1938, The Hercules Myth – beginnings and ends. *Antiquity*, 12, 323–331

Timothy Darvill and Katherine Barker
Enquiry convenors and proceedings editors
Bournemouth
August 1999

List of contributors

Katherine Barker. Senior Lecturer. School of Conservation Sciences, Bournemouth University, Fern Barrow, Poole, Dorset BH12 5BB

Hamish Beeston. Television Producer for BBC Close-Up West. British Broadcasting Corporation, Whiteladies Road, Bristol

Barbara Bender. Professor. Department of Anthropology, University College, Gower Street, London WC1E 6BT

Joseph Bettey. Reader. Clayley Cottage, Compton Dando, Bristol BS18 4NX

Martin Brown. Assistant County Archaeological Officer. East Sussex County Council, Sackville House, Brooks Close, Lewes, East Sussex BN7 1UE

Rodney Castleden. Teacher and writer. 15 Knepp Close, Bevendean, Brighton BN2 4LD

Jeffrey Chartrand. Lecturer. School of Conservation Sciences, Bournemouth University, Fern Barrow, Poole, Dorset BH12 5BB

Sue Clifford. Co-Director of Common Ground.

Timothy Darvill. Professor of Archaeology. School of Conservation Sciences, Bournemouth University, Fern Barrow, Poole, Dorset BH12 5BB

Jan Farquharson. Devon River Poet. Hooten, Branscombe, Seaton, Devon EX12 3DP

John Gale. Lecturer. School of Conservation Sciences, Bournemouth University, Fern Barrow, Poole, Dorset BH12 5BB

Ronald Hutton. Professor of History. Department of Historical Studies, University of Bristol, 13–15 Woodland Road, Bristol BS8 1TB

Hilary Jones. Eco- and Access-Campaigner.

William Keighley. Dorset Area Warden. The National Trust, Wessex Regional Office, Eastleigh Court, Bishopstrow, Warminster, Wiltshire BA12 9HW

Rodney Legg. Author and Publisher. Dorset Publishing Company, National School, North Street, Wincanton, Somerset BA9 9AT

David Miles. Chief Archaeologist. English Heritage, 23 Savile Row, London W1X 1AB

David Morgan Evans. General Secretary of the Society of Antiquaries. Society of Antiquaries of London, Burlington House, Piccadilly, London W1V 0HS

Paul Newman. Writer. 57 Eastbourne Road, St Austell, Cornwall PL25 4SU

Martin Papworth, Regional Archaeologist. The National Trust, Wessex Regional Office, Eastleigh Court, Bishopstrow, Warminster, Wiltshire BA12 9HW

Bill Putnam. Retired lecturer and archaeologist. 1 Mill Lane, Stratton, Dorchester. Dorset DT2 9RX

Sandra Tappenden. Devon River Poet. 8 Abbots Road, Mount Pleasant, Exeter EX4 7AN

David Thackray. Archaeological Secretary, The National Trust. National Trust Estates Office, 33 Sheep Street, Cirencester, Gloucestershire GL7 1RQ

James Turner. Member of the Devon River Poets. 18 Alexandra Terrace, Exeter EX4 6SY

Vivian Vale. Chairman of the Cerne Local History Society. Middle House, 22 Long Street, Cerne Abbas. Dorset DT2 7JF

Tom Williamson. Senior Lecturer. Centre for East Anglian Studies, University of East Anglia, Norwich. Norfolk NR4 7TJ

PART I

Introducing the Cerne Giant

The Cerne Giant: a place in space

Jeffrey Chartrand

Today, the Cerne Giant lies on the south western side of Giant Hill within Ordnance Survey land-parcel 6867 centred on National Grid Reference ST 66650168 (OS 1:50,000 Landranger Map 194). Administratively he is within the civil and ecclesiastical parish of Cerne Abbas, in the district of West Dorset, within the county of Dorset. These details are important in terms of finding and situating the Giant within our modern intricately georeferenced geographies of space, but of little relevance to the people who originally made the Giant or who enjoy its charms today. In the following sections attention is directed towards some of the more physically dominating aspects of the Giant's location: topography, geology, and environment.

Topography

Figure 3 shows a computer-generated terrain model of the varied physical landscape in which the Giant is set. Viewed from above in this way, with light striking the ground surface from the north-west (summer sunset position) the terrain becomes clear and easy to appreciate even though it could never have been experienced in this way. Four contrasting topographic blocks can be seen.

In the west there are a series of roughly parallel east-west orientated ridges separated by incised valleys. The upland blocks are small and rounded; the valleys narrow and steep sided. The valleys link with the second block, the north-south orientated valley of the River Cerne. This flat-bottomed and relatively broad valley in now dominated by the river itself running more or less down the centre. The head of the valley is near Lady's Well at Hermitage some 6km north of the modern village. Southwards flowing, the River Cerne is a north bank tributary of the Frome which eventually empties into Poole Harbour and serves to connect the relatively inland region around Cerne with the coast. The modern course of the river is braided, but in earlier times would have been more so, and there are clues to this in the contours of the valley floor. The incised valleys to the west must once have been tributaries of the Cerne, although most are now dry valleys or 'winterbornes'.

East of the Cerne valley is the third topographic block, a ridge of upland running broadly north to south, narrow at the north but widening significantly to the south. It is cut by very few east-bank tributaries or former tributaries of the Cerne, but one rather significant departure from this is the small river that must once have run through Yelcombe Bottom and is now represented by the stream from St Augustine's Well down to the River Cerne. It is around this stream that

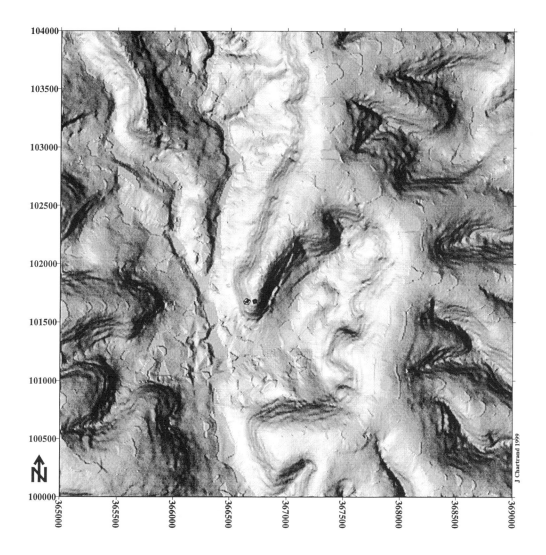

Figure 3. Terrain model of the Cerne Valley and adjacent countryside in west Dorset. (*Elevational data derived from 1:10000 Ordnance Survey digital data, Crown Copyright Reserved, 1995*)

the modern village of Cerne Abbas is clustered, and which must have attracted the monks of Cerne Abbey during the early Middle Ages. Back still further in time, the down-cutting effect of the stream, possibly assisted by glacial action during the Pleistocene Ice Age, created a steep-sided slice into the ridge leaving a small triangular promontory on the north side. It was on the west slope of this promontory, just below the highest point on the ridge, that the Giant was cut.

The fourth topographic block to the east of the ridge mirrors the western-most block and comprises shallow valleys running eastwards off the ridge to join and drain into the Piddle Valley that runs parallel to the Cerne Valley just off the view provided on Figure 3.

The head of the Giant lies at about 182m above sea level, 60m above the valley floor to the west and 38m below the highest point of Giant Hill at 220m. The slope of the hill is about 45° from horizontal where the Giant lies, and stuck mid-slope in this way has a strange position relative to the local terrain. His image dominates the main valley of the River Cerne, looking towards its source or headwaters to the north-west. Although he can be seen from some parts of the medieval abbey, he is invisible from St Augustine's Well and anywhere further east into Yelcombe Bottom. This is perhaps most clear from Figure 4 which shows a close-up terrain model of the area immediately around the Giant. Figure 5 shows a plan of the Giant made in 1996 in preparation for the Enquiry.

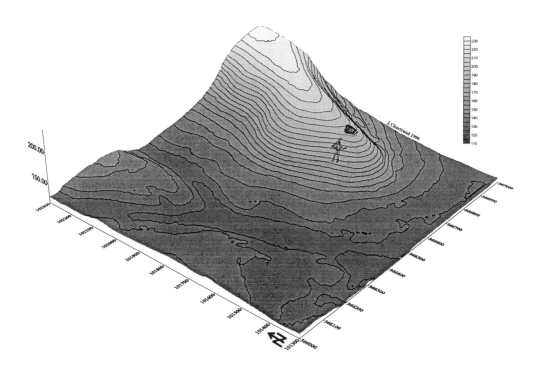

Figure 4. Detailed terrain model of Giant Hill, Cerne Abbas showing the position of the Giant in relation to the hill-slope. The contours at 5m intervals between 110m and 230m OD. (Elevational data derived from 1:10000 Ordnance Survey digital data, Crown Copyright Reserved, 1995)

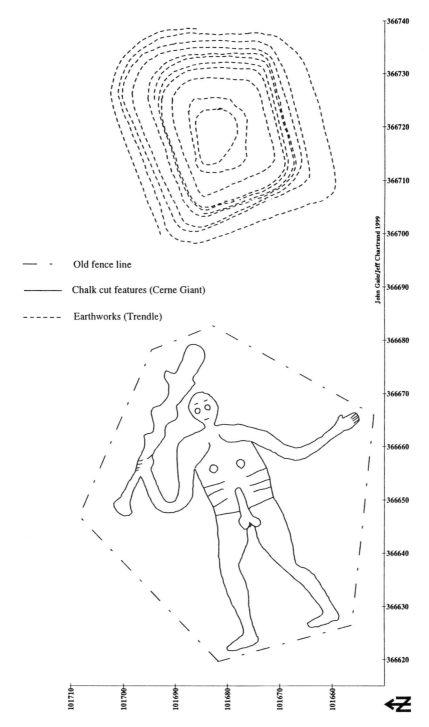

366740
366730
366720
366710
366700
366690
366680
366670
366660
366650
366640
366630
366620

John Gale/Jeff Chartrand 1999

— - Old fence line

——— Chalk cut features (Cerne Giant)

- - - - - Earthworks (Trendle)

101710 101700 101690 101680 101670 101660

Figure 5. *Plan of the Cerne Giant and Trendle, Cerne Abbas, made in 1996.*

Views of the Giant from the valley bottom are inevitable foreshortened because of the angle at which the image lies. Far better, although over a longer distance, are the views from the hills on the west side of the valley, especially Weam Common Hill above Cerne Park and Rowden Hill. Earthworks on Wean Common Hill include hut-circles, a fieldsystem and a trackway (RCHM 1952, 84).

Geology

The whiteness of the Giant's defining outline is a product of the local geology. Giant Hill is dominated by Upper Chalk, but the Giant is actually cut into a band of Middle Chalk which stratigraphically underlies the Upper Chalk. The valley floor below is formed of upper Greensand capped with an accumulated depth of alluvium and colluvium that can be seen to mark the floodplain (Geological Survey 1958; Bird 1995).

The chalk used in whitening the Giant in recent decades is not always taken from the site itself, but is kibbled chalk[1] from the Shillingstone Lime and Stone Company's quarry at Shillingstone in the Stour Valley north-west of Blandford Forum (see Keithley *et al.* below).

The soils covering Giant Hill are thin humic rendzinas.

Environment

Most of Giant Hill and the surrounding land is in agricultural usage. The steeper slopes are mainly permanent grassland, but the lower slopes and flat hill-tops are variously used for short-ley grass and cultivation. Archaeological traces of ancient fieldsystems all along the side of the Cerne valley suggest that in earlier times much more land was in cultivation.

Where long term pasture has been left to develop a species-rich and tough sward exists. Slight traces of soil creep in the form of contour ridges can be seen on some slopes, and cumulatively these will have caused the down-slope movement of substantial quantities of topsoil over the centuries.

Notes
1.   This is river-washed chalk gravel.

Acknowledgements
Kate Anderson kindly assisted with the preparation of Figures 3–5.

Bibliography
Bird, E, 1995, *Geology and scenery of Dorset*, Bradford upon Avon. Ex Libris Press
Geological Survey, 1958, *Geological Survey Sheet 328 Dorchester (Solid and Drift)*. London. Geological Survey and Ordnance Survey
RCHM, 1952, *An inventory of the historical monuments in the County of Dorset. Volume I. West Dorset*. London. HMSO. (Reprinted with amendments 1974)

The Cerne Giant: an English hill-figure

Timothy Darvill

Hill-figures

The Cerne Giant is one of over 30 hill-figures currently known in Britain, most of which are cut into the downs of Wessex. The earliest comprehensive survey of these images was by the well-known Egyptologist Sir Flinders Petrie (1926) who established use of the term hill-figure to describe these sites, and made detailed plans of them. Later, in 1949, Morris Marples published what became the standard text on the hill-figure tradition (Marples 1949) drawing together many disparate accounts scattered through earlier literature, and above all emphasizing the great range in design, purpose and date of these images. No other class of ancient monument could span such diversity as the enigmatic white horses of Uffington, Westbury or Osmington, the menagerie represented by the Laverstock panda and the Bulford Kiwi, the Giants at Wilmington and Cerne, and the clearly identifiable regimental badges at Fovant.

Following the rather idiosyncratic study of hill-figures by Tom Lethbridge (1957), interest in them has slowly gathered pace, and several general surveys were published in the 1980s and 1990s. Notable amongst these are the volumes by Paul Newman (1987; 1997), and the wonderfully succinct *Discovering hill figures* in the Shire Archaeology series by Kate Bergamar (1986). In 1990 the integrity of hill-figures as a discrete kind of archaeological monument was recognized with the production by English Heritage of a monument class description to assist with the definition and identification of suitable examples for protection through Scheduling and site management (Bowman 1990).

Hill-figures are not monuments that fit a closely defined time-span nor a tight geographical spread. It is clear that some, such as the Gogmagog Giants of Plymouth Hoe, have vanished from view during historical times, and there may be others lying hidden from sight that still await discovery. The earliest certain example is the Uffington White Horse, Oxfordshire, which has been the subject of scientific investigation and dated to the later Bronze Age, about 1000 BC (Miles and Palmer 1995; and Part II this volume). Making hill-figures is an on-going tradition. Amongst the more recent was a caricature of Prime Minister John Major by cartoonist Steve Bell on the South Downs in July 1994 (*The Guardian* 8th July 1994), and it has been suggested that a flock of sheep are etched into the pastures of north Wiltshire to celebrate the turning of the millennium.

It is this difficult question of origin and purpose that makes the hill-figure of the Cerne Giant so enigmatic, problematic, and challenging. The main body of this book discusses the issues and presents competing views; here the intention is simply to identify and briefly describe some of the salient features of the image that are touched upon later, and point to some of the main sources that have given rise to the present understanding of the site.

The Giant: a brief life

The Cerne Giant lies on a west-facing hill-slope above the River Cerne. The figure stands 55m high and dominates the hill-side which is actually a promontory overlooking the junction of a dry valley, Yelcombe Bottom, and the valley of the River Cerne. The hill itself is called Giant Hill after the figure rather than the underlying topography. Cerne Abbas village lies in the bottom of the valley with the earthwork remains of Cerne Abbey to the east. The earliest published account of the Giant is believed to be an anonymous letter in *Royal Magazine* for September 1763, although the earliest account in a mass-circulation journal was just under a year later, again anonymous, in *The Gentleman's Magazine* for July 1764 (Anon. 1764; see Evans in Part III below). This last-mentioned account also includes the earliest printed plan of the Giant (Figure 6). Who the author of these

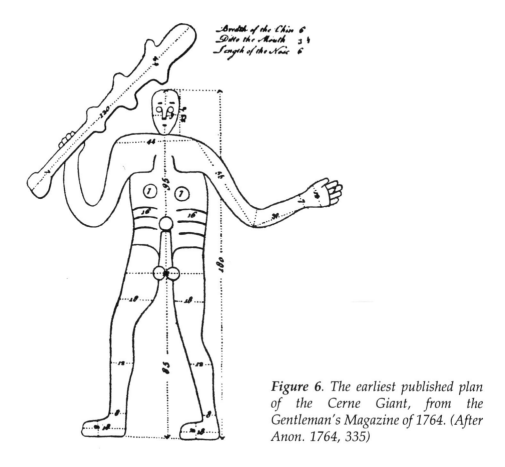

Figure 6. The earliest published plan of the Cerne Giant, from the Gentleman's Magazine of 1764. (After Anon. 1764, 335)

letters and early accounts was is not known, although Bettey (1981, 120–1) has documented a series of correspondence dating to the period 1742 to 1764 between the Oxford antiquary Francis Wise, John Hutchins of Dorset, and Dr Charles Lyttleton Dean of Exeter and later Bishop of Carlisle. Moreover, it may be no coincidence that on 15th March 1764 William Stukeley read a 'Minute of the observations made by him on the Giant of Cerne Abbas in Dorsetshire' to the Society of Antiquaries of London (Stukeley 1764; Evans 1956, 122). When he made these observations is not clear, although it is known that from about 1759 onwards he was re-using earlier papers and notes, and that by 1764 was beginning to loose his faculties. Stukeley died a year later on Sunday 3rd March 1765 (Evans 1956, 122; Piggott 1950, 151).

The apparent absence of seventeenth century and earlier descriptions of the Giant in the works of antiquarians and travellers especially led Joe Bettey to argue for a post-medieval origin (1981), a line of research that he and others have continued, and which forms the basis of the case presented in Part III below.

A number of detailed descriptions of the Giant have been published in the present century, notably by Petrie (1926), Crawford (1929), Darton (1935), Marples (1949, 159–79), the Royal Commission on Historic Monuments (RCHM 1952, 82), Clark (1983), Newman (1987, 72–101; 1997, 68–97), and Castleden (1996). Alongside these substantial texts there are numerous pamphlets, guides, and popular accounts (e.g. Thwaites n.d.). Over the centuries the site has also attracted many visits by national and local archaeological and antiquarian societies, whose descriptions provide a further source of information about the state of the monument at specific times (e.g. Anon. 1897; 1901; Black 1872; Smart 1872). The folklore of the site has been documented by Dewar (1968).

Not all of these accounts agree about the dimensions of the Giant, and there have certainly been changes to his form over the years as Leslie Grinsell documented very clearly (Grinsell 1980). Periods of neglect alternating with periods of interest and renovation seem to have been responsible for these changes, the most notable being the loss of a navel and the related extension by up to 1.8m of the penis. This change may have occurred about 1887, and was perhaps connected with renovations ordered by General Pitt Rivers, then owner of the site, and carried out by Jonathan Hardy (Grinsell 1980, 30).[1] Alternatively, it may be connected with the renovation in 1908 (see Kiethley *et al.* below) which was carried out through public subscription. Renovations in 1924 and subsequently, following the presentation by Alexander and George Pitt Rivers of the Giant to the National Trust in 1920 (Gaze 1988, 78–9), seem to have little altered the overall appearance.

Today, the Giant lies within a rectangular fenced enclosure, although this is a replacement for a six-sided coffin-shaped enclosure built in 1887, traces of which can still be seen on the ground. Since 1920, both enclosures served the dual purpose of defining the land owned and managed by The National Trust and providing the site with a measure of protection. Visitors are encouraged to keep outside the fenced enclosure.

Construction and form

Like the Uffington White Horse and the Long Man of Wilmington, but in contrast to most other hill-figures, the Giant is of substantial constructed. Rather than simply cutting off the turf to reveal the white chalk beneath, as is popularly believed, a trench appears to have been cut into the natural chalk to a depth of 0.6m. This was then filled with rammed chalk up to the height of the contemporary ground surface. In places there is evidence that successive re-cuttings have not exactly followed the lines of earlier cuts, with the result that there is what Castleden (1996, 31) describes as a 'hard shoulder' along the edge of the more recent narrower cuts. There is also some evidence of down-slope movement of chalk silt that can be seen in a build-up of deposit below the lines that run along the contour of the hill (i.e. the horizontal lines). There is considerable relief to the form of the Giant today, his nose, for example, is actually represented as a slight mound.

As currently represented, the Giant is nude, standing upright but striding to the left (Figure 7). The overall form is naturalistic, his nipples, ribs and genitals being boldly represented. A line across the lower torso is taken to be a belt. His penis is erect. His head is small for the size of the torso, but the face is well

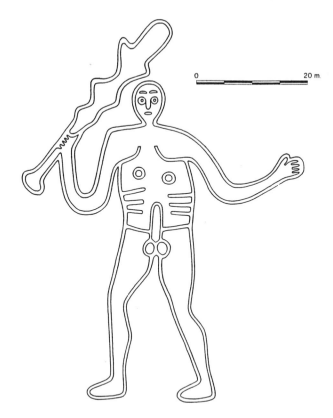

Figure 7. *Outline plan of the Cerne Giant.*

formed with large eyes, eyebrows, nose, and a small mouth. The fingers of both hands are depicted, but no toes are marked on the feet which appear only in profile.

In his right hand he holds a large knotted club, 36.5m in length, raised above his head. This is primitive-looking, although there is some evidence that it is a depiction of a carefully fashioned weapon. The end of the handle is expanded to form a distinct terminal, the hand-grip is shaped and smooth, and the distal end is rounded. This club is not simply a piece of tree pressed into service as a weapon, it is a fashioned object but sadly of a type that is not chronologically distinct and could find parallels almost any time from the fourth millennium BC onwards (*cf.* Piggott 1954, fig. 47.4 for an early example from Ehenside Tarn, Cumbria).

The left arm is outstretched. There have been many suggestions that he originally held something in this hand. There is, in Stuart Piggott's words, 'a suspicious irregularity and slight mound below his hand' (1938, 327). Various suggestions have been made as to what he might have been holding, the favoured explanations being a lion-skin or cloak draped over his arm (Lethbridge 1957, 77–8; Clark 1983, 30; Castleden 1996, 156–9), and/or a severed head held in his hand (Castleden 1996, 162–5).

Hutchins (1774) identified what he believed were some letters and numbers cut in the turf between the legs of the Giant. He transcribed them as three numbers, probably '798', above three letters, perhaps 'IHS'. He suggested that the numbers represented a date, although many other possibilities for the letters and the numerals have been discussed (Marples 1947, 164; Castleden 1996, 173–6). Various other depictions in the vicinity of the Giant have also been suggested, but not verified, including the profile of a dog to the left of the Giant (Legg 1992; Castleden 1996, 170–2).

Interpretations

Since the eighteenth century the Giant has been identified with various mythological and real people. William Stukeley was one of the first to suggest an identity, seeing the Giant as an image of Hercules (Heracles) the Greek athlete-hero, founder of the Olympic games, and the personification of physical strength who played the part of a protector.[2]

Stukeley (quoted in Piggott 1932, 214) also suggested that the Giant was locally known as Helis. Whether this identification, and the texts on which it was based, is correct is a matter of debate (see below Part III), but it gave rise to a series of discussions about names, place-names, and possible oblique references to the Giant in the context of local pagan beliefs. One of the starting points for this was William of Malmesbury, who, in describing the foundation of Cerne Abbey at the end of the sixth century AD, claimed that St Augustine met with a hostile reception in what was regarded as a particularly heathen part of the country. This is taken up by William Camden in the early editions of his *Britannia* (e.g. 1637,

2212) where he claims that St Augustine founded Cerne Abbey to commemorate his having there 'broken in pieces Heil the idol of the heathen English Saxons, and chased away the fog of pagan superstition'. Camden's editor Richard Gough, who continued revising the *Britannia* long after Camden's death, linked Heil with the Giant (Camden 1789).

Another early authority brought into the discussion is Walter of Coventry. Writing in the thirteenth century, he adds that Cerne was in an area in which the god 'Helith' was worshipped (Marples 1924, 166–8 for summary). To these can be added a reference in a twelfth century manuscript which describes how, in the ninth century, St Edwold travelled to Cerne to lead a hermit's life but was troubled by dreams (Lloyd 1982). None of these early sources specifically mentions the Giant, and, as already indicated, alternative readings of the texts are possible and critique can also be applied (see below Part III).

In 1842 another name was added to the list of possible identifications, the Celtic deity Baal (or Bel/Belinus) who was said to symbolize the sun (Sydenham 1842), although there is no iconography or epigraphic evidence to support this suggestion.

Stukeley's original identification was revisited by Stuart Piggott in two papers published in *Antiquity* during the 1930s. First, in 1932, Piggott reviewed the idea that the local name for the Giant was Helis, and through some slightly tenuous argument brought together the identification of Heth, Helis, and Hercules (Piggott 1932, 216). Second, in 1938, Piggott reinforced the link with Hercules through a general study of the Hercules myth that starts with Akkadian cylinder seals dating to the third millennium BC from Tell Asmar, Iraq, runs through pre-Hellenic Greece, and on into classical Greece and Rome. He notes how, in Roman times, 'the popularity of Hercules was as a domestic god with very human attributes, and as such he plays an important part in the religion of the Roman emperors, and from time to time the megalomanic had sought to establish a Hercules cult and to identify themselves with the god' (1938, 325).

In endorsing associations between the Giant and the Roman Hercules, Piggott noted especially the naked form and the club as common characteristics. If the left hand did indeed once hold a cloak, or lion skin, and/or a severed head as has been claimed, then the identification of the Giant as Hercules has still greater force. Archaeological finds from Britain which included depictions of Hercules in similar poses to that of the Cerne Giant were identified by Piggott in support of his argument, and stone altars from Corbridge (Northumberland) and Castlesteads, (Cumbria) can now be used to extend his list (Figure 8; Ross 1967, 382–3).

Piggott suggests a specifically Romano-British context for the Giant as Hercules (1938, 327) because the Emperor Commodus (AD 180–192) was the instigator of a Hercules-Commodus cult. There is no evidence that Commodus himself ever came to Britain, although the province must have been forward in his mind rather often because of numerous difficulties with maintaining the northern border (Hadrian's Wall) in the later second century AD, and because of general unrest amongst the military units stationed here. Peter Salway recounts (1981, 213–4), how Commodus announced that on January 1st 193 he would appear publicly as Hercules returned, assuming the dual roles of consul and gladiator and proving his divinity by invincibility in the arena. However, Commodus never had the opportunity to play out his boast because he was assassinated on the last day of AD 192.

A number of other attributions connected to Celtic and Roman gods have been suggested and fully discussed by Castleden (1996, 136–54), including Jupiter, Mars, Sucellos, Nodens, Cernunnos, the 'Huntsman' and Celtic warrior gods. Some of these are considered further in Parts II and III below.

More recent attributions have also been suggested, principally the Dorset Clubmen who were active during the Civil War (Darton 1935, 319; Bettey 1981, 120) and Oliver Cromwell lampooned as Hercules in the seventeenth century AD (see Part III below).

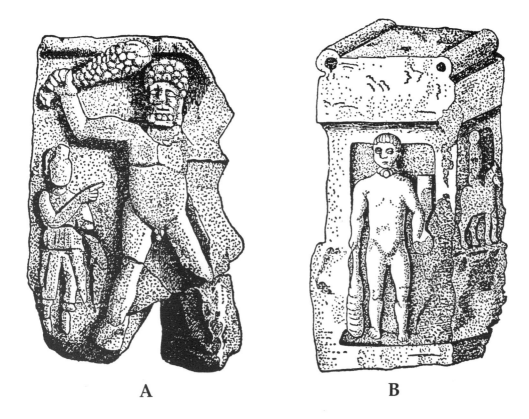

A   B

Figure 8. Carved images of Hercules from Roman sites in Britain. A: club-wielding naked giant from Corbridge, Northumberland. B: torc-wearing naked giant on the front of an altar from Castlesteads, Cumbria. (After Ross 1967, figs. 206 and 207)

Attitudes

Controversy surrounding the Giant is not confined to his origins or identification. Temple Willcox (1988) has documented twentieth century attitudes to the Giant, noting the succession of protestors, notably a Mr Walter Long of Gillingham in Dorset who have, unsuccessfully, tried to convince the owners and general public alike that such a sexually explicit image should be covered-up out of public decency.[3]

Associated structures

On the hill-slope immediately above the Giant lies a rectangular enclosure, about 37m by 30m in extent, known locally as the Frying-Pan or the Trendle. It is described by the Royal Commission on Historical Monuments (England) as being:

> a roughly rectangular enclosure. It consists of an outer bank with a slight outer ditch on the N and E and an inner bank with a slight inner ditch. The inner bank is of sharper profile and more regular form, and is presumably of later date; it is indeed stated to have been a hedge-bank. Within the enclosure is a rise in the ground of quite irregular form. The enclosure is said to have been used for maypole dancing. (RCHM 1952, 82)

The site has never been excavated, and the RCHM account clearly illustrates the difficulties of interpreting the visible field evidence (Figures 5 and 9). Curiously, and perhaps rather importantly, the structure appears to have been levelled into the hill-side, and there is no obvious entrance.

A number of explanations have been put forward to account for the monument, in many cases linked to ideas about the Giant. It is worth noting, however, that there is no evidence at all to associate the Giant with the enclosure beyond the fact that they lie in close spatial proximity.

O G S Crawford, a renowned field archaeologist and close observer of earthworks, suggested that the Trendle was:

> one of those small four-sides enclosures which are so common on the downs and which belong, for the most part, to the early Iron Age. At a later date a small inner bank has been thrown up (from both sides) following roughly the lines of the outer. (1929, 279)

Stuart Piggott takes a slightly different view, emphasizing the way the enclosure is cut into the hill-slope and suggests that it may be considered as the site of a primitive temple (1938, 328). This view has found considerable support amongst later writers, although no more evidence for such an interpretation has been adduced (e.g. Castleden 1996, 100–1).

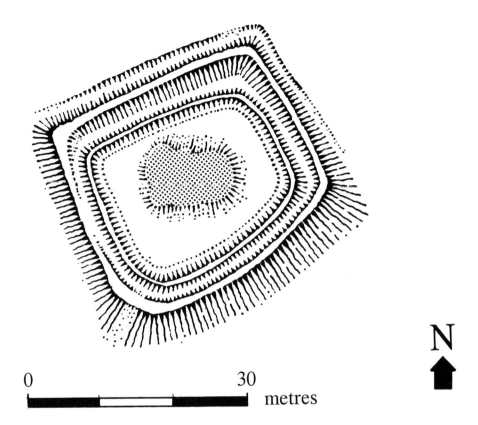

N

0   30
                                    metres

*Figure 9. Plan of enclosure known as The Trendle. The central mounded is shown shaded.
(After RCHM 1952, xxxiv)*

Two other features of the Trendle deserve note. First is the idea that it was
the site of a maypole (March 1901). This has common currency (e.g. Petrie 1926;
Crawford 1929, 280; Piggott 1938, 328; RCHM 1952, 82), although there is no
certain evidence that Cerne's maypole was ever here at all (see Part III below).
There is also the possibility that the site was in origin, or re-used as, a plantation.
Legg (1986, 14) suggests that the inner bank is a modern hedge bank created in
AD 1825 to enclose a little group of fir trees.

Another possible explanation of the field evidence represented at the Trendle
that has seemingly never been explored is that it is a prehistoric barrow, in
particular an oval barrow of third or fourth millennium BC date. Such barrows
typically have small slightly irregular mounds set with oval or sub-rectangular
ditched enclosures. One excavated example at Barrow Hills, Abingdon, had
several phases of construction, but ultimately appeared as a double concentric
ditched enclosure externally 26m by 22m (Bradley 1992). There was no entrance
gap in the enclosure boundary.

Conclusion

Without excavations there is a limit to what can be said about the construction, history, use, and date of the Giant and its associated monuments. Many important and carefully documented observations of the field evidence are available, and these are crucial not only to reaching an interpretation of what is presently known but also in planning future research programmes. Inevitably, some evidence and associated interpretations have been repeated and embroidered so often that their authenticity has sometimes become lost or obscure. In this respect the critical approaches taken in Parts II to IV below provide important perspectives on what has accumulated in the literature to date.

Notes

1. Thompson (1977, 72) notes that during the 1880s Pitt Rivers was recording many interested observations and jottings in his notebook, and that one entry concerns the Cerne Giant as a result of a visit to the British Museum: 'Figure of Hercules in the B.M. for comparison with the Cerne Giant. The figures have always the club in the right hand; it is usually knotted. The left hand is usually turned out like the Cerne Giant but it nearly always has the lion skin hanging on it. The private parts are always shown. Some have a serpent in the left hand.'
2. Heros, who were originally idealized men, became demi-gods and in the hierarchy occupied a position mid-way between men and the Olympians.
3. Protests still continue: see for example *The Guardian* 9th September 1994 (front page) and *The Times* 9th September 1994.

Bibliography

Anon., 1764, Description of a gigantic Figure. *Gentleman's Magazine*, 34, 335–6

Anon., 1897, Report of the Annual Meeting at Dorchester. *Archaeological Journal*, 54, 405–11

Anon., 1901, The Giant. *Proceedings of the Dorset Natural History and Antiquarian Society*, 22, xlii

Bergamar, K, 1997, *Discovering hill figures* (4th Edition; first published 1968). Princes Risborough. Shire Publications

Bettey, J H, 1981, The Cerne Abbas Giant: the documentary evidence. *Antiquity*, 55, 118–121

Black, W H, 1872, The Giant at Cerne. *Journal of the British Archaeological Association*, 28, 234–7

Bowman, A, 1990, *Monuments Protection Programme Single Monument Class Description: Hill figures*. London. English Heritage. [Circulated typescript report] Also available on the internet at <http://www.eng-h.gov.uk/mpp/mcd/hillf.htm>

Bradley, R, 1992, The excavation of an oval barrow beside the Abingdon causewayed enclosure, Oxfordshire. *Proceedings of the Prehistoric Society*, 58, 127–42

Camden, W, 1637, *Britannia*. London

Camden, W, (ed. R Gough) 1789, *Britannia*. London

Castleden, R, 1996, *The Cerne Giant*. Wincanton. Dorset Publishing Company

Clark, A J, 1983, The Cerne Giant. *Archaeological Journal*, 140, 29–30

Crawford, O G S, 1929, The Giant of Cerne and other hill-figures. *Antiquity*, 3, 277–82

Darton, F J H, 1935, *English fabric: a study of vilage life*. London. G Newnes. (see especially Appendix, The Giant of Cerne, 319–31)

Dewer, H S L, 1968, *The Giant of Cerne Abbas* (= West Country Folklore Series 1). St Peter Port. Toucan Press

Evans, J, 1956, *A history of the Society of Antiquaries*. Oxford. Oxford University Press and the Society of Antiquaries of London

Gaze, J, 1988, *Figures in a landscape. A history of the National Trust*. London. Barrie and Jenkins

Grinsell, L V, 1980, The Cerne Abbas Giant: 1764–1980. *Antiquity*, 54, 29–33

Hutchins, J, 1774, *History of the county of Dorset* (1st Edition. Two volumes). London. W Bowyer and J Nichols

Legg, R, 1986, *Cerne's Giant and village guide*. Milborne Port. Dorset Publishing Company

Legg, R, 1992, One Giant and his dog. *Dorset Magazine*, November 1992, 29–30

Lethbridge, T C, 1957, *Gogmagog*. London. Routledge and Kegan Paul

Lloyd, R, 1982, The Cerne Giant: another document? *Antiquity*, 56, 51–2

March, H C, 1901, The Giant and maypole of Cerne. *Proceedings of the Dorset Natural History and Archaeological Society*, 22, 101–118

Marples, M, 1949, *White horses and other hill figures*. London. Country Life Books. [Reprinted with additions, 1981. Gloucester. Alan Sutton]

Miles, D, and Palmer, S, 1995, White Horse Hill. *Current Archaeology*, 12.10 (number 142), 372–378

Newman, P, 1987, *Gods and graven images. Chalk hill-figures of Britain*. London. Robert Hale

Newman, P, 1997, *Lost Gods of Albion. The chalk hill-figures of Britain*. London. Robert Hale

Petrie, Sir F, 1926, *The hill-figures of England* (Royal Anthropological Institute Occasional Paper 7). London. Royal Archaeological Institute

Piggott, S, 1932, The name of the Giant of Cerne. *Antiquity*, 6, 214–6

Piggott, S, 1938, The Hercules Myth - beginnings and ends. *Antiquity*, 12, 323–31

Piggott, S, 1950, *William Stukeley. An eighteenth-century antiquary*. London. Thames and Hudson

Piggott, S, 1954, *The Neolithic cultures of the British Isles*. Cambridge. Cambridge University Press

RCHM, 1952, *An inventory of the historical monuments in the County of Dorset. Volume I. West Dorset*. London. HMSO. (Reprinted with amendments 1974)

Ross, A, 1967, *Pagan Celtic Britain*. London. Routledge

Salway, P, 1981, *Roman Britain* (= Oxford History of England IA). Oxford. Clarendon Press.

Smart, T W W, 1872, The Cerne Giant. *Journal of the British Archaeological Association*, 28, 65–70

Stukeley, W, 1764, [The Cerne Giant]. *Minute Book of the Society of Antiquaries of London*, 9, 199–200

Sydenham, J, 1842, *Baal Durotrigensis: a dissertation on the ancient colossal figure at Cerne, Dorsetshire*. London. W Pickering

Thompson, M W, 1977, *General Pitt-Rivers*. Bradford upon Avon. Moonraker Press

Thwaites, J A, n.d., *The Cerne Giant. Who made him and when?*. [Printed leaflet; no place of publication or publisher noted]

Willcox, T, 1988, Hard times for the Cerne Giant: 20th-century attitudes to an ancient monument. *Antiquity*, 62, 524–6

Owning and managing a Giant

William Keithley, Martin Papworth and David Thackray

Introduction

The Giant is a hill-figure cut into the turf and underlying bedrock to expose a white chalk outline. He is almost 60m tall, and brandishes a club 36m long. His body is outlined and detailed by narrow trenches no more than 0.60m wide, and his condition has been maintained by periodic scouring by local people, an activity traditionally separated by long intervals. This short account summarizes a little of what is known of the scouring activities in recent centuries, and especially since the Giant came into the ownership of the National Trust in 1920. Attention is also directed to other issues connected with the management and maintenance of such a popular and poignant site.

Early scourings

Gerald Pitman of Sherborne has carefully chronicled the history of the Giant, and has assembled records of scourings in 1694, 1868, and 1887, when the fence was placed around the figure. There are records of five scourings in the twentieth century at intervals ranging from 11 to 23 years. During that of 1908, the Giant's navel, which by then must have become almost completely obscure, appears to have been incorporated into his phallus (*cf.* Grinsell 1980, 30). However, there is now no clear record of what his condition was when the property was given to The National Trust in 1920 by Alexander and George Pitt Rivers, although this was the year that Flinders Petrie carried out his survey of the Giant, published six years later (Petrie 1926). The gift to the Trust was endowed by Henry Hoare of Stourhead, Wiltshire, in 1924.

The 1920s to the 1950s

Much of the detail of what happened to the Giant between 1920 and the mid 1950s is now obscure. As with so many buildings and monuments, management activities were not recorded systematically, and, sadly many of the archive records have disappeared. A scouring is recorded in 1924 at a cost of £5.00, but by 1934 the Giant was again overgrown. Pitman records that the Giant's whole outline was obscured by brushwood in 1940 to hide it from enemy aircraft. Following the war, in 1945-6, a scouring took place in which Stuart Piggott was involved as archaeological adviser. The Trust's records pick up the detail again in 1956 when Messrs E W Beard of Swindon carried out a re-chalking of the outline (Figure 10).

The firm had previously gained experience in this sort of work by their employment on the Uffington White Horse, another chalk-cut hill-figure, also belonging to the National Trust. The detailed specification for this work required cutting out decayed chalk, and replacing it with fresh, rammed, white chalk, a specification that has guided subsequent work.

The problem of the fences

Difficulties in maintaining the Giant's outline were exacerbated by the previous fence-line, which, coffin-shaped, tightly constrained the Giant. It was hexagonal in shape, with two strands of barbed wire positioned near the top of the posts, thus allowing access for sheep and young stock underneath. Severe erosion was taking place around the fence-line, as visitors and stock hugged the line. Particularly serious was the erosion caused by rain water scouring the outline of the Giant's left foot, forming a deep, white scar connecting his outline to his coffin-shaped fence-frame.

Young stock, visitors and rabbits were all having a serious effect on the outline of the Giant himself. It was, therefore, decided in 1977 to re-fence the figure, enclosing a much larger area of the hill-side, and including the terraced

Figure 10. The re-scouring team from Messrs Beard & Co of Swindon at the Cerne Giant in 1956. (Photograph courtesy of the National Trust. WCEG/18. Copyright reserved)

earthwork enclosure of the Trendle above the Giant's head. With the agreement of Lord Digby of Minterne, the owner of the Trendle and adjacent land, rabbit and stock-proof fencing was put up and initial remedial work was carried out on the erosion scars along the line of the earlier fence. A small flock of downland sheep, Dorset Horns, was allowed within the fence to reduce the intensity and provide a level of grazing compatible with the conservation of the herb-rich chalk downland and with the impact on the Giant. Grazing now takes place in June and again in the autumn, and the enclosure is full of flowers and butterflies throughout the summer.

The 1979 scouring and re-whitening

It was soon realized that the re-fencing alone was not going to solve the problems associated with the conservation of the Giant himself. Erosion and frost action had broken up the surface of the chalk in the trenches, and subsequent natural scouring had caused the lowering of the level. At the same time the trench sides had begun to collapse, and moss and grass were growing in the trenches. As a result, the figure had lost a great deal of clarity when observed from the road. A major re-whitening programme was again required. It was also realized that

Figure 11. Re-whitening the Giant in 1979. General view up-slope showing the temporary trackway across the Giant's left side. (Photograph courtesy of the National Trust. WCEG/22. Copyright reserved)

Figure 12. Re-whitening the Giant in 1979. Close-up view of the chalk being put into the trenches and rammed down. (Photograph courtesy of the National Trust. WCEG/20. Copyright reserved)

facilities for viewing from the road were totally inadequate. This led to discussions between the National Trust and Dorset County Council, and the development of a scheme to provide a suitable lay-by and an information panel at the road junction on the other side of the valley where the best views of the Giant could be had.

In 1979, therefore, after consultation with the Department of the Environment, Directorate of Ancient Monuments, and the County Archaeologist, Laurence Keen, a scheme was approved, consent obtained, and a schedule of work compiled. Messrs E W Beard of Swindon were again approached to undertake the work, and were able to draw on the experience of a member of their staff who had been involved in 1956.

The scouring and re-whitening took place over a period of about three months starting in May 1979 (Figures 11 and 12). It involved the construction of a light timber track to allow access for a small, winched waggon to transport materials from the hill-top above the Giant's head, down the hill-slope, and across his left arm. The decayed chalk was cut out to a maximum depth of about 0.25m, carefully, so that there was no change to the edges of the trenches, and fresh chalk was introduced and rammed down hard to the level of the tops of the trenches. The task was completely successful, the weather was marvellous, and an innovative trade was developed in the sale of Cerne Giant tee-shirts over the fence to curious visitors. The chalk used then, and subsequently, was a local material, known as kibbled chalk. This is a small chalk gravel from a quarry at Shillingstone worked by the Shillingstone Lime and Stone Company Ltd. Amongst other benefits, this material provides an almost burnished surface when puddled and rammed, allowing better flow-off of water.

Management objectives

This broad programme of work, including the re-fencing, scouring and re-whitening of the outline, the modified grazing regime, the construction of the lay-by, and the provision of an information panel at the lay-by, all contributed to the fulfilment of the Trust's management objectives for the Giant. These were defined at the outset as:

- Conservation, primarily to ensure the preservation of the monument, but also to preserve the surrounding downland flora.
- Careful control of access to the site in order to lessen the problems of erosion caused by both visitors and stock.
- Provision of information for the public, both to encourage their interest in the history of the place, and to make them aware of the sensitivity of the site and the need for conservation.

These objectives remain as the long-term conservation framework for the Giant, and to which we might now add the protecting the setting of the Giant. Realistically, the setting was unlikely to be threatened or compromised whilst in the ownership of Lord Digby and controlled by a range of local and national designations: the County and District Development Plans; Cerne Abbas Conservation Area; both the Giant and the adjacent site of the Abbey are Scheduled Ancient Monuments; the sites lie within an Area of Outstanding Natural Beauty; and Giant Hill is a Site of Special Scientific Interest.

In addition, the improvements to the conservation and presentation of the Giant won for the National Trust a Civic Trust Commendation in 1980, the result of successful and satisfactory partnership between the National Trust, Dorset County Council, the village of Cerne Abbas, and the Directorate of Ancient Monuments, Department of the Environment.

Routine maintenance since 1979

Further routine maintenance work took place almost annually throughout the 1980s, under the supervision of the Trust's Dorset Wardens, initially Major Ian Davey who retired in 1981 and thereafter William Keighley, who continues to maintain responsibility for the care of the Giant. The scouring of 1983 was sponsored by the brewers, Heineken, and carried out by a team from The British Trust for Conservation Volunteers (Figure 13). On this occasion over 4 tons of chalk were used in maintenance carried out mainly on the Giant's arms. Although Heineken did not use this sponsorship directly in their advertising, press releases were issued and a tee-shirt (again!) produced with a picture of the Giant and underneath a caption reading 'Refreshes the parts!'

Figure 13. *Re-whitening the Giant in 1983. Work in progress ramming down the new chalk in the trenches forming the Giant's head. (Photograph courtesy of the National Trust. Copyright reserved)*

The Giant's nose

Amongst the longest-running correspondence in the files is that relating to the Giant's nose. In 1990 Gerald Pitman drew the National Trust's attention to the fact that the Giant's nose had deteriorated since the 1970s. This is of great interest, as it drew attention to the fact that the Giant was not simply a two-dimensional engraving in the chalk, but a figure with three-dimensional relief, of not inconsiderable sculptural sophistication. Photographs taken in low light show the relief of the nose very clearly, and it is generally assumed that this was what Flinders Petrie tried to showed in his single-line convention used for the nose in his 1920s survey (Petrie 1926). After some deliberation, which reached the National Trust's Council, the National Trust sought Scheduled Monument Consent to restore the nose. The delicate surgery was carried out under the close scrutiny of television cameras on 6th April 1993.

Using the 1970s photograph as the guide, the turf was carefully lifted over his nose, and the feature was remodelled using chalk rubble to raise it by approximately 0.2m. The turf was then relaid, and pegged down, the task completed in a matter of hours (Figure 14). Inevitably, the media interest, including the usual *double entendre*, was remarkable and persisted for months.

Figure 14. *Reconstructing the Giant's nose in April 1993. (Photograph courtesy of the National Trust. Copyright reserved)*

The Giant in public affairs

The Giant has always been a major public affairs challenge for the National Trust. Nearly any event that takes place there causes great media interest. Whatever the subject of the report, it seems journalists cannot avoid a passing reference to the Giant's central and most obvious feature. This is often to the great embarrassment of the poor archaeologist and warden blushing excruciatingly whilst being interviewed by a skilful journalist who seems to have spent hours swotting up innuendoes!

The 1993 work on the Giant's nose was billed as 'restoring another important organ to prominence'. When the work took place, camera crews from rival local television companies fought for the best pictures as the pile of chalk rubble was moulded into shape.

The Giant is a potent symbol for advertisements, and the National Trust's Public Affairs Department keeps a close eye on applications to use the figure in this way. They are mindful of the offence that insensitive advertising might create; even quite low-key use of the Giant inspires letters of protest. If an advertisement is approved a donation towards the upkeep of the figure is agreed with the advertiser.

The National Trust is, however, sympathetic towards charities who wish to use the Giant to help publicize their cause. In 1993, a fertility celebration was organized by the Dorset Infertility Support Group, who came together and formed a human chain across the hill-side to link hands with the Giant. Later the same year, to advertise the 'Great Dorset Clean-Up' campaign, a logo was created to show the Giant holding a broom instead of his club.

Giant research

In addition to the management and maintenance of the Giant, the National Trust has an active interest in research on the Giant, to improve understanding. Geophysical surveys have been undertaken, often with the active involvement of the National Trust's archaeologists. Tony Clark's 1980 survey of the area beneath the Giant's left arm (Clark 1983), was followed by more extensive surveys by Rodney Castleden in 1988. The results of these are noted elsewhere in this volume. Martin Papworth, the National Trust's Wessex Regional Archaeologist has undertaken a detailed contour survey of the mound beneath the Giant's left hand, and has participated in further geophysical surveys carried out by John Gale of Bournemouth University, also described later in this volume. Further research, including investigation of the potential for buried soils, and to develop an understanding of the construction, and possibly the date of the figure by careful excavation are currently being discussed (1997).

Greater knowledge promotes greater attention to detail in care and conservation, and maintenance work is never ending. The Giant is carefully cleaned using dustpans and brushes after each grazing to remove the accumulation of sheep droppings and to control the build up of soil on the outlines. The grass is frequently trimmed, particularly beneath the horizontal lines, to keep the figure visible from the lay-by and viewpoint. The whole figure is carefully edged every year, using shears and spades, to prevent the encroachment of the turf, and the outlines are also sprayed annually using a knapsack sprayer with a spray shield to further prevent the outline from grassing over. The rabbit and stock-proof fence is maintained and visitor access is limited to prevent the recurrence of the severe erosion that characterized the Giant as recently as the 1970s.

Community involvement

The involvement of the local community is of the greatest importance as traditionally the scourings were undertaken by the villagers of Cerne Abbas. Today much of the annual maintenance is carried out as an Acorn Project, a National Trust working holiday, employing ten volunteers for a week. The Parish Council are always informed by the Warden, who welcomes local participation. On the occasion of the project in 1995, the year of the National Trust's Centenary, local people provided a most welcome party for the volunteers to celebrate the event.

No doubt this famous hill-figure will continue as a source of pride and interest to his fellow parishioners and Dorset folk, and will inspire diverse responses from individuals, commercial companies and organizations. The National Trust's appreciation of the site will continue to be a blend of archaeology, conservation, local character, modesty, and a sense of fun steeped with the mystic qualities the figure inevitably evokes.

Acknowledgement

The authors would like to acknowledge, most gratefully, the help and advice given to all three of us and to the National Trust more widely by Gerald Pitman, who has unfailingly made his research and experience available to us.

Bibliography

Clark, A J, 1983, The Cerne Giant. *Archaeological Journal*, 140, 29–30
Grinsell, L V, 1980, The Cerne Abbas Giant: 1764–1980. *Antiquity*, 54, 29–33
Petrie, Sir F, 1926, *The hill-figures of England* (Royal Anthropological Institute Occasional Paper 7). London. Royal Archaeological Institute

PART II

The case for an ancient Giant

Figure 15. *Aerial view of the Cerne Giant looking north-west. The Giant's situation of a steep-sided promontory can clearly be seen. Above right of the Giant is The Trendle, to the far right of the picture earthwork remains of Cerne Abbey are visible. (Photography courtesy of Cambridge University Committee for Aerial Photography. AAU-2. Copyright reserved)*

A prehistoric warrior-god?

Timothy Darvill

Introducing the case

The Cerne Giant, languishing mute on the turf-covered slope of Giant Hill, is without doubt one of the most enduring and important marks left by early communities once occupying what is now south Dorset (Figure 15). The Giant has been much maligned in recent decades by historians and others overly concerned with the antics of post-medieval landowners and eccentrics in the area. But if the grinning lips of the Giant could speak he would certainly put the record straight and tell of his origins at the very dawn of history, sometime in the period between 1000 BC and 250 AD, probably well before Roman soldiers brought this area into the great Roman Empire. But of course the Giant cannot speak for himself, and instead we must rely on the interpretation of archaeological evidence, academic reasoning, and structured argument to establish the antiquity of the Giant.

The proposition that the Giant is Romano-British or prehistoric in origin is not new; it has been the orthodox view for more than two centuries, even though elements of the argument have been challenged and amended from time to time and the pendulum of probability has swung between the second millennium BC and the early first millennium AD. The antiquarian William Stukeley was the first to report seeing the image of Hercules in the form of the Giant back in the mid eighteenth century (Stukeley 1764). More than 150 years later another distinguished archaeologist, Sir Flinders Petrie, surveyed the Giant accurately and argued for a date back in the Bronze Age on the basis of alignments with nearby prehistoric earthworks (Petrie 1926, 11), but these connections have since proved groundless (Crawford 1929, 279–80). In the early 1930s, Stuart Piggott pulled together various pieces of hearsay and circumstantial evidence to suggest a link between Helis, which Stukeley recorded as the local name for the Giant, a reference to a local god Helith in a thirteenth century version of the legend of St Augustine's visit to Cerne in the sixth century AD set down by Walter of Coventry, and the image of the Greek mythological god Hercules (Piggott 1932). Six years later Piggott reinforced his view that the Cerne Giant was Hercules, concluding that:

> I feel it almost inevitable that the Giant of Cerne must be Romano-British, and that it may possibly date from the years immediately following 191. (Piggott 1938, 327)

Since the 1930s a prehistoric/Romano-British origin has been perpetuated and repeated many times over (e.g. Marples 1949, 169; RCHM 1952, 82; Powell 1958, 122; Putnam 1984, 75; Pinder *et al.* 1998, 36).

In restating, revising and updating the orthodox view of an early date for the creation of the Giant I will introduce a wide range of experts to discuss their evidence, most of which has been gathered and assembled through much painstaking research and analysis. Some of this material, by its very nature, is technical and must of course be used with due care.

Two main lines of enquiry will be pursued. First there is a need to dispense with the negative evidence suggesting that because there is no historical account of the Giant before the early seventeenth century he was not in existence before this time. Such an argument is philosophical non-sense: an absence of evidence can never be taken as evidence of absence. Nonetheless, I will deal with the point and show how such views are misplaced.

The second line of enquiry relates to the Giant himself. In this I shall seek to demonstrate the antiquity of the tradition of creating hill-figures in England before going on the examine the original form of the Giant, its iconography, and the attributes it represents. Taking these identifications we will look at the local context of the Giant in relation to contemporary later prehistoric and Roman life, and finally bring forward evidence which suggests that the figure was lost sight of in early historic times before being re-established as the feature we see today.

History, prehistory, and the development of intellectual enquiry

The Cerne Giant has not always been seen as prehistoric. It cannot have been, because the very idea of prehistory is a relatively modern concept (Chippindale 1988). Closely connected with the development of the so-called Three Age System (Stone, Bronze and Iron), the word prehistory was first used in English in 1851 by Daniel Wilson in the title of his book *The prehistoric annals of Scotland* (Wilson 1851). Before this time the ancient past was, chronologically speaking, relatively undifferentiated. Instead it was populated by culturally or historically situated communities such as the Danes, Saxons, Romans, Celts, and Druids. At various times, and for various reasons, the Giant has been attributed to all these peoples and others beside. Only since the mid nineteenth century has a more solid conceptualization of the ancient past been applied to the Giant, with the consequence that any records set down before Daniel Wilson's time cannot be expected to be very interested in the absolute dating of the site *per se*.

More confusion arises at the end of prehistory when, in AD 43, Roman troops began an invasion of Britain. Although it is tempting to say that after the mid first century AD the country was Roman, it is now widely recognized that in most areas, Dorset included, life continued for most people much as it did before being annexed to the Empire, especially in the countryside (Putnam 1984).

These two examples show how the development of intellectual perspectives on the understanding and interpretation of the past effect views of it and what is regarded as interesting: in other words how we construct history.

This is important for the Cerne Giant because its recent history, recorded through historical accounts, runs parallel to a series of changing intellectual positions and perspectives. This applies equally to the way iconography and images are used and understood, and to the kinds of things that are recorded by travellers, antiquarians, and scholars. To explore these strands of evidence further I would like to call my first expert witness, Paul Newman. Mr Newman is a writer who has been researching the problem of hill-figures in general and the history of the Cerne Giant in particular for many years. In 1987 he published *Gods and graven images: the chalk hill-figures of Britain*.[1]

* * * * * * * *

In defence of antiquity

Paul Newman

The image of the Cerne Giant stands as antiquity's rebuke to political correctness. Naked, angry and aroused, he wields a club – an outdated, not particularly effective weapon even at the time of the Iron Age to which he has been attributed. Back then a club was something of an archaism, during a time of slings, swords and spears. Possibly the Giant was a nod to traditional masculine values, a strong man able to fight his way through the world equipped with nothing save his block of wood and rampant virility.

Who carved the figure? The Phoenicians? The Celts? The Romans? The Saxons? Successive waves of invaders or settlers have been posited at different times by different writers. But not every scholar or expert has invariably assumed that the Giant dates from distant antiquity. The poet Geoffrey Grigson (1966) suggested that the carving might have been 'the obscene jest of a ribald free-thinking eighteenth century nobleman making fun of the antiquaries'. However, if there existed a Dorsetshire wing of the Hellfire Club, it has escaped the notice of contemporary chroniclers. Furthermore, if the carving had been incorporated in a park or artificially contrived wilderness – a scandalous centrepiece, say, outlined by statues of naked nymphs – one would have little difficulty in placing it squarely in the eighteenth century.

But the Giant is very much as isolated gesture, standing alone on a sheep-cropped hill-side, and the issue does not end with designing and cutting. We are dealing with the inauguration of a continuous, arduous obligation to scour and maintain the figure down through the centuries. It is this prolonged effort that makes one assume that the figure arose from the collective concerns of the community rather than impulse or whim or playful prank.

Yet a custom must start at some point. It is mere sentimentalism to assume that new traditions could not arise in the seventeenth century or earlier. The problem is that the primary themes expressed by the Giant – violence, nakedness, sexual arousal – stand as blatant affronts to Christian values. Of course, in their daily lives, people were frequently violent, often seen naked, and knew all about erections; but such commonplaces were not perpetualized on hill-sides.

A proud physique and an enormous club had little relevance to the Age of Monasticism or the Enlightenment. Neither would the Giant relate to Cavaliers and Roundheads, or the subsequent Restoration. The Age of Elegance offers no suitable niche either. Jane Austen might have admired his rude enthusiasm or primitive honesty, but would not have dwelt overmuch on the social possibilities embodied in his stance.

Unabashed phallicism

To seek a period where the qualities expressed by the Giant belong, where he does not stand out as a gross anomaly, it is necessary to look back two thousand years and more, to a time when his primary features corresponded closely with the outlook and practises of many communities.

Let us first deal with the obvious aspect of the Giant; those qualities that Aristophanes parodied in the fifth century BC in *The Archarnians* as being comic and quaint: the rampant, unabashed phallicism, a concept as old as creation or, should one say, procreation?

Figure 16. Rock-art images of club-wielding humans from Northern Bohuslän, Sweden. A: Kasen Lövåsen; B: Torp; C: Säms Utmark (After Coles 1990, fig. 11)

Figure 17. (Left). The Dorset Ooser. (After Newman 1987, 90). Figure 18. (Right). Hercules depicted on the reverse of a silver tetradrachm of the second century BC from the Danube region of central Europe. (After Allen 1980, plate 7)

There is a Bronze Age carving from Lofasen, Sweden, showing a figure half-man, half-bull, wielding a mallet and, simultaneously, experiencing a turbulent erection (Figure 16A; J Coles 1990, 42). One imagines that this figure stands for fertility in men and cattle, and there are several hammer-wielding Celtic equivalents, like Sucellus the good striker, to whom he might loosely relate (Green 1986, 136; Ross 1967, 246). Other depictions in Scandinavian rock-art show similar individuals (Figure 16B and C).

Ox-like qualities are locally reflected in the Ooser, a bull-masked man who used to caper through the streets of Dorset, demanding refreshment and kisses from the women (Figure 17; Dewar 1968). In Shillingstone he was called the Christmas Bull, for he appeared at the coldest, most blighted time, when the spirit of fertility and growth struggled against the hanged year.

So initially we have an animal god, erect and brandishing a mallet. Centuries later, man has established supremacy over oxen and bulls, and we are presented with the Cerne Giant, a hero of animal appendages but retaining the upraised weapon and phallus. No longer is he a beast but a tamer of beasts: the hero-god Hercules.

This must be qualified, however. Hercules is a loose rather than a strict identification (Piggott 1938). For the Celts were great incorporators and copiers of the styles and icons of other cultures, and the figure of Hercules – a warrior-god, virile and brave – fitted unobtrusively into their pantheon. Incorporated within their myths, he might have acquired a Celtic name and additional qualities, but that is presently less significant than establishing his widespread acceptance (*cf.* Ross 1967, 381; Webster 1986). Evidence for this is prominent in the third example, an imitation of the Macedonian tertradrachms of Alexander III (336–323 BC), minted by Celtic tribes in central Europe during the second century BC and later (Figure 18; Allen 1980, plate 7, 71–2). On the obverse side, they show a head of the young Dionysius with leaves and grapes in his hair; on the reverse, the standing figure of Hercules, holding a club in his left hand and the skin of the Nemean lion over the arm of his right.

Consider the three depictions, noting stages of transition. Starting out with someone who is half-man, half-beast, erect and brandishing a mallet. We later find that he has shed his horns, evolving into a Hercules-figure, discrete from the animal, yet still emphatically virile and wielding a weapon. Centuries pass and finally Hercules the tamer has himself been tamed by civilization and imprinted on a coin. He is no longer phallicly excited. Neither does he wield his club; the implement is at rest like a furnishing. In fact, the coins show a stylized, formally posed Hercules, a civilized role model.

What we find at Cerne, however, is no dead piece of classical statuary, but a native interpretation, a halfway house between blatant animality and restrained formality. The Giant is a hero who preserves the virile qualities of an earlier tradition. He is a mediator between the Bronze Age and the classical period – not necessarily in strict chronological time, for icons and beliefs, especially in the folk tradition, overlap and thrive contemporaneously, but in terms of how civilization was developing – a hero-god, if you like, reflecting the concerns of warriors and cattle rearers.

Seasonal magic-making

When trying to reach back into a period in which many gods and spirits were of local origin – assigned to individual springs, hill-tops and tribes – it may be misleading to draw extensively on classical and continental comparisons and forget that the Giant should be seen as something special to Cerne Abbas and Dorset (Sydenham 1842; Legg 1978). Whatever deity he recalls – Hercules, a sun-god, a Celtic warrior holding a cloak-shield – it is subsidiary to his role as Cerne's local Dagda or 'Daddy' whose overpowering presence was preserved down through the centuries. He was the Great Village Elder, occupying the hill below the Trendle (maypole enclosure), the place where the *duende*, or earth pulse of the village, beat clearest and loudest.

The significance of drawing a figure is different from that of erecting a building; the resultant outline is not meant to entrap or enclose a congregation. A hill-figure has a function closer to myth, drama and seasonal narrative. One draws it on the earth like stage scenery, and despite its considerable size and avowed age, it may be wrong to see the Giant in terms of the monumental figure he has become, but more as a talismanic gesture, a piece of seasonal magic-making intended to urge men and crops around the bend of the Celtic year.

Proximity, of course, does not always imply unity of intent. A bank may be situated next to a church, though their outlooks and aims are quite different. Similarly the (alleged) placement of the maypole in the earthwork called the Trendle, immediately above the Giant, might be an accident, but because there is a unity of meaning – both stand for the vegetational cycle and the procreative thrust of existence – many writers have been inclined to look on the two as at least complementary if not contemporaneous (March 1901).

Lateness of record

Much has been made of the comparative lateness of records relating to the Giant. In particular, Joe Bettey (1981) found no mention of the Giant previous to Frances Wise's letter of 1742.[2] Even so, the hill-figure was acknowledged before the Long Man of Wilmington in East Sussex; here the earliest known sketch was for long held to be that by Sir William Burrell in 1776, although in 1993 a drawing of 1710 by one Thomas Rowley, surveyor, was discovered and established a deeper antiquity (Holden 1971; Farrant 1993). Yet the Long Man must have been scoured and maintained down through the centuries; traces of Roman brick were mixed up in the subsoil beneath the figure who also stands in the vicinity of an ancient Abbey (Heron Allen 1939).

Even in the far more populous town of Plymouth there were ancient hill-figures hardly ever referred to. The Giant figures of Gogmagog or Gogmagog and Corineus, whom John Leland, incidentally, omitted to mention in his *Itinerary*, had been re-cut in 1486 and were regularly maintained by the town council. Some brief references in an old audit and receiver's book are all that is left of the two huge carved figures that guarded the Hoe for centuries (Newman 1987, 102–10).

The evidence of eloquent omission – absence of documentation equalling non-existence – places a heavy responsibility on the shoulders of a small literate segment. It is akin to arguing what is not recorded by clerks or antiquaries have no role in historic time, an argument that coils around and, ultimately, strangulates itself. For the absence of record also applies to the core event – the actual cutting of the figure. One could argue with equal strength that, if such an extraordinary, learned, satiric spoof as the Giant had been co-ordinated during the Middle Ages, or in the middle of the seventeenth century when people were becoming increasingly antiquity-conscious, some memory or explanation might have been expected to survive. But no such survival has been found.

Revolution in perception

It is easy to forget that a revolution in perception is often required before things are properly seen or grasped as possessing intrinsic value. Educated Europeans did not bother overmuch about mountains, lakes, and long country walks until thinkers like Rousseau awakened Europe to the beauties of nature, and then, decades later, we have Worksworth, Coleridge, De Quincey and a host of minor poets flocking to the Lake District, observing and praising each waterfall, crag, and tarn.

Similarly John Aubrey had not heard of Avebury until he visited it in 1649, comparing it to a place where giants had 'fought with huge stones against the gods' (Aubrey 1663; and *cf.* Hunter 1975, 157). The monument was regarded as a haphazard structure until the Reverend William Stukeley, a century later, had a flash of perception and conceived it as a patterned unity (Stukeley 1740). In subsequent decades other antiquaries followed suit, combing the British landscape, finding new henges and arrangements of stone upon almost every high outcrop and declaring them Druidical altars or rude temples to Thor or Odin. In their enthusiasm, antiquaries began to discover patterns where none existed; many believe that this is exactly what Tom Lethbridge did when he uncovered the missing Sawston Giant in 1953 (Lethbridge 1957) but at least the clay had been washed from their eyes.

Antiquaries were never fired by hill-figures in quite the same way that there were by henges and burial mounds, presumably because the former were not considered proper 'monuments' – neither did they hoard the promise of uncovering valuable artefacts. Thus, while many stone monuments were surveyed and their associated folklore recorded, the same consideration was not applied to hill-figures, save the Uffington Horse which, because of its visual prominence, has always been thought an important landmark. Even the solid red figure of the Horse of Tysoe, praised by Michael Drayton in his poem *Polyolbion*, was neglected and allowed to grass over and fade from sight (Newman 1987, 62).

It must be borne in mind that hill-figures are very much a 'now-you-see-me, now-you-don't' type of artefact. A lapse of scouring for a couple of decades, to which may be added the work of sheep's hooves and men's footprints, and a once-splendid figure is no more than a faint outline. If we see the Giant as among the prehistoric wonders of Britain – a startling, overpowering presence – it is only because decades of historians, archaeologists, and scholars, plus the guardianship of the National Trust, have given us the spectacles.

'Works of this sort', Dr Maton wrote of the Giant in 1796, 'especially when contiguous to encampments, were the amusement merely of idle people, and cut with as little meaning as shepherd boys stripping turf off the Wiltshire plains' (1796). Despite its tone of dismissal, it is interesting that Dr Maton alludes to such a custom, as if it were a recognized diversion to strip away turf and doodle on the landscape. What designs did these shepherd boys trace out in the ground? Horses? Dragons? Sheep? Men? Buxom ladies?

This is a diversion about which little is known and, contrary to Dr Maton's views, it can no longer be disparaged as having 'little meaning', for the Giant survives as an image redolent with meaning, concerning warrior-heroes, fertility, aggression, the tenacious adherence of rural communities to a totem, a Father-Protector. He has handed us back a portion of the past that would have otherwise grassed over and been lost forever.

* * * * * * * *

Parallels and the antiquity of the hill-figure tradition

TD: The implications of Mr Newman's evidence that the Giant has an ancestry back before the Age of Enlightenment but was not noticed, allows a clearer understanding of the few texts that do exist from the late seventeenth century through to the mid eighteenth century, after which accounts are more common and wide-ranging. The very earliest documentary reference, the entry in churchwardens' account dating to 1694 (see Vale in Part III below) is a statement of fact and has little real context. It simply records expenditure of parochial funds on repairing the Giant. All that can really be said is that the Giant existed by this time and was considered sufficiently important for the expenditure to be made. The various mid eighteenth century accounts by Stukeley (1764), Hutchin's (1774), and anonymous authorities writing in *The Gentleman's Magazine* (Anon. 1764), *St James's Chronicle* (Anon. 1763a), and the *Royal Magazine* (Anon. 1763b) all suggest clearly enough that the Giant had been in existence for a long time. So often these texts are quoted selectively by proponents of the argument for a medieval or later origin. The historian John Hutchins and his successors appear to have checked their sources and consulted locally about the origin of the Giant between 1774 and the publication of the third edition of his history in 1870, so that it is quite clear what is reported as hearsay and what is considered more likely:

> This figure has been reported to have been made by Lord Helles' servants, during his residence here. But it is more likely he only caused it to be repaired, for some people who died not long before 1772, 80 or 90 years old, when young, knew some of the same age that averred it was there beyond the memory of man. (Hutchins 1861–70, IV, 35)

This kind of writing is a classic antiquarian device, a diversion, in order to appear authoritative about something for which there is no written record or local gossip. The situation here is made worse because associated legends are tantalizing but difficult to match with the evidence (*cf.* Lloyd 1982), and the folklore and tradition is insufficient to fall back upon. Nobody could say what its origins were, only that it was customarily repaired from time to time.

If an ancient origin for the Cerne Giant is possible it is unlikely that it was unique in England. Thus it becomes important to consider whether similar things were present elsewhere in Britain during prehistoric times, and if so how they related to the landscape, associated monuments, and the iconography and symbology of their times. The majority of hill-figures in England are certainly of recent date, but of the few possibly older examples the only one that has been examined in detail is the Uffington Horse in Oxfordshire. Like the Cerne Giant it is situated in an archaeologically rich landscape, a point to which we shall return. To outline the results of recent scientific studies at and around the Uffington Horse I would like to call on my second expert witness, David Miles. Mr Miles was, until recently, the Director of the Oxford Archaeological Unit, and the author of many books and articles reporting excavations and surveys on settlement sites of the first millennia BC and AD.

* * * * * * * *

Figure 19. *Aerial view of the Uffington White Horse, Oxfordshire, and its position relative to Uffington Castle (centre) and the Ridgeway (right). (Photography courtesy of Cambridge University Committee for Aerial Photography. BOV-64.* *)*

The Uffington Horse and its antiquity

David Miles

Before the gods that made the gods
Had seen their sunrise pass
The White Horse of the White Horse Vale
Was cut out of the grass ...
from *The Ballad of the White Horse* by G K Chesterton (1911)

The Uffington White Horse is one of the best known icons of the English landscape (Figures 19 and 20). Its elegant and abstract form, nearly 110 metres in length, stretches across the most dramatic scarp of the Berkhire Downs (since 1974 in Oxfordshire).[3]

The Horse is carved at the head of the Manger, a spectacular combe which is also the source of the River Ock. Both the horse and the river give their names to the Vale below – the Vale of the White Horse or the Ock Valley – which stretches between Swindon in the west and Abindgon on the Thames in the east. The hill-figure is just below the summit of White Horse Hill; the highest point on the Downs (261m), which is capped by the ramparts of the prehistoric hillfort of Uffington Castle. The Horse faces west-north-west and is visible from about 30km across the Vale, particularly when lit by the setting sun. The distinctive outline of the hillfort ramparts is even easier to locate at a distance.

The Uffington White Horse is the only English hill-figure which is known to be ancient. It was first recorded in an Abingdon Abbey cartulary of the mid twelfth century and in the catalogue of the Wonders of Britain (which also includes Stonehenge) The earliest representation of the Uffington Horse may be the image of a horse accompanied by a dragon, on the fourteenth century tenor bell of St Birinus in Dorchester Abbey.

For the past three centuries antiquarians, archaeologists, poets and politicians have speculated about the Horse's origins. This is a classic example of a contested landscape, claimed by Whigs, Tories, muscular Christians and neo-pagans alike. Antiquarians have seen the Horse as a creation of the Celts, pagan Saxons or King Alfred. However, until recently surprisingly little scientific examination had taken place.

In 1980 several members of the Oxford Archaeological Unit spent a weekend surveying the White Horse. This started a dialogue with the National Trust, the owners of the Horse, and English Heritage, its legal guardians. The timing was opportune because David Astor had just given to the National Trust a block of Downland around the Horse, which contained a number of other monuments. This extension released the Horse from its tightly bounded corral and also

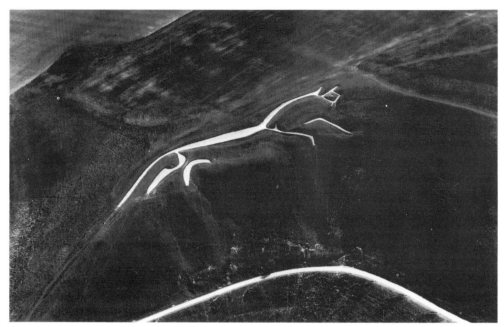

Figure 20. *Close-up aerial view of the Uffington White Horse, Oxfordshire. (Photography courtesy of Cambridge University Committee for Aerial Photography. LK-46. Crown copyright reserved. RAF photographs)*

allowed visitors to roam more widely. For the National Trust and English Heritage the gift provided an opportunity to create new management plans for the wider landscape. For the archaeologists there was the persistent question 'who built the White Horse; why and when?'. However, the removal of its fences was a physcial reminder that the hill-figure was part of the wider landscape. Could it be better understood in this context, not simply as an isolated icon?

The White Horse Project aimed to test several propositions: that the Horse was constructed, not simply etched into the chalk; that it contained stratigraphical layers build up over the centuries; that its shape may or may have changed over time. The trenches cut into the head, belly and legs of the figure clarified these issues. The architects of the Horse made the figure by cutting a trench up to one metre deep into the hillside – into colluvium or hillwash as well as chalk. They produced a clean white image by ramming chalk, probably taken from visible quarries on the hilltop, into the trench. As erosion, silt and weeds blurred the white image new layers of chalk were superimposed. In the eighteenth and nineteenth centuries great scouring festivals took place, recorded in local newspapers and by Thomas Hughes, notably in his novel *The Scouring of the White Horse* (1859). Unfortunately there are no earlier records of such events. However, unless maintained about every decade the image would possibly disappear. On the other hand, if the location were remembered, the figure could be revived by cleaning over the surface to reveal the chalk-filled trench.

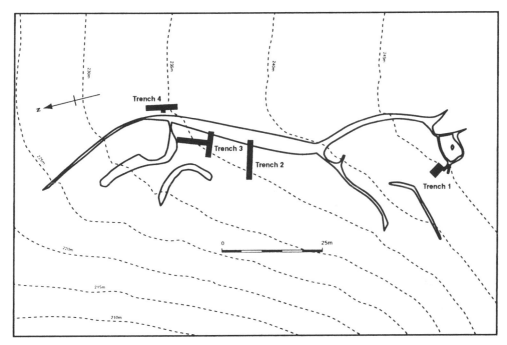

Figure 21. Plan showing the position of trenches cut to examine the stratigraphy around the horse. (Oxford Archaeological Unit)

The excavation confirmed that the segmented, abstract shape with a beaked head had not substantially changed over the years. This disproved the theory, set out by Diane Woolner, that the Anglo-Saxons carved a more prosaic, naturalistic and heavier beast as at Westbury. Because of its trench construction the Horse can be curated with relatively little effort and is, to some extent, resistant to change.

Delays in mounting the excavations were fortuitous. By the time fieldwork started the Oxford University Research Laboratory for Art and Archaeology's work on Optical Stimulated Luminescence had reached a stage where it could make a vital contribution. The 1994 excavation in the belly of the Horse located sediments containing feldspar and quartz in the lowest levels. From these Julia Rees-Jones was able to date three samples: two quartz dates indicate an earliest date for the existence of the Uffington White Horse of approximately 1300-600 BC at the 68% confidence level. These OSL dates suggest that the Horse was created in the late Bronze Age or early Iron Age, a period of particularly intense activity on the Berkshire Downs.

The White Horse Project aimed not only to date the figure; it also emphasized the study of the Horse in its landscape, using non-destructive survey methods and minimal targeted excavation. As a result it became clear that this spectacular area of the Downs had been a highly symbolic focus for local communities for millennia; a landscape constantly re-invested and re-worked to reflect changing ideologies and cultural identities.

On the false crest above the Horse geophysical survey located an early Bronze Age round barrow re-used for sixth century Anglo-Saxon burials. A second mound – oblong in shape and 120m south-west of the Horse also hangs on a false crest above the Manger. Its construction date is uncertain; possibly it belongs to the Neolithic or Bronze Age. However, it was re-used for burial in the later Romano-British period, when at least 50 burials were placed in the ancient mound.

Small-scale excavations have, therefore, confirmed that White Horse Hill was associated with burials before the construction of the Horse and during periods of its lifetime. This is a tradition which continues, unofficially today: the scattering of cremations ashes and the placing of wreaths on the Horse are not uncommon rituals.

The White Horse Project has indicated a construction date for the hill figure close to the early first millennium BC. This is a time of extraordinary activity in this areas of the Downs. A string of hillforts (including the adjacent Uffington Castle) was constructed; the Downland was divided, for the first time, by major, parish-like linear land boundaries. The Project also located other settlements nearby such as Tower Hill, a large open settlement on the adjacent hill to the west where a late Bronze Age hoard of palstaves and scrap metal was found in the round house doorway. Earlier excavations at the nearby Wayland's Smithy chambered tomb also located similar metalwork and late Bronze Age settlement evidence. The White Horse may, therefore, have been constructed to mark an ancestral burial ground at a time of extreme pressure on land, along with dominant fortifications and territorial enclosures to emphasize territorial control and group identity.

Remarkably, the White Horse has survived for some four millennia. Mythology, folk memory and literature provide some indication of the changing traditions, symbolism and sense of ownership which may explain this extreme example of long-term curation. There is evidence for the ritual use of White Horse Hill in the Roman period. Place-names suggest that this was a complex Anglo-Saxon landsape suffused with mythical significance. In the Middle Ages the Horse and the spectacular and enigmatic mound of Dragon Hill was appropriated for Christianity and the nationalistic myths of St George and King Arthur. In the eighteenth and nineteenth centuries rival antiquarians promoted King Alfred and the Celts as the White Horses creators. At the same time local people used it as a place for games, competition, rivalry with neighbours and a degree of bloodletting and anarchy. Today the hill is still a contested landscape – argued over by scientific archaeologists, managerially-minded authorities, neo-pagans, mountain-bikers, ramblers, four-wheel drive enthusiasts and Berkshire patriots. The White Horse is not a passive beast: it generates its own history.

* * * * * * * *

Regression to original form and iconography

TD: Clearly, the work at Uffington emphasizes two points. First is that the hill-figure is associated with many other distinctive kinds of monuments and structures. This is a matter we shall return to later. Second, is the very clear evidence that the tradition of creating hill-figures was an established aspect of prehistoric life, and if one exists there are likely to be others of different kinds. Some will have been lost permanently or temporarily, while those that survive are likely, from the evidence of Uffington, to have gradually changed details of their shape and design. Leslie Grinsell (1980) illustrated very clearly how this has happened at Cerne since the mid eighteenth century, but this 200 year span is only a small proportion of the total history of the site. Thus to get a more complete understanding of the original form of the figure it is necessary to turn the clock back further. As already noted, in 1938 Stuart Piggott reasserted an earlier suggestion that the Giant was a representation of Hercules, but this is an argument that needs to be re-examined and carefully checked. Images of anthropomorphic male figures with arms held high feature widely in prehistoric rock-art in northern Europe, specially Scandinavia (*cf.* J Coles 1990; Figure 16 above), although remain unknown in British rock-art. Wooden figurines holding clubs and shields, some with detachable genitalia, are however known from many parts of the British Isles (B Coles 1990). Stone images of warriors naked except for a belt are also known from the Humber basin in north-eastern England (Stead 1988; Cunliffe 1991, 520). To help assess the iconographic evidence represented by the Cerne Giant I would like to introduce my third expert witness Rodney Castleden. Mr Castleden is a geography teacher at Roedean School and an amateur archaeologist who has published a number of books on the Neolithic and Bronze Age of Britain. He has been researching the Cerne Giant for many years and in 1996 published an extended account of his findings as *The Cerne Giant* (Castleden 1996).

* * * * * * * *

Iconography and the identity of the Giant

Rodney Castleden

It should be possible to tell who the Cerne Giant is. We recognize people fairly easily. We usually pick up someone's racial group, culture, and social rank instantly from a range of signals. We see the shape of their physical features, we notice which parts of their bodies they choose to cover and which to expose, we see the style of their clothing, the gestures they make and the badges, emblems or insignia they carry. We apply this technique continually, often unconsciously, in twentieth century Britain when we distinguish a judge from a barrister, a police

sergeant from a gas meter man; we apply it equally to people in the past when
we look at portraits of Tudor dignitaries and aristocrats, or the heraldry on
medieval tombs. We know, at a glance, the difference between the Black Prince
and a Knight Templar. I believe, as a result of my research on the Cerne Giant,
that the image of the Giant itself contains a surprisingly large amount of encoded
information of the kind I have described. I believe it gives us enough to place him
firmly in a specific culture and a specific time frame, and enough to allow the
probably wholly illiterate audience for whom he was drawn to 'read' his image
like a book.

I will come back to the Giant's visible features later, after considering the
possibility that some of them may have been altered and some completely lost.
Before we can read it we need to restore the image to its original form, at least on
paper, to make sure we are seeing it as it was originally intended to be seen. If
we do not, we risk misidentifying the Giant, seeing him as a sergeant when he is
really a superintendent or, more seriously, as a Tudor when he is really a
Plantagenent.

Reconstructing the Giant

In 1989 I started searching for lost features on the Giant, using a resistivity meter
to locate filled and grassed-over trenches (*cf.* Castleden 1996, 155). The natural soil
depth on Giant Hill is only 0.12m, and electricity passes more easily through the
soil where it is deeper, so a soil-filled trench as shallow as 0.2m deep might show
up as a line of low readings. I took resistivity readings unusually close together,
every 0.25m, across an area 10m by 14m below the left elbow. This produced in
the region of 2000 readings, which were computer-processed using two different
systems, GEOPLOT and SURFER, to generate a wide range of visual presentations
including block diagrams and contour maps.

Two conspicuous lines of low readings were visible. The longer of the two
lines snakes down from close to the left armpit to a point level with the middle
of the thigh: from there it sweeps up to the left wrist. Above this is a second,
roughly parallel, line; a third, and less obvious, line runs along the contour
towards a low knoll below the left fist. The lines clearly indicate a cloak folded
over or wrapped round the left arm, and its curving shape suggests that the cloak
is moving about, either because the Giant is running or because he is waving his
arm like a matador.

The smoothness of the lines means that the feature cannot be a lionskin. A
lionskin, with its head, four paws and dangling tail, would have to be represented
by a ragged outline, as seen on some Roman coins. The discovery of the precise
form of the cloak seriously weakens any interpretation of the Giant as Hercules.
There is no need to associate him with the Hercules cult at the time of the Roman
emperor Commodus, nor to attach to him the dates of Commodus' reign; the date
traditionally given to the Giant of around AD 190 therefore no longer has any
force.

It is also worth pointing out that it is un-characteristic for Hercules to be shown with an erection; if anything his genitals are de-emphasized, as in the many representations of Hercules at Baccarat in France (Figure 22; Moitrieux 1992). The Giant could therefore only be Hercules if the erect phallus was added later, but to argue in this way would be desperate.

The computer image of the cloak was surpris-ingly clear, particularly in view of the rather blurred patch of resistivity highs showing on Anthony Clark's 1979 survey (Clark 1983). It was important to check that the meter was working properly and really showing the positions of silted trenches. There was reason to believe that a ring had once represented the navel and that this had been incorporated into the phallus; it seemed likely that the grassed-over lower limb of the navel might be a metre down from the tip of the phallus, and that another curved line marking the original tip of the phallus was half a metre below that. It was likely there were two lost lines crossing the phallus, both potentially retrievable by resistivity survey, so this was a promising place to test the meter. Readings were taken every 0.1m to get max-imum detail.

The resulting computer map shows two lines of resistivity lows 1.25m and 2.4m down from the present tip of the phallus (Figure 23), proving three things. First, that Gerald Pitman's observ-ations about the lost navel (Pitman 1978) were absolutely correct; second, that the meter was working properly and detecting sections of lost outline; and third, that the phallus was originally not only shorter but a lot shorter. We know, from an early picture postcard of the Giant, that the navel was still visible around 1900 or 1902 (see Castleden 1996, plate 32). The navel had dis-appeared by 1920, so the most likely time for the alteration is the one scouring that happened between those two dates, in 1908. This mistake has been perpetuated ever since – the National Trust has rejected a recent proposal to correct it – and the effect is to emphasize a feature that was not

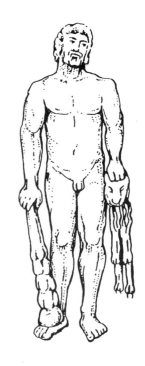

Figure 22. Bas-relief of Hercules from the Sanctuary at Baccarat in Gaul, second to fourth century AD. (After Castleden 1996, 94)

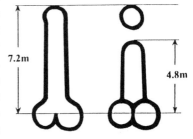

Figure 23. Left, the phallus today. Right, the pre-1908 phallus, reconstructed from resistivity anomalies.

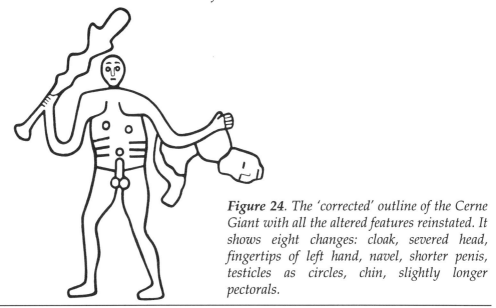

Figure 24. The 'corrected' outline of the Cerne Giant with all the altered features reinstated. It shows eight changes: cloak, severed head, fingertips of left hand, navel, shorter penis, testicles as circles, chin, slightly longer pectorals.

originally intended to stand out. The pre-1908 phallus was 2.4m shorter: 4.8m (15.5 feet) long, not 7.2m (23.5 feet) long as today. Given the Giant's overall height of 55m (180 feet), his erection was not exaggerated, and this fact should give pause for reflection that, although it has long been assumed that the Giant was a fertility figure, it would now seem more likely that it was not.

These surveys revealed two of the changes that need to be made. What should we make of the changed composition (Figure 24): the nudity, the erect but correctly proportioned phallus, the huge club brandished above the head, and the cloak wrapped round the half-extended arm? And there is another feature that is often overlooked because people are distracted by the phallus that stands in front of it: a belt depicted as single line around his waist. Each of these attributes is a clue to the Giant's ethnic group, the customs and beliefs of his time, even his social status; together they speak of a particular phase of Britain's past, and tell us when and why he was made.

Identifying the Giant

The search for images with similar attributes leads to Iron Age Europe. In a zone running across Europe from Britain to Romania, many images of warriors or warrior-gods were made with varying combinations of the Cerne Giant's features (Van Hamel 1934; Green 1989). Andreae (1991) has discussed in some detail the way in which Celts were depicted in Etruscan, Greek, and Roman art, and a small sample of these and other traditions will demonstrate very clearly the Giant's credentials as an Iron Age warrior.

Two warriors are shown on a bronze belt-plaque made in Slovenia around 500–450 BC and found in Barrow IIB at Magdalenska Gora (Figure 25; Megaw and Megaw 1989, 39); they fight naked, they wear only belts and they are shown with erections. A life-size stone statue from Hirschlanden, Kr. Leonberg, Germany dating to about 500 BC shows another naked warrior (Figure 26) wearing only a helmet and a belt: the belt has a dagger tucked into it, which reveals the belt's purpose (we shall see later for what specific purpose the dagger was used). He too has an erection (Megaw and Magaw 1989, fig. 40). Two bronze figurines made in France in the late Iron Age show variations on the Cerne Giant's cloak. Both individuals are completely naked, even to the point of beltlessness: both brandish a weapon of some kind in their raised right hands. One has his cloak draped over his left arm and the two ends are clearly shown

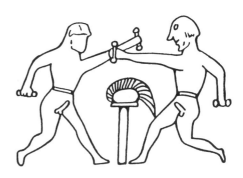

Figure 25. Two Celtic warriors with dumb-bells on a belt-plaque from Magdalenska Gora in Slovenia, now in Vienna. (After Castleden 1996, 150)

hanging down (Figure 27); the other (Figure 28) has his cloak wrapped more tightly round his left arm to make a ball of padding. In both the left arm is half extended as if parrying a blow.

Figure 26. (Left). A life-size sandstone statue from Hirschlanden, Germany, carved in about 500 BC. Now in the Wurttembergisches Landesmuseum, Stuttgart. Figures 27 and 28. (Centre and right). Two Bronze Gaulish figurines, probably first century BC, now in the Bernard Pickard collection. (After Castleden 1996, 147 and 160)

Roman commentators assumed these Celtic tribesmen had undressed and put their cloaks aside to avoid being impeded by undergrowth. However, Diodorus Siculus (*Book V, 29*) assumed the nudity signalled bravado: 'Certain of [the Gauls] despise death to such a degree that they enter the perils of battle without protective armour and with no more than a belt about the loins.' There may have been an element of bravado, but the Gaulish figurines show that the cloak was required for a specific use: it was wrapped round the half raised left arm as a primitive shield, effective in absorbing the impact of a blow from a club, stave, or spear shaft. In Iron Age Europe generally, this type of cloak-shield was the routine equipment of non-professional soldiers, of men pressed into military action by circumstances (Figure 29); probably only aristocrats and mercenaries could afford solid shields. A terracotta figurine made in Egypt in the second century BC shows what a Gaulish mercenary looked like when ready for action (Bailey 1995); he was naked apart from a cloak and a belt to hold his sword but, unlike the Cerne Giant, he carried a substantial solid shield (Figure 30).

The low knoll below the left fist of the Cerne Giant looks from its position as if it might once have been part of the hill-figure design, perhaps as a bag or purse swinging from the hand. Because its relief is so slight (it projects from the hill-side only 0.4m) no surface detail can be made out on the ground. A close contour survey was undertaken by Martin Papworth, and when a computer programme was used to plot the data as contours at 0.03m intervals it revealed traces of a human face modelled into its surface, the eyes and mouth indicated by shallow depressions, the nose by a subdued ridge 1.5m long (Castleden 1996, 165).

Head-hunting was a routine part of the Iron Age world. Warriors regularly took home the heads of important enemies as trophies, as Diodorus Siculus describes:

> They cut off the heads of enemies killed in battle and attach them to the necks of their horses ... while singing a song of victory; and they nail up these first fruits on their houses, just as do those who lay low wild animals in certain kinds of hunting. (*Book V, 29*)

Livy (*Book XXIII, 24*) wrote that, 'the consuls had no news of the disaster until some Gallic horsemen came into view with heads hanging at their horses' breasts ... and singing their customary song of triumph.' He also reported that the head of a prized enemy chieftain was placed in one of their temples by the Boii in 216 BC. Archaeological evidence (e.g. sculpted reliefs, shrines with skull niches, finds of severed heads) confirms that such things happened (Ross 1967, 111–3). That the Cerne Giant was proudly displaying a severed head shows that he is returning victorious from battle, silently singing his song of triumph. Unlike some of the depictions described above, he seems to have left his decapitating knife on the battlefield, but the tribe is safe.

From all these attributes, the Cerne Giant is plainly identifiable as an Iron Age warrior-god of a pan-European type that the Romans sometimes referred to as Mars. From the iconographic parallels, he could have been cut any time

Figure 29. (Left). *Tetradrachm of Poliorcetes, 300-295 BC, from Salamis. The god Poseidon with trident and cloak-shield. (After a coin in the Museum of the Coinage of Cyprus, Nicosia, Cyprus).* *Figure 30.* (Right). *Terracotta figurine of a Gaulish mercenary in the Ptolemaic army, third or second century BC to judge from the style of the shield. This view of a Celtic warrior was made by an Egyptian craftsman, the piece is now in the British Museum. (After Castleden 1996, 151)*

between 500 BC and the time of Christ, the nearest we can get to a date without an excavation.

The god's nudity shows him ready for battle. He is minimally armed, with only a simple wooden club and his cloak-shield to defend him: he is equipped as an ordinary man. God he may have been, with supernatural powers at his command, but his tribespeople gave him minimal weapons, so that he took part in the fray on the same footing as the poorest of them. The Cerne Giant's attributes suggest that he was the guardian-god of the tribe living in the Cerne valley, perhaps even the principal protector-god of Iron Age Dorset as a whole. Every Iron Age tribe had its guardian god, who was often a warrior: hence the nudity, belt and raised club, which would have told an illiterate Iron Age onlooker his function straight away. He was there to defend his people and their livestock with his cloak-shield and fend off their enemies with his club.

The phallus symbolically showed his power, vigour, wholeness: this was not the Freudian idea of sexuality, but something closer to the Jungian concept of libido. The Giant's phallus, in common with other phallic images from the Iron Age and early Romano-British period (*cf*. Hawkes 1948), was a good luck charm, succinctly symbolizing life force. It could be presented in the face of evil just as the crucifix was later held up to ward off the powers of darkness. Having a phallus visible about the place was rather like hanging up garlic against vampires.

It was the severed head that ultimately proved his potency against the enemy.

It has been suggested more than once (e.g. Harrison 1973; Rudd 1986, 70–71) that the Cerne Giant is Cernunnos, a Gaulish god of hunting and healing, but a glance at his insignia reveals that this cannot be right. Cernunnos is often accompanied by a stag, his main cult animal; he often wears a torc, holds a ram-headed serpent and wears antlers on his head; he always sits cross-legged. We see none of this in the figure at Cerne.

It could be argued that the Giant may once have had horns or antlers that were later allowed to grass over. Certainly some Celtic representations of human heads with horns are known, for example the stone head from Holzgerlingen, near Württemberg, Germany (Powell 1953, 137), but they are relatively rare. The Dorset Ooser, the horned mask that used to exist at Melbury Osmond, suggests that a horned pagan god was once worshipped in this area (Dewer 1968). No doubt the mask, lost around 1900, was the last in a series of copies the prototype for which was made many centuries before; but, even if the Ooser had its beginnings back in the Iron Age, does it have any proven connection with the Giant? For the Giant and the Ooser to be one and the same, the Giant would have to be fitted with horns. A resistivity survey across the top of the Giant's head showed no sign that the Giant has ever had horns, so from that evidence it seems clear that he is neither Cernunnos nor the Ooser.

The Giant as a warrior

The Giant is best seen as an Iron Age warrior, an icon of either the local (*pagus*) or the regional (*civitas*) tribal protector-god. With no more than a mortal's simplest weapon and the flimsiest shield, he is ready to join battle. This is a god to inspire even the poorest and most disadvantaged in the community to fight on bravely. He is prepared to shape-shift into mortal form in order to inspirit people and provide them with an example of the way their lives ought to be lived. The god at Cerne identifies himself with the poorest members of society, and they in their turn could easily identify with him in his mythic battles with the forces of evil on their behalf. He is the god not of a ruling elite but of Iron Age Everyman.

* * * * * * * *

Regional context and setting

TD: The tentative identification of the Giant as an Iron Age 'god of the people' finds resonance in depictions of Celtic gods elsewhere in Britain. The carved chalk figurines of the Parisi have already been mentioned; the representation of an erect phallus and belt on several of these providing close parallels with the iconography of the Cerne figure. It is also noteworthy that where the chalk figurines are equipped with weapons (a sword or knife) they are shown tucked into the belt at the back in a position invisible to someone viewing the image from the front (Stead 1988). The form of head and the representation of the eyes, mouth, and nose in the chalk figurines also has similarities with the Cerne hill-figure, and it may even be significant that chalk is the raw material available and used in both areas. Carved stone heads, many of which show artist similarity to the Cerne Giant's head and facial features, are amongst the most widely distributed cult objects in later Iron Age Britain (Ross 1967). One showing remarkably similar facial characteristics was found at Deal in Kent in 1986 (Parfitt and Green 1987).

The presence of a large-scale depiction of a local god in the landscape raises a number of important questions about the local settlement pattern in later prehistoric and Roman times. In 1926, Sir Flinders Petrie tried to argue that the Giant was of Bronze Age date because of associations with earthworks that at the time he had wrongly identified. Another great field archaeologist, O G S Crawford, put him to rights in 1929, preferring instead a later prehistoric date for the associations. To shed light on this archaeological context for the Giant I would like to call on my fourth expert witness, Bill Putnam. Bill has recently retired from being senior lecturer in the School of Conservation Sciences at Bournemouth University, but is continuing his researches into the later prehistoric and Roman period of Dorset, a subject on which he has published many articles and a very useful book entitled *Roman Dorset* (Putnam 1984).

* * * * * * * *

The Cerne Valley in prehistoric and Roman times

Bill Putnam

In later prehistoric and Roman times a tribal grouping of dispersed communities known as the Durotriges inhabited the area approximately equivalent to that of modern Dorset. Their name is first known to history in the Roman period (AD 43–410), but their identity can be established from the distribution of distinctive material culture from a considerably earlier date. For perhaps a thousand years, the Durotriges were responsible for the character and development of the landscape. The distribution of their coins and their distinctive burnished hand-made pottery confirm the extent of the tribal area as extending from the River Avon in the east to the River Otter in the west, and from the south coast northwards perhaps as far as Taunton (Putnam 1984, 11–13). The Cerne Valley stands roughly in the centre of such a territory (Figure 31).

It is likely that the Cerne Giant was constructed by the Durotriges, whether during the Roman period or before. He should be regarded as a powerful symbol of tribal authority and beliefs, perhaps representing a native god of fertility which, as Stuart Piggott has argued (1938), was conflated with the Roman god Hercules.

His presence at Cerne may well originally have been connected with religious observance at the copious and reliable spring which rises here on the valley floor.

In spite of two millennia of cultivation and other human activity, it is possible to reconstruct many aspects of the Durotrigian landscape in which the Giant takes his place. Specific figures cannot of course be given, but the population was substantial. Aerial photography has shown the extent of cultivation. Celtic fields cover much of the upland chalk, and farms and villages occur at frequent intervals. This is particularly true of the Cerne area, where at least seven settlements are known on the higher ground of the parish, together with their fields, as a result of detailed surveys by the Royal Commission on the Historical Monuments of England and others (RCHME 1952).

The tribal leaders of the Durotriges had developed a tradition of major hilltop fortifications on a grander scale than any other region of Iron Age Britain (*cf.* Sharples 1991, 260–3). These appear to have been the focus of political and military activity, and the primary object of attack from the invading Roman forces from 43 AD onwards. They even merit a specific mention by the Roman historian Suetonius as he describes the Roman assault led by the future emperor Vespasian (Putnam 1984, 17).

Hillforts like Maiden Castle (near Dorchester) and Hod Hill (near Blandford) may have been developing into towns when the process was brought to an end by the Roman conquest, and an existing pattern of urban society imposed on the tribe.

The Durotriges have unfortunately left no written record of the names of people, though we have the names of some geographical locations from Roman sources. *Durnovaria* was the name of their Romanized capital at Dorchester, and was almost certainly the name of that location prior to the building of the town. The hillfort at Hod Hill may have been called *Dunium*.

Even prior to the Roman conquest a tribal coinage circulated extensively, made of both bronze and silver. It is widely found, showing that it was in every day use, rather than bullion in the hands of the wealthy. The Durotrigian potters of Purbeck manufactured a dark brown or black burnished pottery of considerable sophistication, which was sold even beyond their own tribal territory. During the Roman phase of their history this industry changed the style of its products to suit Roman taste and went from strength to strength. It held major contracts with the Roman army, and its pots are found in enormous quantities even on Hadrian's Wall.

The Durotrigian farmers of the Cerne area will have owed allegiance probably to the lord of Maiden Castle during the Iron Age, and later to the Roman style Durotrigian administration of *Durnovaria*. Life will have been hard at times, though the building of *Durnovaria* will have brought new opportunities to sell produce to the markets of the town.

The major settlements of this period near Cerne are Black Hill, Smacam Down, and Giant Hill itself, though almost all the land of the parish shows some signs of ancient settlement.

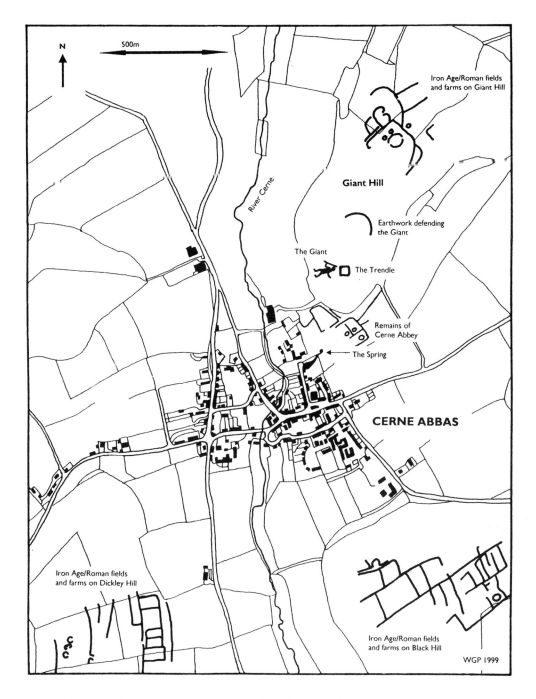

Figure 31. *Map of the Cerne area with ancient features shown.*

At Black Hill there is a farmstead and nine or ten of its fields (RCHM 1952, 83). At Smacam Down, which is a Scheduled Monument, there is a complete farming landscape of the Iron Age and Roman period covering a whole valley and the hilltops adjacent to it. A circular farmstead lies in its own enclosure, and around it is an extensive pattern of small fields. The downhill movement of soil has created lynchets or banks which still define the farmer's fields with great clarity (RCHM 1952, 83–4).

On Giant Hill itself, not only are there areas of Celtic fields and an Iron Age farmstead in its own enclosure, but also a defensive ditch and bank, a so-called cross-ridge dyke of Iron Age or earlier type, cutting off and perhaps protecting the sacred area of the Giant from intrusion (RCHM 1952, 82). The significance of cross-ridge dykes in relation to the definition of ceremonial or 'special' places in prehistoric times has only recently been recognized (Vyner 1994; and *cf.* RCHM 1970b, xl–xli), and the existence of this earthwork at Cerne is one of the most powerful arguments for placing the Giant in a Roman or earlier context (Figure 32).

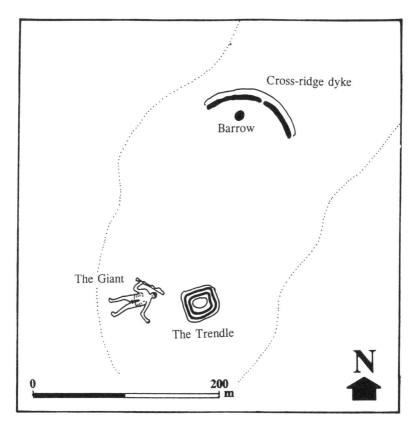

Figure 32. Detail of Giant Hill showing the position of the Giant and the Trendle in relation to the cross-ridge dyke. The approximate edge of the spur is shown as a dotted line.

The Durotriges worshipped a multitude of gods (Green 1986). It is clear that springs, wells, woodland glades, and other landscape features were regarded as the homes of spirits of one sort or another, and their propitiation was an important aspect of life, especially in relation to the farming cycle (Ross 1967). Other gods related to love, war, wisdom, and all sorts of human activity. There may well have been gods related to the family and to political identities.

The worship of these gods involved sacrifice (sometimes human) and all sorts of ceremonies designed to gain their intervention in human life. Every disaster could be put down to failure to pay enough attention to the relevant spirit. Images of the gods played an important part in their worship. There were many shrines throughout the countryside. Some of these have been identified, especially where they later took on Roman form and acquired features in stone.

There was no dramatic change to these beliefs when Roman authority was imposed (Webster 1986). Roman gods, and their Greek equivalents, were identified with native Durotrigian gods according to their characteristics. Hercules may have been identified with an unnamed Durotrigian fertility god, and worshipped at Cerne under a joint name. In the same way the native god Sulis at Bath was equated with the Roman Minerva, and the temple became one of the most popular religious complexes in Roman Britain. Other such arrangements have been identified at Heathrow, South Cadbury, and Hayling Island. In Maiden Castle itself the fourth century Romano-Celtic temple may well have been built on the site of a shrine dating from the Iron Age (Woodward 1992, 17–30).

The archaeological features of the Cerne site include the Giant himself, the spring, and the small enclosure above the Giant known as the Trendle (RCHM 1952, 82–3). The exposure of the chalk which forms the figure of the Giant is discussed elsewhere in this book, but it is important to remember that recent study of the Uffington White Horse shows that substantial changes may have taken place to the Giant's appearance over the centuries. There were probably many other chalk figures in the Iron Age and Roman periods, but only where systematic cleaning has taken place over the centuries do they survive into more modern times.

The spring, known as St Augustine's Well, lies in a large boggy area. All the masonry features at present visible belong to periods later than the Giant, particularly that of the Benedictine Abbey of Cerne. However, the buried wet deposits offer the best opportunity to discover the history of the spring, should an excavation ever become possible.

The Trendle, also known as the Giant's Frying Pan is a small enclosure with two banks around it, on a piece of specially levelled ground high above the Giant himself. It is not easily visible from below, and thus becomes an almost secret place. The inner bank appears to be recent, and used to have trees on it. The outer bank is much older and represents the original enclosure which is remarkable for being so neatly terraced into the hill-side (RCHM 1952, 82). There has been no excavation here. The Trendle does not fit any domestic or agricultural explanation. There is a tradition that the site has to do with May Day ceremonies, but it seems unlikely that these would take place in such a secret location.

It is possible, though no more than that, that it carried a small temple for the worship of the Giant in Iron Age times, or was at least a levelled area for conducting ceremonies. It is unlikely to have been used for this purpose in the Roman period as masonry structures would be expected. If such buildings existed they might have been built below on the present village site.

The Cerne Giant fits well into an Iron Age and Roman context in which ostentation was commonly embodied in the construction of massive ramparts at hillforts, roads, and fortifications. The surrounding landscape is inhabited and cultivated on a large scale by Durotrigian farmers and villagers. A defensive ditch and bank protect the Giant from intrusion and set it apart from the secular world of crop production, livestock and settlement. Fertility deities played an important part in religious activity in the pagan world. This is the world of the Cerne Giant.

* * * * * * * *

Local context and survival

TD: The presence of multiple local cults and religious sites in south Dorset during later prehistoric times carrying on through into the Roman period provides a very appropriate regional context for the Giant. Despite numerous excavations in Roman Dorchester itself, no major temple or shrine has been identified and there is very little religious sculpture (RCHM 1970a, 531–92). By contrast, the surrounding area has a number of temple sites, including the excavated example within Maiden Castle possibly dedicated to Minerva (Wheeler 1943) and Jordon Hill above Weymouth (RCHM 1970a, 616–7), and shrines associated with the larger villas. In this sense, the region was truly pagan in later prehistoric and Roman times, the word itself originally referring to the religions of the countryside.

At Cerne itself, the formal separation by the cross-ridge dyke of the Giant from settlements and fieldsystems to the north is rather important in this context. The similarities with what David Miles and his team have found at Uffington are striking: the enclosure and barrows above both hill-figures are especially clear, and similar associations are also known at Wilmington in East Sussex (see Brown in Part IV below). A possible connection between the Giant and the sacred spring at Cerne is also a powerful local context.

Of course clinching dating evidence of these associations is illusive as the Giant has never been excavated. But stratigraphic and spatial associations are important and can sometimes be found using other techniques than excavation. Here I would like to call on the work of my final expert witness, John Gale who has recently carried out a detailed geophysical survey of the slope on which the Giant lies with a view to finding evidence of associated features. Mr Gale is a lecturer in the School of Conservation Sciences at Bournemouth University and an expert in geophysics.

* * * * * * * *

The 1996 geophysical survey of the Giant

John Gale

During the last 30 years a number of geophysical surveys of the Cerne Giant have been carried out mainly using soil-resistance techniques. One of the most extensive was in 1979 by Tony Clark, Alastair Bartlett and Andrew David for Yorkshire Television, although the detailed results have never been published (Clark 1983). More recently, Rodney Castleden has used geophysical techniques in an attempt to resolve specific questions about the former appearance of the Giant (Castleden 1990; 1996 and see above). However, all these surveys provide only partial coverage of the figure, or were carried out using systems that have since developed considerably. Accordingly, as a preliminary study for the Cerne Enquiry, a new series of surveys was carried out in February 1996 by the author, on behalf of the School of Conservation Sciences, Bournemouth University, with the support of the National Trust, licensed by English Heritage.[4]

The objective of these new surveys was essentially evaluative, both in terms of archaeological feature definition and the efficacy of the two techniques chosen (magnetometry and resistivity). However, there are also certain issues regarding the Giant for which the application of non-destructive methods may prove to be illuminating.

Speculation as to the temporal integrity of the Giant's outline in relation to its original lay-out and any subsequent alteration can theoretically be resolved by geophysical techniques given suitable ground conditions (Clark 1990). In addition, it may be possible to establish a relative, and approximate, date for the Giant if identifiable archaeological features can be located either underneath or overlying the figure. One might quite reasonably expect, for example, some evidence of the land-use on the site prior to the figure being constructed.

The site

The site occupies a prominent position on the steep south-west facing slope of Giant Hill at an approximate elevation of 200m above sea level. The degree of slope on the hill around the Giant is approximately 42–45°, which affords it excellent potential as a natural canvas and allows extensive visibility for anything displayed on it, even from the low elevation of the valley floor below. The Giant is cut through a shallow (0.1–0.2m) humic rendzina with chalk underneath. The trenches which outline the Giant cut into the underlying Middle Chalk which is the major stratum of Giant Hill (Bird 1995). They now contain imported chalk which has been rammed into the outline trench after recutting and scouring. The figure of the Giant has in recent years been subject to a maintenance programme implemented by the National Trust, but whatever its degree of antiquity it will have undergone many repairs over the centuries.

The scouring, re-chalking, and re-cutting of the figure, as well as natural erosion and soil creep, has led to a complex earthwork where soil and silt overburdens vary considerably across the hill-slope occupied by the Giant. This is particularly noticeable down-slope where the outline trenches of the figure run parallel with the contour. Here small lynchets have accumulated where soil creep has been localized and to some extent accelerated by the cutting and maintenance of the figure.

The 1996 survey

In an attempt to maximize the information obtained during the surveys, two survey methods were applied: magnetometry and resistivity. However, because of time constraints the survey area covered was slightly less for the resistivity survey than the magnetometry (Figure 33). A grid comprising 20m by 20m squares was established for both surveys from the same origin; both grids have an identical alignment so that cross-technique evaluation and comparison could be made during fieldwork and in post-survey processing. The total survey area for magnetometry was 1100 square metres and for resistivity 600 square metres.

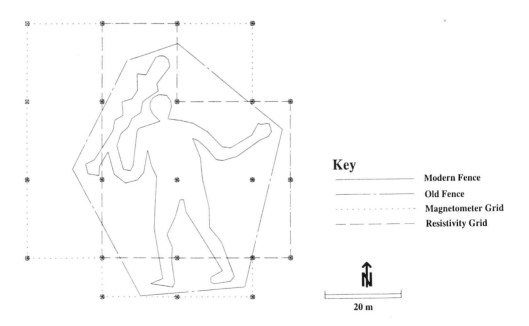

Figure 33. Plan showing the edges of the geophysical survey grids used for gradiometry and resistivity in relation to the outline of the Giant and the hill-slope on which it is set.

The magnetometry survey used a Geoscan FM36 fluxgate gradiometer with a sample interval of 0.5m along traverses 1.0m apart. This was followed by the resistivity survey using a Geoscan RM15 meter (twin electrode configuration) with sample and traverse intervals set at 1.0m. The data was subsequently downloaded from the field equipment's on-board dataloggers to personal computers running Geoplot v2.01, for data processing and storage.

Both survey methods are well established archaeological prospection techniques, and each has the capability of detecting a wide range of anthropomorphic features (Clark 1990). In this instance the features being sought will have been cut into the natural lithology and subsequently either been deliberately back-filled or have silted up over time. As discussed above, ditches or trenches either from agricultural or settlement activity, or from previous cutting of the Giant, are a distinct possibility, and in conducive conditions could be detectable by either or both methods.

Enhanced levels of magnetic susceptibility (MS) in the fills of potential ditches or previous cuttings of the Giant remain a distinct possibility. Such enhancement might be derived from domestic or industrial thermoremnant activity associated perhaps with the use of The Trendle or other occupation sites above the Giant. In such a scenario material will have migrated down-slope into the Giant's outline trenches, particularly those running along the contour. The artificial enhancement of MS of soils because of settlement activity is well documented (Tite 1972; Cole 1995) but may be compromised in this instance because of the repeated scouring of the figures' outline. The extraction of silt build-up in the current outline trench of the Giant from the recent maintenance programme will have almost certainly removed any significant concentration of magnetically enhanced deposits. On the other hand, any previous articulation of the figure which is now no longer visible may have been less assiduously cleaned, and consequently may have accumulated deposits which could be detectable by the magnetometer.

The identification of similar features by resistivity survey is heavily dependant on variable moisture levels between background values and those within the features themselves (Clark 1990; Scholar 1990). At the time of survey the weather was dry and there had been no rain for the preceding two days. However, the thin soil cover was noticeably wet suggesting that the moisture balance between the topsoil and any chalk cut fills was likely to be in a state of relative equilibrium.

The physical implementation of both surveys was complicated by the steepness of slope. A 42–45° angle necessitated that both surveys be undertaken by traversing along the contour. Although this made for an uncomfortable and slow survey in both techniques, the quality of data would appear to be error free, made possible by extra care (specifically of time taken) in data recovery.

The grid lay-out, usually a simple affair accomplished with tapes, had to be undertaken by total station to ensure accurate positioning of grid intersection points.

Magnetometer survey

Figure 34 shows plots and interpretations based on the magnetometer survey. It is immediately noticeable that the outline of the Giant is almost completely unrepresented. The Giant's outline trench would appear not to contain any magnetically enhanced material. For the most part, the frequency distribution of the data indicates that the majority of the readings are uniform lying within 1.5nT of each other.

There are, however, a number of magnetic anomalies which are generally weak but locally enhanced by more extreme values. Anomaly E (Figure 34) in grid squares 2, 7, 8, 9 and 13, is a group of continuous linear anomalies in a recognizably polygonal shape. The characteristics of this feature illustrate a consistently weak anomaly interspersed by intermittent sharp peaks which are characteristic of ferrous material. The outline of this feature is partially identifiable on the ground, and can be associated with the fence which, until recently enclosed the Giant. The intermittent peaks which occur within the feature are most probably small ferrous items associated with the fence for example as nails and staples.

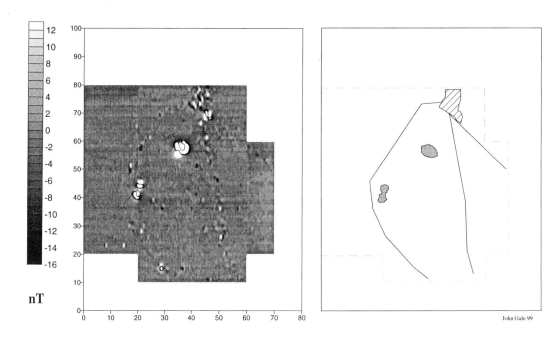

nT

John Gale 99

Figure 34. Gradiometer survey represented as a grey-scale plot, stacked trace plot, and an interpretative diagram. The distribution of readings has been clipped at +7nT. The plot highlights magnetic anomalies associated with the current articulation of the Giant. The 'coffin' shaped old fence line can clearly be seen. The shaded anomalies are ferrous spikes. The hatched area to the top of the plot is disturbance from recently grubbed out scrub.

The largest single anomaly in terms of gradient change is that located at the Giant's nose (anomaly A in squares 2 and 6 on Figure 34) and is a direct result of recent work whereby the nose was physically rebuilt as a small mound covered in galvanized metal chicken wire for stabilization. The wire registers strongly on the magnetometer because of its high iron content which disturbs the local magnetic field up to a radius of 4m from its centre.

At the extreme eastern limits of the plot there is a very disturbed area of ground (anomaly D) with readings fluctuating wildly; many display the characteristically steep gradients of ferric material. It is unclear at this stage whether this is associated with the now removed coffin-shaped fence which appears to delimit the western extent of the anomaly (perhaps where the old fence was piled up during demolition prior to its removal off site?). Alternatively, pre–1960 photographs indicate the presence of a small collection of trees between the Giant's club and the Trendle which is approximately where the anomaly occurs. As this topographic feature is no longer present the anomaly may be associated with its removal.

Anomaly C, located at the junction of squares 6, 7, 8 and 9, is primarily two isolated readings both of which have steep gradients and once again are likely to be caused by buried ferric material. They are, however, associated with a small mound approximately 0.25m in height and 5m in diameter and are probably contained within it.

Archaeologically, the most interesting anomaly identified by the magnetometer is anomaly B, a linear feature which runs approximately east-west through squares 3, 5 and 2. The magnetic response throughout the anomaly is relatively weak, never exceeding 2nT above background and generally much less. As with anomaly E there are intermittent readings of a steeper gradient which may be explained in a similar manner. This feature runs almost directly at right angles to the contour of the hill and is detectable just above the Giant's head, continues across the left shoulder, down the left side, and appears to fade in the vicinity of the left calf. It is unclear whether this anomaly pre-dates or post-dates the current outline, although its significance may lie in the fact that this line does not appear to respect the presence of the Giant's left shoulder. This anomaly probably results from the construction of a wooden chute along which to move chalk during the restoration works in 1979 (see Figure 11 and Part I above).

Resistivity survey

Although the ground conditions were not entirely suitable for resistivity survey (see above) the results were surprisingly good. Figure 35 shows a plot and interpretation of the results. The approximate outline of the Giant can be seen quite easily in certain areas. The club, extended left arm, and portions of both legs are quite visible as areas of lower resistivity. The large amorphous areas of high resistivity values above the extended left arm and to the north-west corner of the plot are likely to reflect natural variations in topsoil thickness with better moisture retention in areas of greater depth, and vice versa.

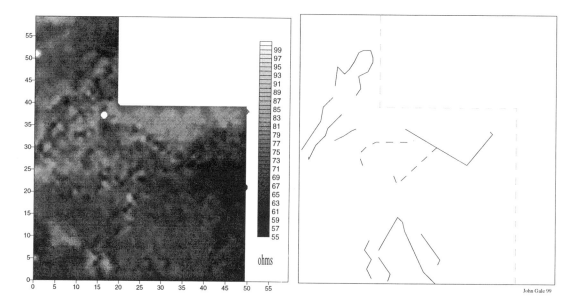

Figure 35. Resistivity survey represented as a grey-scale plot and interpretative diagram. The plot highlights anomalies associated with the current articulation of the Giant (bold line), with less distinct or quantified anomalies in a dashed line.

There is no evidence within this survey for additional features recorded by previous resistivity surveys (Castleden 1990; 1995; Clark 1983). However, this absence of corroborative evidence does not disprove their existence, and could simply reflect the poor ground conditions already mentioned.

Conclusion

This short programme of geophysical prospection has had limited success in identifying previously unknown archaeological activity which might throw some light on the past development or chronology of the Giant. However, the results do demonstrate that feature location is possible with both instruments, and that a further campaign of survey with increased sample resolution might provide better definition of recorded features and perhaps the identification of others. The potential for effective prospection is probably best met with resistivity, especially considering the results apparently obtained on other occasions (Castleden 1990; 1995; Clarke 1983).

* * * * * * * *

Summing up

TD: The results of the geophysical surveys highlight some of the archaeological difficulties inherent with using evidence which relates to remote antiquity. Most of all, however, they emphasize the rather insubstantial nature of the monument that is the Giant. Its modern impressive character as a highly visible feature is, in large measure, a consequence of active management and curation over recent years. The geophysical surveys shows areas of disturbance, some related perhaps to the presence of a clump of trees above the figure. Immediately after cleaning and scouring the Giant would have been bold and white; during intervening periods it would have been dull, overgrown, and perhaps covered in tree litter and leaves. The state of the site at various times in its history is something that needs careful consideration.

In bringing this case to a close I would like to draw out, reiterate, and emphasize five points. First, is the fact that intellectual traditions were evolving in parallel with the later history of the Giant and this bears heavily on what we read and see in the historical sources. Here we have argued that the Giant is carried along in the development of intellectual traditions from the seventeenth century onwards: the earliest we would reasonably expect it appear.

Second, we have established that there were prehistoric hill-figures in England: one has been proved beyond doubt and others almost certainly exist.

Third, we have shown that although the Cerne Giant has changed its exact form in recent centuries, the basic outline remains and can, in part at least, be detected by scientific study. In its original form, the characteristics of the Giant conform to recognized iconography and show a 'warrior god' in an image common in many parts of Europe during later prehistory. Some of the features of these gods later became associated with Roman images of Hercules and perhaps also Mars. In representational terms the Cerne Giant fits within a tradition of later Iron Age depictions of warrior gods that elsewhere find expression as figurines and carved stone heads.

Fourthly, south Dorset is an appropriate context for the Cerne Giant, and there is firm archaeological evidence for the existence of numerous rural cult centres in the area. The position of the Giant on the side of Giant Hill below a cross-ridge dyke, round barrow, and enclosure shows strong similarities with the arrangements at Uffington and Wilmington.

Fifth, the state of the site at various times in its past is critical to the matter of who could have seen what, when, and where. The detail needs sorting out, but the clear implication is that at times the Giant may have disappeared from easy view. Its more recent history may, in this sense be a history of rediscovery rather than creation.

Taken either individually or collectively, these five points, and the supporting evidence for each presented by the expert witnesses, show very clearly that the Giant is ancient, and that its construction must lie in the first millennium BC or first 200 years AD.

As asserted in the opening comments to this case, the possibility of the Giant being ancient goes back almost as far as the definition of a prehistoric timescale itself. In 1896 no less authoritative a body than the Royal Archaeological Institute met in Dorchester and visited the Giant on Monday August 9th. The party was led by Professor Boyd Dawkins who, the account tells us, 'observed that he was in ignorance as to its date' but then proceeded to show how it lay within an area covered with prehistoric burial mounds and settlements, concluding: 'by its surroundings the figure was in a position which would make one pause before assigning to any particular modern time' (Anon. 1897).

Ancient monuments do not feature widely in early histories or accounts, especially the very ancient ones. Stonehenge, for example, only features a couple of times before the seventeenth century (Chippindale 1983). The mid-eighteenth century drawing of the Cerne Giant published in 1764 in the *Gentleman's Magazine* may seem paltry, but it makes this monument a relatively well-documented early site: there are not so many ancient monuments in England with good pictorial evidence from that antiquity. Moreover, ephemeral sites that were wholly or partly invisible for some of the time would have escaped the attention of many antiquaries. It is argued here that the Cerne Giant was periodically invisible. Scourings have certainly been a regular feature of recent centuries but were not always effective (Anon. 1924). In support of this I shall leave the last word to the local archaeological community of the later nineteenth century who really should know what they were meant to be looking at. Yet, during a visit to Cerne by the Dorset Natural History and Archaeological Society on Thursday 28th June 1888, they deferred an inspection of the Giant 'until the proprietor, General Pitt Rivers, should have undertaken the necessary work of cleaning it up' (Stuart 1889, xxii). Perhaps they were making a political point, but, more likely, in common with many others who passed that way before them, they just couldn't see the Giant on the hill-slope despite his presence there!

Notes

1. Subsequently issued as a second edition under the title *Lost Gods of Albion. The chalk hill-figures of Britain* (Newman 1997)
2. Now amended, the parish accounts of 1694 having subsequently come to light, referring to a bill of three shillings for repairing the Giant (see Part II).
3. Thanks to the co-director Simon Palmer, Julie Rees-Jones who carried out the OSL dating, and the National Trust and English Heritage, the principal funders of the project.
4. This survey would not have been possible without the support and co-operation of the National Trust and English Heritage. In particular I would like to thank David Thackray, Martin Papworth and William Keighley for both allowing access to the monument and providing access to their files on the Giant. I would also like to express my deep gratitude to Julie Gale and Martin Papworth for assisting in the fieldwork in what were not always ideal conditions, and to Professor Timothy Darvill for his valuable comments on a draft of this report. Assistance in the production of the illustrations was provided by my colleague Jeff Chartrand.

Bibliography

Allen, D F, 1980, *The coins of the ancient Celts*. Edinburgh. Edinburgh University Press

Andreae, B, 1991, The image of the Celts in Etruscan, Greek and Roman art. In S Moscati (ed), *The Celts*. London and Milan. Thames and Hudson / Bompiani. 60–71

Anon., 1763a, [Anonymous letter]. *St James's Chronicle*, 404 (Tuesday, 4 October to Thursday 6 October 1763)

Anon., 1763b, [Anonymous letter]. *The Royal Magazine*, 9, 140–1

Anon., 1764, Description of a gigantic Figure. *Gentleman's Magazine*, 34, 335–6

Anon., 1897, Report of the Annual Meeting at Dorchester. *Archaeological Journal*, 54, 405–11

Anon., 1924, The Giant of Cerne Abbas. *Country Life*, October 18th 1924

Aubrey, J, 1663, *Monumenta Britannica*. Unpublished manuscript in Ashmolean Museum, Oxford [First published: J Fowles (ed), 1982. Milborne Port, Dorset Publishing Company. 2 vols.]

Bailey, D M, 1995, Gaulish and Nubian mercenaries in Ptolemaic Egypt. *Minerva*, 6.3, 36–39

Bettey, J H, 1981, The Cerne Abbas Giant: the documentary evidence. *Antiquity*, 55, 118–121

Bird, E, 1995, *Geology and scenery of Dorset*, Bradford upon Avon. Ex Libris Press

Castleden, R, 1990, Report on the geophysical survey of the Cerne Giant 1989–90. (Unpublished typescript report)

Castleden, R, 1995, The Cerne Giant Project, Phase 2: surveys undertaken in 1995. (Unpublished typescript report)

Castleden, R, 1996, *The Cerne Giant*. Wincanton. Dorset Publishing Company

Chippindale, C, 1983, *Stonehenge complete*. London. Thames and Hudson

Chippindale, C, 1988, The invention of words for the idea of 'Prehistory'. *Proceedings of the Prehistoric Society*, 54, 303–314

Clark, A J, 1983, The Cerne Giant. *Archaeological Journal*, 140, 29–30

Clark, A J, 1990, *Seeing beneath the soil: prospecting methods in archaeology*. London. Batsford

Cole, M A, Linford N T, Payne, A W and Linford, P K, 1995, Soil magnetic susceptibility measurements and their application to archaeological site investigation. In J Beavis and K Barker (eds), *Science and Site* (= Bournemouth University School of Conservation Sciences Occasional Paper 1). London and Bournemouth. Archetype. 144–162

Coles, B, 1990, Anthropomorphic wooden figures from Britain and Ireland. *Proceedings of the Prehistoric Society*, 56, 315–33

Coles, J, 1990, *Images of the past. A guide to the rock carvings and other ancient monuments of Northern Bohuslän*. Uddevalla. Bohusläns Museum

Crawford, O G S, 1929, The Giant of Cerne and other hill-figures. *Antiquity*, 3, 277–82

Cunliffe, B, 1991, *Iron Age communities in Britain* (3rd Edition). London. Routledge

Dewar, H S L, 1968, *The Dorset Ooser* (= Dorset Monographs 2). Dorchester. Dorset Natural History and Archaeological Society

Farrant, J, 1993, The Long Man of Wilmington, East Sussex: the documentary evidence reviewed. *Sussex Archaeological Collections*, 131, 129–38

Green, M, 1986, *The Gods of the Celts*. Gloucester. Alan Sutton

Green, M, 1989, *Symbol and image in Celtic religious Art*. London. Routledge

Grigson, G, 1966, *The Shell country alphabet*. London. Michael Joseph

Grinsell, L V, 1980, The Cerne Abbas Giant: 1764–1980. *Antiquity*, 54, 29–33

Van Hamel, A G, 1934, Aspects of Celtic mythology. *Proceedings of the British Academy*, 20, 3–44

Harrison, M, 1973, *The roots of witchcraft*. London. Fredrick Muller

Hawkes, C F C, 1948, A Romano-British phallic carving from Broadway, Worcestershire. *Antiquaries Journal*, 28, 166–9

Heron Allen, E, 1939, The Long Man of Wilmington and its Roman origin. *Sussex County Magazine*, 13, 655–60

Holden, E W, 1971, Some notes on the Long Man of Wilmington. *Sussex Archaeological Collections*, 109, 37–54

Hunter, M, 1975, *John Aubrey and the realm of learning*. London. Duckworth

Hutchins, J, 1774, *History of the county of Dorset* (1st Edition. Two volumes). London. W Bowyer and J Nichols

Hutchins, J, 1861–70, *History of the county of Dorset* (3rd Edition. Four volumes). London. J B Nichols and Sons

Jacobsthal, P, 1944, *Early Celtic Art*. Oxford. Clarendon Press

Legg, R, 1978, Dorset and Cerne's God of the Celts. *Dorset County Magazine*, 66 (special issue), 7–41

Lethbridge, T C, 1957, *Gogmagog*. London. Routledge and Kegan Paul

Lloyd, R, 1982, The Cerne Giant: another document? *Antiquity*, 56, 51–2 (includes comment by J Bettey)

March, H C, 1901, The Giant and maypole of Cerne. *Proceedings of the Dorset Natural History and Archaeological Society*, 22, 101–118

Marples, M, 1949, *White horses and other hill figures*. London. Country Life Books. [Reprinted 1981. Gloucester. Alan Sutton]

Maton, W G, 1794–6, *Observations relative chiefly to natural history, picturesque scenery and antiquities of the western Counties of England*. Salisbury. (2 vols)

Megaw, R, and Megaw, V, 1989, *Celtic art*. London. Thames and Hudson

Moitrieux, G, 1992, *Hercules Salutaris*. Nancy. Presses Universitaires de Nancy

Newman, P, 1987, *Gods and graven images: the chalk hill-figures of Britain*. London. Robert Hale

Newman, P, 1997, *Lost Gods of Albion. The chalk hill-figures of Britain*. Stroud. Alan Sutton

Parfitt, K, and Green, M, 1987, A chalk figurine from Upper Deal, Kent. *Britannia*, 17, 295–8

Petrie, Sir F, 1926, *The hill-figures of England* (Royal Anthropological Institute Occasional Paper 7). London. Royal Archaeological Institute

Piggott, S, 1932, The name of the Giant of Cerne. *Antiquity*, 6, 214–6

Piggott, S, 1938, The Hercules Myth – beginnings and ends. *Antiquity*, 12, 323–31

Pinder, C, Wallis, S, and Keen, L, 1998, *Dorset from the air. The county's heritage in aerial Photographs*. Tiverton. Dorset Books

Pitman, G, 1978, Navel. *Dorset County Magazine*, 70, 27

Powell, T G E, 1958, *The Celts*. London. Thames and Hudson. (Reprinted 1980 in Revised format)

Putnam, B, 1984, *Roman Dorset*. Wimborne. The Dovecote Press

RCHM, 1952, *An inventory of the historical monuments in the County of Dorset. Volume I. West Dorset*. London. HMSO. (Reprinted with amendments 1974)

RCHM, 1970a, *An inventory of the historical monuments in the County of Dorset. Volume 2. South-east*. London. HMSO. (Three parts)

RCHM, 1970b, *An inventory of the historical monuments in the County of Dorset. Volume 3. Central Dorset*. London. HMSO. (Two parts)

Ross, A, 1967, *Pagan Celtic Britain*. London. Routledge

Rudd, C, 1986, Cernunnos: Celtic god and Christian devil. *Dorset Year Book*, 77, 69–75

Scholar, I, 1990, *Archaeological prospecting and remote sensing*. Cambridge. Cambridge University Press

Sharples, N M, 1991, *Maiden Castle. Excavations and field survey 1985–6* (= Historic Buildings and Monuments Commission for England Archaeological Report 19). London. English Heritage

Stead, I, 1988, Chalk figurines of the Parisi. *Antiquaries Journal*, 68, 9–29

Stuart, M G, 1889, The Proceedings of the Dorset Natural History and Antiquarian Field Club during 1888. *Proceedings of the Dorset Natural History and Archaeological Society*, 10, xv-xxxiii

Stukeley, W, 1740, *Stonehenge. A temple restor'd to the British Druids*. London. W Innys and R Manby

Stukeley, W, 1764, [The Cerne Giant]. *Minute Book of the Society of Antiquaries of London*, 9, 199–200

Sydenham, J, 1842, *Baal Durotrigensis: a dissertation on the ancient colossal figure at Cerne, Dorsetshire*. London. W Pickering

Tite, M S, 1972, The influence of geology on the magnetic susceptibility of soils on archaeological sites. *Archaeometry*, 14, 229–36

Vyner, B E, 1994, The territory and ritual: cross-ridge boundaries and the prehistoric landscape of the Cleveland Hills, northeast England. *Antiquity*, 68, 27–38

Webster, G, 1986, *The British Celts and their Gods under Rome*. London. Batsford

Wilson, D, 1851, *The archaeology and prehistoric annals of Scotland*. Edinburgh. Sutherland and Knox

Woodward, A, 1992, *Shrines and sacrifice*. London. Batsford/English Heritage

PART III

The case for a post-medieval Giant

A seventeenth-century marvel?

Ronald Hutton

The notion of the Giant as a relic of the ancient pagan past is so familiar, so long established, and so firmly embedded in the popular consciousness, that it is probably natural to many people to view a challenge to this idea as a typical piece of aggressive modern academic revisionism. In fact, doubts concerning it have been expressed ever since the local records of Cerne Abbas were first studied, over 60 years ago; I would go so far as to suggest that they are natural to anybody who considers those records. It was F J H Darton who first pointed to the problem, in the mid–1930s (Darton 1935, 319–21). His warnings were not forgotten, but set aside, until two colleagues of mine at Bristol, Leslie Grinsell and Joseph Bettey, repeated and reinforced them at the beginning of the 1980s (Grinsell 1980; Bettey 1981). Dr Bettey's work, in particular, was so forceful that it ensured that a proper debate of the matter could not be postponed indefinitely; although it took a further one and a half decades, and the enterprise of the new University of Bournemouth, for one to develop. He provides further arguments for questioning the orthodox dating of the Giant, amounting at last to a full-scale rejection of it.

The crux of the problem may be illustrated neatly by contrasting it with another very famous English hill-figure: the Uffington White Horse. As has been made plain (Miles in Part II), the Horse is an undoubtedly ancient piece of work, and now dated firmly to prehistory by scientific processes which have yet to be deployed upon the Giant of Cerne. Any use of it as an argument for comparable antiquity for the Giant, however, rebounds immediately, for there was never any suspicion that the Uffington figure could be medieval or early modern. From the eleventh century AD onwards it is well recorded, in estate documents and then in travellers' tales as well. It is exactly the absence of this sort of reference which makes the case of the Cerne carving so glaringly different.

Establishing the date and nature of the earliest record of the Giant known at present is an important consideration, and I would like to here to introduce my first witness, Vivian Vale. Mr Vale is a local historian and Chairman of the Cerne Local History Society. For many years he has been investigating the early history of the parish of Cerne Abbas.

* * * * * * * *

Churchwardens and the other God

Vivian Vale

Whatever the disposition of the professional archaeologist, a layman may well find it more prudent to approach the quaking bog of Giant legend from the comparatively firm ground of a more recent age. Indeed, in this particular context he may do worse than begin by cutting into the saga at a point early in our own century: to be precise, with an item from the *Daily Mail* of the 22nd of August 1905 – an item which, in front of the entire nation, pointed an accusatory finger at the host village. 'Vanishing Giant' it is headed and continues:

> An interesting survival of prehistoric England is threatened with destruction owing to neglect ... The antiquity of the figure is accepted by all archaeologists ... It is several hundred years since the furrows which outline the figure were scoured and relined with chalk. Gradually the latter has been washed away by the winter rains, and it is now barely visible. Grass has so encroached on the channels that, seen from a distance, the details of the gigantic figure are hard to trace, though the uncouth human form is still recognisable. The cost of renovating is estimated at about £12, but no-one in the locality knows where the money is to come from.

There follows a list of his dimensions (all save one).

Thus the *Mail* in its best 'Wake up England' vein. Two questions suggest themselves. First, did the village deserve this public reproach? Seemingly, yes. One has to go back some twenty years, to May 1886, to find the local newspaper – usually pretty assiduous in noting such things – recording the previous clean-up of the figure: though in January 1889 he had been enclosed by iron fencing – the first time His Mightiness was confined within a metal playpen.

Second question: what was Cerne's response to journalistic obloquy? Prompt but unprofessional, one might judge. Within two months the *Dorset County Chronicle* could report that:

> On Thursday a party of ladies and gentlemen, armed with spades, hoes &c, took Cerne by storm, but the fears of the inhabitants were soon allayed, for it transpired that they had only come to clean out the trenches of the Giant. In a very short time they were hard at work, and before the end of the afternoon the long grass was removed and the figure is now more easily discerned.

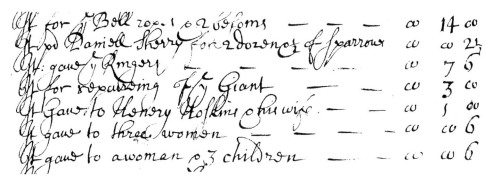

Figure 36. *Extract from the Cerne Abbas Churchwarden's Accounts for 1694. (Reproduced courtesy of the Dorset County Record Office)*

But more than another two years were allowed to elapse before the experts arrived on the scene (30th January 1908) backed by subscribers including the landowner himself (Alexander Pitt Rivers), the Dorset Field Club, and the Geological Survey Office. In the presence of their representatives the site was professionally restored under the direction of Jonathan Hardy, who had done this before in the late General Pitt River's time.

Now, these two contrasted approaches may serve to remind us that preservation of the Giant has never followed a consistent pattern of expertise. In between professionally conducted operations have been interspersed attacks in which, with the acquiescence of the landowners but the agony of archaeologists, willing but unskilled folk have just pitched in and had a go. Bearing in mind, then, that the site has suffered both long periods of neglect and many assaults by amateurs, let us take another cut into the saga, this time a good three hundred years back, in fact to the earliest substantive reference to the deity this writer has come upon. It is a single entry in the churchwarden's accounts for St Mary's church dated the 4th November 1694 (Figure 36). It is quite terse: 'For repairing of ye Giant 3s'. However, that contribution would compare with the £12 needed in 1905, it was certainly more than the sum periodically dispensed for cleaning St Augustine's Well; rather less than that laid out for (say) the construction of a cucking stool. But recorded without comment. A routine matter, one might infer.

One could not be more wrong. From Cerne's earliest surviving parish accounts for the year 1628 to the present, that entry is unique. By tradition the site of the Giant was and always has been the responsibility of the landowner, from Abbey to National Trust. Whatever its state of neglect by the 1690s, how (one wonders) could the vestry conceivably have been moved to cross the line separating parish obligations from private on this solitary occasion? Churchwardens did not lie awake nights thinking up new ways of spending the rate money so painfully extracted: unless, perhaps on some project which might incidentally commemorate themselves – and there are indeed a number of examples where past wardens' names or initials are memorialized in and over and around St Mary's. *A fortiori* it is inconceivable that any part of the hard-gotten parish fisc would be allotted to underwrite the whimsy of some gentleman of the manor with a talent for Romano-British pastiche. Whatever was executed on that hill in the 1690s was no *jeu d'esprit* or folly.

So, we ask: what possible accumulation of circumstances, together (we are entitled to presume) with no slight sense of historical responsibility, could have compelled the wardens to commit, and the vestry to sanction, that which strictly speaking was a malversation of funds? Three such contemporary circumstances may strike one as relevant and plausible. The first arose directly from the Civil War. At mid-century the lord of Cerne Manor and landowner was Denzil Holles, MP for Dorchester (Figure 37). In 1651, while he was a refugee in France, the Council of State ordered the sequestration of his estates, on the unlikely supposition that he was conspiring with old cavaliers. Though the order was never executed, it hung over his head until the Restoration, a persistent disincentive (one must suppose) to development and maintenance.

Figure 37. Denzil Holles (1599–1680)

Secondly, while briefly revisiting his seat after the sequestration order, Holles heard from, his wife strong complaints about the mismanagement and neglect of the estate by his agent of some years past, one Ezekias Lambe. When he arranged for an audit, Lambe's papers mysteriously went up in smoke. A formal complaint as to his conduct was subsequently filed in Chancery, but by then Lambe, guilty or not, clearly had other, and more lucrative, fish to fry. Surviving deeds show him to have acquired in 1649 a principal interest in the operation of the Cerne mills (formerly the Abbey mills), a proprietorship maintained until 1713 when he sold it on in extreme old age.[1] That Mill Lane was for many years known as Lambe's Lane testifies to the durability of his family fortunes there – a more attractive prospect certainly for Ezekias than managing an estate under sentence of sequestration.

Thirdly, there was the death in 1666 of Holles's wife, widow of the previous lord of Cerne Manor and estates, John Freke. It was this marriage (his second, her third) which had brought to Holles the house and land but not (as it seems) as a simple dowry. Whatever the terms of her jointure, her son Thomas Freke immediately on her death laid claim to the reversion of the estate 'fearing it wd run away'. 'Done like a Dorsetshire country gentleman' commented Holles bitterly and once again *in absentia* abroad, though this time as ambassador and ennobled. Here was the germ of lengthy contention: for Holle's sojourns in France, at first prudential, then official, were further prolonged from personal choice and by marriage to a third, French wife. Indeed, his biographer (Crawford 1979) has inferred that death in 1680 found him still abroad, judging by the long interval between that occurrence and the bringing back of his body for burial in St Peter's, Dorchester. Thereafter, wrangling over the estate continued between his family and his step-family, to cease only with the extinction of the Holles peerage on the death of the 3rd Lord in 1694 – coincidentally the year of the churchwardens' intervention and subvention.

After fifty and more troubled years, then, had passed over and around the Giant, the problem of restoring whatever had survived neglect was one which the parish of St Mary's. though themselves bearing no official responsibility, felt it exceptionally incumbent upon them to help address. In so doing, it is reasonable to surmise, they believed they were contributing to an enterprise of integrity. But was it with a sense of restoring a work of indefinite antiquity? Or simply with a mind to uncover again a spectacle of which their grandfathers and great-grandfathers had preserved a folk memory they valued? We can only conclude that some kind of revival occurred in the 1690s, exactly what was revived remaining ultimately a matter for the archaeologists; and that their rescue of something from obscurity was timely not only in that it remedied the neglect of immediately preceding years, but inasmuch as it thereby made feasible the speculations of the great antiquarians – Pococke, Stukeley, Hutchins – of the following century.

To the churchwardens, their pens marching stiffly across the pages of their ledger, let us devote a postscript. In a little more than a century after that three-shilling entry of 1694 arrived evidence that they had (as it were) domesticated their Giant. The leads of the aisle roofs of St Mary's church bear a sequence of inscriptions each denoting, from 1682 onward, an occasion for repair. The panels commemorating the repairs of 1800 and 1843 bear as usual the names of the contemporary wardens, but now surrounded in relief by stylized figures of – the Giant. Their successors, offering Sunday by Sunday their praises to the Three-in-One, may reflect with satisfaction that overhead is represented, in sextuplicate, the ancient alternative deity.

* * * * * * * *

Where the Giant is not

RH: My concern, and that of Joseph Bettey (1981 and below), is more with the very large number of earlier sources which ought to have mentioned the Giant, had it existed in their time, and did not. Dr Bettey provides below a host of Tudor and Stuart travellers who knew northern Dorset well and provided descriptions of the area, without a single reference to the figure. To this class of negative evidence, can be added the case of John Aubrey, the antiquarian who has often been called England's first field archaeologist. He grew up in the neighbouring county of Wiltshire, went to school at Blandford, and in his huge output of published and unpublished works made many references to the ancient monuments of the Wessex chalklands, without ever including one to the Cerne Giant.

More disturbing still is the testimony of estate and other local records. It must be stressed that Cerne Abbas is unusually well provided with them for the period between the thirteenth and early seventeenth centuries, and it was the remarkable absence of any appearance of the figure in these documents which first alerted Darton to the problem. To review all of this evidence I would like to introduce my second witness Joseph Bettey. Dr Bettey's work has already been mentioned several times in this case and he is well-known through the published literature on the Giant (Betty 1981).

* * * * * * * *

The Cerne Giant revisited

Joseph Betty

In an article published in *Antiquity* in 1981 I discussed the wealth of documentary evidence relating to Cerne Abbas and the remarkable absence of any mention of the Giant until the very end of the seventeenth century. At that time I avoided the conclusion that the Giant did not exist earlier, only emphasizing that he is not even hinted at in all the numerous surviving records, and I was at pains to stress the point which has frequently been made since that 'absence of evidence is not evidence of absence'(Betty 1981). Since that time I have pursued much detailed research on the documentary sources relating to the landscape, agriculture and rural society of Dorset in the sixteenth and seventeenth centuries, and have assiduously followed any references to Cerne Abbas in the records of the Court of Augmentations and in Courts of the Chancery and the Exchequer. As a result of this further research, I feel sure that the figure of the Giant was not there in the sixteenth century and only appeared at some time in the mid-seventeenth century, possibly during the upheavals of the Civil War and its aftermath.

The following account reviews this further research and again marshalls the arguments for believing that the Giant did not exist earlier. It goes on to suggest that all the evidence points strongly to the fact that the Giant was cut at the orders of Denzil Holles whilst he was in enforced exile or when he was living at Cerne Abbas during the 1650s.

The first and possibly the strongest argument against the existence of the Giant during the Middle Ages is the antiquity, wealth, and prestige of the Benedictine abbey which had been founded in the tenth century and continued to dominate Cerne and provide the main reason for the existence of the town until the dissolution in 1539. Like the numerous other ancient Benedictine foundations in the west country, Cerne abbey was very well endowed and at the time of the dissolution the abbot and his sixteen monks enjoyed the very large income of nearly £600 a year (Record Commission 1810–34, I, 253–7; Hutchins 1861–70, IV, 15–37). The widespread abbey estates stretched across Dorset, and included all of Cerne and the surrounding lands, as well as control of the weekly markets and annual fairs in the town. Contrary to common belief, there is no firm evidence of laxity or neglect of religious duties at the abbey during the later Middle Ages. The bishop's registers of the diocese of Salisbury contain no criticism of the abbey or of its monks, and the extensive estates seem to have been well administered and profitable (Horn 1982; Timmins 1994; Wright 1985).

There was a monastic school at which local boys were educated and the abbey appears to have lived up to the intentions of its founders and provided a focus for religious life and culture in the district. In Cerne itself the survival of the long row of timber-fronted houses in Abbey Street dating from *c.* 1500 and constructed during the time of Abbott Thomas Sams (1497–1509) to form a row of shops by the market place, provides evidence of the way in which the abbey continued to husband its resources and exploit its opportunities during the decade before the dissolution (RCHM 1952, 77–80). The fact the Abbott John Vanne (1458–70) rebuilt the Guest House which still survives suggests that accommodation was needed for visitors to the abbey and for travellers along the road. Its estates and income are listed in the *Valor Ecclesiasticus* of 1535 where the abbey is shown as possessing a flock of over 2,000 sheep at Cerne a further 700 at nearby Nether Cerne and another 3,000 on other manors. (Record Commission 1810–34, I 253–7).

Several *Inquisitions Post Mortem* survive in detail: the possessions of the abbey, its estates, properties, rights and privileges but none of these late-medieval records gives any hint of a hill-side figure, and the hill overlooking the abbey continued to be known as Trendle Hill from the small prehistoric earthwork at its summit (Fry 1916–23).

All the stories concerning the alleged depravity of the last abbot, Thomas Corton, which have served to blacken the reputation of the abbey, are based upon the obviously biased statements of a disgruntled monk, William Christchurch. His charges against the abbot and his fellow monks are so exaggerated as to be quite unbelievable, and in particular it is incredible that an elderly abbot could have been so sexually active as William Christchurch accuses him of being. Christchurch's real motivation appears in his final statements when he complains of the harsh discipline imposed upon him by the abbott, of his imprisonment and final expulsion from the abbey.[2] This hardly suggests an unruly and misgoverned household. Moreover, in spite of the pensions offered to the monks and the extremely generous inducements to the abbott, Thomas Corton and his monks refused to surrender their house to the King until finally forced to do so by the royal commissioner, John Tregonwell. Not until March 1539 was the abbey suppressed, and then not before the monks had offered to pay large sums to the King and to Thomas Cromwell if they could be allowed to continue their religious life at Cerne.[3]

It is inconceivable to suppose that throughout its long history, successive generations of celibate monks in this wealthy Benedictine house would have continued a life dedicated to prayer, praise and abstinence beneath the figure of a sexually-exultant Giant looming above them on the neighbouring hill-side. Nor is it credible that the religious would have sanctioned or supported the regular scouring necessary to maintain a large chalk-cut figure. It is true that some carvings on parish churches have obvious sexual references, but these are quite different in scale and character from the Giant, and are clearly designed as a warning against the dangers of unbridled lust and sexual activity. They are certainly not intended as a glorification of sexual power (Weir and Jerman 1986).

It is also important to realize that Cerne was not an isolated settlement in a remote valley. Apart from the wealth and importance of the abbey, the town was on the main road between Sherborne and Dorchester, while its markets and fairs were crucial to the economic and social life of the surrounding area. Many travellers journeyed through the valley and past the abbey gates, and the huge figure of a Giant would hardy have gone unnoticed. In the summer of 1542 John Leland stayed with the Strangways family at Melbury House, only seven miles from Cerne, and his hosts, knowing of his passion for topography and antiquities, would surely have discussed the nearby abbey and its site with him. Leland wrote at length about the early history of Cerne and about the legends connected with the foundations of the abbey, but he makes no mention of any Giant (Smith 1906–8, I, 247–8 and IV, 73, 107–9; Chandler 1993, 1334). Even more remarkable is the absence of any mention by Thomas Gerard who wrote a *General Description of the County of Dorset* early in the seventeenth century. Thomas Gerard (1592–1634) was a member of a wealthy family who lived at Trent near Sherborne. In 1618 he married Ane, daughter of Robert Coker of Mappowder, which is some seven miles from Cerne. It is clear from his detailed account of the topography, agriculture, markets and ports of Dorset, that Gerard had visited all parts of the country to collect material for his survey, and he wrote with obviously first-hand knowledge of the places he described. His section on Cerne mentions the recently-completed house built at Upcerne by Sir Robert Mellor, and dwells on the scanty remains of the abbey buildings 'nowe whollie ruinated and onlie a small parte of the House standing, with a faire Tower or Gatehouse over which you maye see graven the Arms of Richard, Earle of Cornwall'. Clearly Gerard had visited Cerne, and it is totally incredible that he would not have mentioned the Giant if it had existed (Gerard 1980).

The dissolution of the abbey at Cerne, the destruction of its buildings and the dispersal of its lands produced many records, including surveys, rentals, descriptions, legal disputes and depositions concerning land-use, grazing rights, buildings and manorial customs, but careful examination of all these sources has revealed no hint of a Giant. Not all of these records could be expected to mention a hill-side figure, but some would surely have referred to the Giant if only as a boundary mark in the landscape, if he had existed. A survey of the abbey lands made for the Court of Augmentations in 1540 lists all the fields and downland, while an account roll of the same date includes all the field names, but the hill on which the Giant now stands continued to be listed as 'Trendle Hill'.[4]

During the decades after the dissolution the former abbey lands passed through many hands in a complex web of leases and sub-leases. In 1541 a lease was granted to Philip Vanwilder who immediately sub-let much of the land and also began the long process of demolishing the abbey church and other buildings. Shortly afterwards Vanwilder died and the lease passed to his widow and thereafter to her second husband. The result was a series of legal disputes between tenants and sub-tenants over rights, title, custom and rents, and a mass of evidence was produced, including numerous depositions. It is not necessary to pursue these complex disputes of the 1550s and 1560s beyond the fact that nowhere in all the documents is there any reference to the Giant (Dugdale 1846, II, 621024). In 1565 the lease from the Crown was acquired by John Fowler; in 1574 it passed to John Dudley, John Ayscough and others; and in 1579 to Edmund Downing and John Walker. Early in the 1580s a major interest in Cerne was obtained by Thomas Freke of Iwerne Courtney. None of these men lived at Cerne, regarding it simply as a source of profit, and sub-letting all the land.[5]

Further legal disputes during the 1570s also produced a mass of detailed depositions about many aspects of the landscape at Cerne and about the former abbey. The depositions of elderly witnesses concerning a dispute over rights of way through the former abbey grounds and over burials in the churchyard which adjoined the abbey precinct are particularly informative. The witnesses were all men who had known the monastery before its dissolution. Some had been monastic servants, others had attended the monastery school, while one, Henry Wiliams of Hilton, had for 20 years after the dissolution lived in the gatehouse of the former abbey. William Tyser of Sydling St Nicholas, aged 90, had been a scholar at the abbey for 13 years; John Wheaton of Dewlish, yeoman, had known the abbey for the previous 57 years and had been a 'servant in th'abbie to the sexton of the church and after served the Abbot in the butterie three yeres'. Most interesting of all was William Dyer of Hermitage, a former monk, whose pension of £5 6s 8d per annum was still being paid by the Crown in 1575. The witnesses provided a great deal of detailed information about the abbey and its precincts. They described the graveyard which measured 35 perches or 'luggs' and 'is adjoining to the house of the said late monastery uppon the north and bounded by a wall on the west and by a way by which the late Abbot brought his carriages and his horses to a ground called the Bever on the south while the Abbey stode with the churche which now ys downe on the easte'. The Abbot had allowed the parishioners of Cerne to be buried there and had provided nearby another burial ground for the inhabitants of Nether Cerne, while the monks' cemetery called Muncken Lytten adjoined both. Now the new owners were refusing access and denying other ancient customs and rights of way.

The witnesses also described the north and south gates of the abbey, the porter's lodging and 'a little wicket through which men passed'. The north gate led to 'convenient high waies from and to all partes of the cuntrye adjoininge the said abbey'. By the north gate stood the abbey brewery. The south gate was destroyed in riots during the reign of Edward VI which 200 men from Cerne and neighbouring parishes rose in protest against the enclosure of lands by the new owners and 'tore down the hedges about Cerne and did break or shake in pieces the south gate'.[6]

This mass of evidence about the former monastery and its surroundings contains no suggestion of a Giant on the hill-side overlooking all the lands in question. It would surely have been mentioned by one of the witnesses and we can only conclude that it did not exist at that time.

By the early 1590s the Cerne lands were being leased by Robert Freke of Iwerne Courtney, and when he died in 1593 his *Inquisition Post Mortem* listed all his property in great detail, but again with no mention of any Giant.[7] Another notable Elizabethan figure who knew Cerne Abbas and would undoubtedly have referred to the Giant in both prose and verse if it had existed was Sir Walter Raleigh. In 1592 he had acquired his estate at Sherborne and for the next twelve years spent must time in Dorset. At Sherborne castle the colourful friends who gathered around Sir Walter and his indiscreet brother Carew Raleigh, and their wide-ranging discussion of religion produced numerous local rumours of atheism. A summer party in Sir George Trenchard's house at Wolfeton, a few miles south of Cerne on the road to Dorchester in 1593, attended by several leading Dorset gentlemen and clergy, including Sir Walter Raleigh and his brother, led to a lengthy discussion of religious matters. Such conversations and rumours were to lead to a Privy Council enquiry into atheism which was conducted at Cerne

Abbas in 1594 before numerous witnesses. Raleigh would already have been well acquainted with Cerne, for he had tried to obtain a lease of nearby Upcerne, from where today there is a clear view down the attractive valley to the Giant. Raleigh's wayward spirit would have delighted in the Giant, and he would not have failed to make use of his startling image in his writing if he had seen it. But like all other sixteenth-century writers, Raleigh makes no mention of the Giant (Lloyd 1967, 233–94).

This wealth of sixteenth-century evidence and detailed description of the lands and property at Cerne, and the complete absence of any reference to the Giant, would be sufficient to convince most people that the figure did not exist at that time. Some who are wedded to the notion that since the figure looks old it must be old might still try to argue that, apart from the incontrovertible evidence of the field names, many of the sources so far considered *could* have ignored the Giant. But they can hardly disregard the final piece of evidence from this period.

Early in the seventeenth century the lands at Cerne reverted to the Crown and became part of the possessions of the Prince of Wales. A detailed, professional survey was conducted in 1617 by the two most reputable surveyors of the time, John Norden the elder and his son, also John Norden, of 'divers Manors, Landes and Tenements lately granted unto Prince Charles by our Sovereigne Lord James his most loving father'. The Nordens carefully listed the tenants, their holdings, rents and services, the arable and meadow, the customs of the manor of Cerne, and commented on the inadequacy of the manorial officials and the poor government of the town:

> ...the towne is most unorderlie governed, and as unrulie as if there were
> no Magistrates, for the officers are weake men, and they that injoye the
> prinicpall howses of the towne dwell from them, and lett them to a
> masse of base people, meere mendicantes...

They also mentioned the weekly market and three annual fairs and described the 'ancient and spatious' Guildhall in the market place, with various shops beneath it 'and places convenient for manie uses touchinge the Markett'. Like much else in Cerne at this time, the Guildhall was falling into ruin, and the Survey provides a vivid picture of the poverty and social problems in the town which, with the departure of the monks and the destruction of the wealthy abbey, had lost the principal reason for its existence. Most notably, the Survey lists the pastures and common sheep grazing around Cerne including:

> 3 Sheep Downes, viz Rowdon about 90 acres Weame Hill about 120 acres
> and Trendle Hillabout 130 acres.[8]

It is impossible that a figure so large as the Giant would not have given his name to the hill on which he now stands, if he had existed at that time. Had there been any sign of a Giant or even a faint outline in the grass, it is certain that the Nordens would have mentioned it, just as in the same survey they noted that at

Bere Regis the earthworks of an Iron Age hillfort were visible on the summit of Woodbury Hill.

It remains true that 'absence of evidence is not evidence of absence', but the fact that so many different sources and such a variety of observers throughout the sixteenth century did not mention what is now by far the most dramatic feature of the topography if Cerne Abbas, can only mean that it was not there, and that it appeared in the landscape at a later date.

If we accept that all the evidence, negative though it is, points to that fact that the Giant did not exist in the sixteenth century, the next question is obviously when was he created and who is responsible? The first definite documentary reference to the figure occurs in the Cerne Abbas churchwardens' accounts for 1694 when 3s 0d was paid 'for repaireing of the Giant', so obviously he had already been there for some time.[9] In what follows it will be argued that the Giant was made during all the upheavals and confusion of the Civil War and its aftermath, and that the man responsible for his creation was Denzil Holles.

The Civil War had a devastating effect upon Dorset, for although no major battle was fought in the county, it had considerable strategic importance for both sides in the conflict. Not only did it posses a number of well-fortified castles and strongholds such as Corfe, Portland, Sherborne and Lulworth, but the county also formed an important link between London and the royalist west. During the course of the war, Lyme Regis withstood a protracted siege, Beaminster was burnt as were some of the houses in Cerne Abbas and Shaftesbury, the castles at Sherborne, Corfe and Lulworth saw major conflict, while great damage was done to the mansions at Cranborne, Chideock and Abbotsbury (Bayley 1910).

The passing and re-passing of the armies of both sides through the county caused immense damage, plundering and requisitioning of goods, cattle, horses and foodstuffs. Estate accounts for the period are full of references to the sufferings of tenants and to the continued fear of the armies or of the numerous, small and ill-disciplined bands of soldiers which roamed the countryside (VCH 1908, 150–9). It was the feeling of helpless outrage among the rural communities of Dorset at the loss of their goods, livestock and crops which led to the remarkable rising of the Clubmen in the county during 1645. The Clubmen claimed to be neutral in the struggle between King and Parliament, and were concerned only to protect themselves and their property against the damage caused by both sides.[10] Following the defeat of the royalist cause and the execution of the King, government by Parliament and the minute supervision of daily life which this involved provoked strong reaction in many parts of Dorset, and many of the leading county officials proved to be very unpopular (Mayo 1902). It was against this background that the Giant was created on the land belonging to Denzil Holles, who had played a leading role in the political life of the nation since 1620s and who represented Dorchester in Parliament (Crawford 1979).

Denzil Holles (1599–1680) was the younger son of John Holles, first earl of Clare. As a younger member of Parliament during the 1620s he fiercely opposed the royal policy, and in 1629 he was one of the members who held the Speaker in his chair while the House passed resolutions against the King's proposals. For this typically rash and passionate action Holles was imprisoned in the Tower for a year. He lived abroad for much of the 1630s, but in the Parliaments of 1640–42 Holles was again a leading critic of the King, and was one of the five members impeached on charges of high treason. When the Civil War began, Holles raised his own regiment for Parliament and fought at Edgehill. But gradually Holles began to dread the supremacy of the Parliamentary army more than the pretensions of the King, and in face of the suffering which the war brought to the civil population of the country, he became a steady advocate of peace, urging a reconciliation with the King. This brought him into conflict with his former colleagues, and particularly with Cromwell, for whom he conceived an intense hatred as the main obstacle to a settlement of the conflict. Having failed in his attempts to secure a treaty between Parliament and the King, Holles fled to Normandy in 1648 and stayed there until after 1654. Following the Restoration he was created a baron as Lord Holles of Ifield. During the period 1663–66 he was the English ambassador in Paris.

To appreciate that Holles was certainly capable of a grand gesture of defiance such as the creation of the Giant it is important to appreciate his fierce unyielding temper. All contemporaries agree that Holles was a proud, passionate man, unwilling to compromise his views, unable to bear contradiction and with an intense sense of the justice of his own cause. It was said of him by Gilbert Burnett, Bishop of Salisbury, that he was:

> a man of great courage and as great a pride...He... argued well, but too vehemently, for he could not bear contradiction. He had the soul of an old stubborn Roman in him... (Burnet 1833, I, 177)

Holles was intensely conscious of his position as son of an Earl, and the unruly episode in Parliament in 1629 when he held down the speaker and which brought him national fame as well as imprisonment, was in keeping with his quick temper and proud refusal to accept defeat. A letter written by Holles to the Earl of Salisbury in 1638 illustrates his fiery nature and inordinate pride. Through his wife Holles had acquired the tenancy of a house and lands in Damerham in Hampshire, part of the Cranborne estate of the Earl of Salisbury. In 1638 the Earl's steward at Cranborne, Samuel Stillingfleet, delivered to Holles a letter from the Earl complaining of the waste of timber trees and other misdemeanours which he alleged that Holles committed on the land. The letter produced an immediate and violent response from Holles who complained bitterly and at length about the Earl's letter:

> ... The style is such as I cannot believe yourself did dictate it, who better do know how to write to the son of one of your own rank, nor do I think but that you have so bred your younger sons that there is none of them but would stomach the receiving of such a letter... for beginning, middle

and end, inside and outside, are all below me, who am it seems above your secretary's level, that he knows not how to write to me in such a manner as is fit.

Holles went on to claim that any timber he had taken had been used in repairing the dwelling house on the property, 'a rotten house not fit for a gentleman to live in', and he continued:

> Dont't think I will run to your officer in Cranborne, or I know not where, to beg a tree and tarry his pleasure to assign it to me. I use my own tenants better. To a gentleman, or one I respect, I am not so nippy a landlord to stand strictly on assigning him every tree... [11]

Through out his long life Holles continued to be involved in similar fierce quarrels brought about by his pride, fiery temper and unyielding spirit. Another manifestation of his stubborn insistence upon his own rights is the number of law suits which he initiated, especially during the 1650' when he became involved in long and acrimonious disputes over lands and property at Damerham (Hampshire), Ifield (Sussex) Hermitage, Cerne Abbas, and other places in Dorset.

In 1626 Holles married Dorothy, the only child and sole heiress of Francis Ashley, the Recorder of Dorchester, and became the member of Parliament for Dorchester. On Ashley's death in 1635 Holles also acquired a considerable estate including the house formed out of the former Franciscan friary in Dorchester.[12] Dorothy died in 1640, and in 1642 Holles married Jane, eldest daughter of Sir John Shirley. She had already been married twice, first to Sir Walter Covert and secondly to John Freke of Cerne Abbas, and it was through her that Holles acquired his interest in Cerne and the surrounding lands. Apart from the years he spent in France, Holles lived at Cerne until Jane's death in April 1666 when the lands at Cerne reverted to her son Thomas Freke of Iwerne Courtney. In September 1666 he married Esther, daughter of Gideon le Lou of Columbieres, Normandy who outlived him (Hutchins 1861–70, IV, 86–7).

It is clear from the few fragments of Holles's surviving correspondence that he was very attached to Cerne, and yearned to be there during the long years of his exile abroad during the period 1648 to 1654.[13] These years were the low point of Holles's life, when all his attempts to secure reconciliation had failed, the King had been executed, Cromwell was triumphant and the Parliamentary army was all-powerful. In exile Holles saw all of his greatest fears for his country realized. Above all, he blamed the intransigent attitude and ruthless determination of Cromwell for what he regarded as the unnecessary bloodshed and destruction which had occurred and the Parliamentary tyranny which had resulted.

In 1648 during the early months of his enforced exile in Normandy, Holles wrote a long *Memoir* recording in detail the events of the period since 1641, justifying his own part in them and making a vitriolic attack on Cromwell and the Parliamentary Army. This is not so much a memoir as a defence on his own actions and a total condemnation of his political opponents. The *Memoir* was printed in 1699 and runs to more than two hundred printed pages (Holles 1699). Its tone is evident at the outset, since it is addressed as follows:

> To the Unparalleled Couple, Mr Oliver St John, his Majesty's Solicitor General, and Mr Oliver Cromwell, the Parliament's Lieutenant General, the two grand designers of the Ruin of three kingdoms.

The *Memoir* is a violent, intemperate attack on the Parliamentary leaders, their refusal to compromise with the King and the desolation which they have brought to the country.

> The meanest of Men, the basest and vilest of the Nation, the lowest of the people have got the Power into their Hands; trampled upon the Crown; baffled and misused the Parliament; violated the Laws; destroyed or supprest the Nobility and Gentry of the Kingdom; oppressed the Liberties of the People in general; broke in sunder all Bands and Tyes of Religion, Conscience, Duty, Loyalty, Faith, common Honesty, and good Manners; cast off all fear of God and Man; and now lord it over the Parsons and Estates of all sorts and ranks of Men from the King on his Throne, to the Beggar in his cottage...

The King had chastised the people with whips, but Parliament was chastising them with serpents. Holles suggests that the excesses of royal power have now been curbed and cannot be revived, so that only the evil schemes and base ambition of the parliamentary leaders prevents them reaching a peaceful settlement with the King. Holles accuses them of base depravity in allowing the Army to become more powerful even than Parliament:

> They looked upon the Army as even at their doors, *Hannibal ad portas*, and all of them Children of Anak, armed Giants not to be resisted.

The result had been burdens upon the people even greater than those imposed by the King. He concludes the *Memoir* with:

> I shall not trouble myself any more with blazoning their Coat Armour, which is nothing but false colours and base metals; their Impostures, Contradictions, Falshoods, Hypocrisies, and Damnable Delusions being beyond all Heraldry and not to be tricked within the compass of any Scutcheon.

In a significant passage in his impassioned and almost hysterical attack upon Cromwell, Holles accused him of villainous, evil designs and wrote that:

> the people are ruined and inslaved to a rebellious Army, they deliver up themselves and Kingdom to the will of their Enemies; prostitute all to the Lust of heady and violent Men. Suffer Mr Cromwell to saddle, ride, switch and spur them at his pleasure.

No-one reading these wild accusations and long denunciation of Cromwell and all his works could doubt that Holles, fretting in exile and watching with horror the train of events in England, could have authorized the creation of a grand gesture of defiance towards Cromwell on his land at Cerne Abbas. Elsewhere in the country supporters of Cromwell were depicting their leader as the British Hercules, for example, at Highnam in Gloucestershire, the Parliamentarian Colonel William Cooke included a large statue of Cromwell as a burly half-naked Hercules, complete with club, above the doorway of his new house (Figure 38; Mowl and Earnshaw 1995, 186–8).[14] What could be more apposite therefore for an opponent to show him as a rampant Giant, the ultimate symbol of total domination? Alternatively, Holles may have ordered the Giant to be cut during the period after 1654 when he had returned to England and was living quietly at Cerne Abbas. From there he would have been infuriated to learn of the triumphant progress of Cromwell, the increasingly regal grandeur of his life-style, the pressures from Parliament for him to accept the title of King, the over-blown salutations of poets such as Marvell and Milton, with Milton writing in 1652 of 'Cromwell, our chief of men...'

Figure 38. Oliver Cromwell as a burly half-naked Hercules, complete with club, originally above the doorway to Highnam Court, Gloucestershire. The house was built by Colonel William Cooke. The statue is about 2m high overall. (Photograph by Paul Stamper. Copyright reserved)

and what Holles perceived as the replacement of the former royal tyranny by a Cromwellian dictatorship. With the country controlled and regulated as never before, it is understandable that Holles's fierce temper and passionate feelings would have sought an outlet in a massive public response, but one which nonetheless avoided any charge of overt hostility to the regime.

Having been prominently involved in politics since the early 1620s and because his views were well known, Holles was at pains to avoid too blatant a display of opposition, and it is significant that he took no part in the ill-fated Penruddock rising in the west country in 1655, even though he was related by marriage to the leader, John Penruddock, whose estate at Compton Chamberlayne was only a few miles from Cerne (Crawford 1979, 182).

During the period after his return to England in 1654 Holles was involved in numerous legal suits about his lands and property. Upon his return he had found his affairs in disorder, apparently due to the neglect of his agents Ezekias Lambe and Arthus Shirley. During the next few years Holles and his wife, Jane, pursued a number of actions in the Court of Chancery, complaining a mismanagement by Lambe and Shirley. During a complex legal dispute in 1655 concerning lands and woods at Hermitage in Dorset, it was alleged that Ezekias Lambe of Cerne Abbas who had served Holles for many years had entered into a plot to defraud him, that the estate papers had fallen into total confusion and that many had been burnt in a fire in Lambe's house, 'casually burnt by fire accidently happening in his dwelling house at Cerne'. This explains why there is such a dearth information abouth the lands at Cerne during Holles's residence there, and why no direct evidence concerning the creation of the Giant can be found.[15]

In 1666 while Holles was still serving as ambassador to France, his wife Jane died. The lands at Cerne immediately reverted to her son Thomas Freke, and Holles was distressed to learn that Thomas had taken immediate possession of the property including the estate papers. According to Holles this unseemly haste was 'done like a Dorsetshire country gentleman'.[16] During the later seventeenth century the lands at Cerne passed from Frekes to the Pitts of Stratfield Saye and thence to Lord Rivers, eventually becoming part of the Pitt-Rivers estate. The figure of the Giant was no doubt neglected by these non-resident owners, and in 1694 the churchwardens at Cerne were moved to spend 3s 0d on repairing this remarkable feature of their local landscape, thus providing in their accounts the first documentary evidence of its existence.[17]

The final piece of evidence comes from 1751 when the meticulous Dorset historian, the Revd. John Hutchins (1698–1773), was engaged upon his life's work collecting material for his magisterial *History of Dorset*.[18] In his thorough research he travelled throughout the county, and at Cerne he naturally enquired about the origin of the Giant. He related the information he was given to Charles Lyttleton, then Dean of Exeter and later Bishop of Carlisle, and in a letter of 28th August 1751 wrote that:

> I have heard from the Steward of the manor it is a modern thing, cut out
> in Lord Hollis' time, who lived here while it continued his 2nd Lady's
> Jointure.[19]

Later Lyttleton asked the Oxford antiquary, Francis Wise, for his opinion of the Giant, and Wise replied that, having seen it, he was of the opinion that it was modern 'only a humble imitation of the Saxon manner'.[20] In his *History of Dorset* which was first published in 1774, just after his death, Hutchins wrote that the figure was made by Lord Holles's servants, although he also added that some local people 'averred it was there beyond the memory of man' (Hutchins 1861–70, IV, 35). By this time the Giant would have been a century old, and, as is well known, local memory is notoriously unreliable on such matters.[21]

All we know about Holles, his patrician attitudes, his passionate feelings, his exile, his furious contempt for Cromwell and his rage at the sorry course of English affairs leading to the execution of the King and the establishment of what he regarded as a tyrannous Republic, make it evident that such a grand gesture of defiance in the form of a rampant Giant was precisely in keeping with his character. If a diligent researcher and clergyman such as John Hutchins, who spent his whole career in Dorset and devoted himself to the study of its history, could accept that the Giant was made by Holles there is no reason why we should doubt it, even if, like Hutchins, we continue to be perplexed by the antique appearance of the figure. When Hutchins was told by a credible local witness that the Giant had been made by Lord Holles's servants, this was clearly the true explanation of its origin. The Giant exists as a massive satire on Cromwell's government and pretensions, and as a reminder of the failure of the short-lived Republic.

* * * * * * * *

Naming places and the role of the landscape

RH: What is especially significant about way the area around the Giant is perceived is that after the late seventeenth century the whole landscape around the area subsequently occupied by the Giant was named and defined in relation to the huge figure; before then, it was literally as if the figure did not exist. Field names, boundary markers, and descriptions alike referred to two other monuments, at the crest and foot respectively of what is now Giant Hill. One was that still enigmatic earthwork at the summit, which until the nineteenth century was called Trendle, after the circular frame used for rotating sacred candles for blessing at the medieval Christian feast of Candlemas. It was this which gave the whole hill-side its traditional name. The other human feature conspicuously mentioned in the records is the holy well in the valley below.

This well also became the focus of a local legend concerning St Augustine, a misunderstanding of which has become responsible for one of the most widely-diffused twentieth-century myths about the Giant; that a late thirteenth-century source establishes that the pre-Christian population of the Cerne district worshipped a god called Helith, whose image the figure might plausibly be taken to represent. This was first suggested by Sir Flinders Petrie in 1926 (Petrie 1926, 10). The source concerned is the *Memoriale* of Walter of Coventry, who indeed states that St Augustine converted the people of Cerne to Christianity from the veneration of a heathen god of that name. The problem with this entry was noticed within a few years of Petrie's reference; that Walter appears to have based his account upon one in the *De Gestis Pontificorum Anglorum* of William of Malmesbury, written over a hundred years before. However, in William's work, the reference to Helith is missing.

It is illuminating to see how an archaeologist and a historian dealt with this problem in precisely opposite ways. The archaeologist was Stuart Piggott, who argued that since William had talked of virtually everything else in Walter's story, the absence of any mention of Helith was not significant (Piggott 1932, 214–15). The historian was Darton, who pointed out that the difference between the accounts was very important, suggesting that the figure of Helith was a later addition to the legend, made between the time of William and that of Walter (Darton 1935, 319–31). It seems to have been Piggott's view which has prevailed among most works upon the Giant ever since; but a simple explanation for the problem can be offered when the two references are compared. Both have long been accessibly edited in the Rolls series, *De Gestis* in 1870 (the Cerne entry being on p.184) and the *Memoriale* in 1872 (in which see vol. I, p. 60). William speaks of how Augustine, having converted the heathens, renamed their settlement 'Cerno' (I see) 'Hel' (the Hebrew for God); from whence the name of Cerne. It may be argued that Walter of Coventry, a much less meticulous scholar than William, misread this passage to signify that Hel was the name of the pagan deity of the place.

Once this particular puzzle is removed, the early and high medieval records for Cerne turn out to be as barren of evidence for the existence of the Giant as those from the subsequent period. But what if we turn the clock right back to the very earliest period for which historical sources exist? Here I would like to introduce my third expert witness, Katherine Barker. Mrs Barker, a senior lecturer in the School of Conservation Sciences at Bournemouth University has for many years been researching the Anglo-Saxon landscape of north-west Dorset. Here she unfolds the issue of Giants in relation to the development of the idea in both Christian and Pagan ideologies, and links these to the evidence of land Charters and documentary records.

* * * * * * * *

Medieval Giants:
Bible, history, heritage and landscape

Katherine Barker

'Immoderate curiosity is a grave sin ...' declared Aelfric the Grammarian, first Abbot and Mass-priest of Cerne Abbas (Thorpe 1844–6, II, 375). If simple inquiry will not yield an answer we are advised, it seems, to leave well alone. To Aelfric, answers were sought through revelation, and if revelation is not forthcoming we should accept unknowing with good grace. To later medieval scholarship the route to enlightenment still lay in revelation, skillfully developed by way of allegory and exposition. Through a network of complex resemblances the natural world was held to correspond with the spiritual. It was a route finally consigned to extinction by the new experimental philosophy which saw the old order as 'knowledge (condemning) itself to never knowing anything but the same thing' (Foucault 1970, 30). Questions and answers had become connected in an ever-closed loop of aprioristic reasoning.

Happily freed from tradition and dogma, the inquiring mind was re-directed to join company with analytical, deductive science, towards open-ended knowledge. As heirs to the empirical method we are licensed to be immoderately curious. In exercising that curiosity about the origins and identity of the hill-figure at Cerne Abbas we may now not only undertake systematic and inductive work in the physical sciences on the hill-side, but evoke the social sciences in exploring the power of images and the mechanics of forgetting – how is it no one can remember what the hill-figure is or when it was. We no longer fear the strictures imposed by Aelfric because we ask different questions. But the strictures remain nevertheless. Whatever the approach or technique, whatever the method, the pursuit of *impeccable* – literally sinless – scholarship, still remains a laudable aim. Peccability, as Aelfric would have agreed, is to overreach to expect more from a source of information than it can yield.

Whoever it was plotted out and cut the giant hill-figure at Cerne Abbas knew full well when it was done and in what spirit it was done. But the people implicated did not convincingly bequeath their story to posterity and the Giant does not yield secrets easily. John Hutchins noted that the figure:

> has been reported to have been made by Lord Holles' servants, during his residence here, but it is more likely he only caused it to be repaired; for some people who died not long since, 80 or 90 years old, when young, knew some of the same age that averred it was there before the memory of man. (John Hutchins 1774, II, 293).

Memory is notoriously unreliable; averrals of custom or usage going back 'before the memory of man' are not infrequently encountered in other documentation relating to the period. But Hutchins was uncertain and set down the conflicting views.

In good antiquarian style he included in his work a scale drawing of the figure first published a few years earlier by Stukeley in *The Gentleman's Magazine* of 1764, incorporating some minor internal changes (Grinsell 1980, 31). Hutchins also included three figures between the feet, which Stukeley had been unable to read. 'It is plain' writes Stukeley, 'there were but three figures, so that supporting the first to be 9, it must have been formed a long while ago. Some think it was cut by the Antient Britons ... others believe it to be the work of Papists ... I hope some of your ingenious correspondents will favour us with an account of its orgin and use ...'. He then lists the dimensions of the figure 'which I took myself' and which Hutchins gives in a slightly different order. The latter gives the figures between the feet as '798'. Both writers were faced with a hill-figure which, to an antiquarian eye, presented an image which was undoubtedly archaic. It was certainly manmade – belief in fabled origins was no longer acceptable. As additional evidence in favour its antiquity however, Hutchins includes the tradition that the area had once been terrorised by a local giant who, having:

> regaled himself with several sheep, retired to this hill and lay down to sleep. The country people pinioned him down and killed him, and then traced out the dimensions of his body, to perpetuate his memory. (Hutchins 1774, II, 293)

Fabulous as this story is, notes Hutchins, it is perhaps proof of the great antiquity of this figure.

Writing towards the end of the eighteenth century he separated myth and history but interpreted myth – as did the later generation of folklorists – as something likely to result from long gestation – not just the result of tall-story telling.[22] He was, however, still prepared to leave the question of its origins open while drawing the reader's attention to some field monuments of a similar type including the White Horses in Berkshire and Wiltshire, the Whiteleaf Cross in Buckinghamshire and noting the reference made by John Aubrey to the effigy of a giant cut on Shotover Hill, north of Oxford before the Civil Wars. By putting such sites in a comparative perspective, he may be one of the first writers to see hill-figures as a distinct class of field monument:

> Most antiquaries agree that [the Cerne Abbas Giant] is a monument of high antiquity, and make little doubt but that it was a representation of the Saxon god Heil; so that it must be more ancient at least than AD 600 ... Dr Stukeley was of a singular opinion, that it was the figure of Hercules ... not so much an object of religious worship, as a memorial. (Hutchins 1774, II, 293)

This hill-figure continues to present a bizarre and powerful image, at its best from the air, difficult to categorize, with no obvious provenance and no apparent purpose. Such an image evokes a puzzled fascination – expressed here as 'worship' or 'memorial'. To help understanding it has to be assigned an identity – 'Heil' or 'Hercules' – and then an age, 'more ancient than AD 600'. And when the age is decided, sources are checked and later generations have proceeded to provide it with a selection of contexts and iconologies usefully collected by Castleden (1996). The next stage is to go back through that period between AD 600 – or high antiquity – and the present, looking for references to help narrow the field (Bettey 1981). The flaw in the argument is to assume at the outset that something can be dated and provenanced on stylistic grounds alone. And then set out to prove it. If something *looks* old, does it have to *be* old?

Aelfric

Aelfric the Grammarian, first Abbot and Mass Priest of Cerne and later Abbot of Eynsham, is our first narrative source emanating from Cerne Abbas and with him we start our inquiry. If the Giant is indeed old, then it was there in the tenth century. Aelfric was an accomplished and prolific writer. Educated at Winchester under Bishop Aethelwold who played a major part in the tenth century monastic revival, Aelfric has been described as 'one of the great luminaries of Benedictine letters' (Swanton 1975, xviii), his sources 'were very much the new theology of the day' (John 1996, 127). The greater part of his work dates from the 15 years he spent at Cerne between 987 and 1002. Here he completed two volumes of sermons or *Homilies*, translated six books of the Old Testament and composed a series of *Lives of the Saints*. For his pupils he wrote a Latin primer, a *Grammar*, and a useful book with parallel phrases in Latin and English, the *Colloquy*, a short work cast in the form of a set-piece dialogue between a teacher and his pupil. He thus provided what has been described as a Christian Curriculum for his day and he wrote in English. Late tenth century royal patronage approved Biblical exegesis expounded in the vernacular; learning made accessible.

Does Aelfric mention the Cerne Abbas Giant? The short answer is no, he does not. But the question is not an appropriate one to ask of material not composed to provide an answer to that kind of question. We are making a fundamental mistake if we attempt to wrest information from a source not constructed to provide it and then expect to come away with insight. We can, however, begin by approaching the late tenth century thought-world through Aelfric's work and learn a little of his sense of the meaning of the evil and outsize – the gigantic. And then something of the approach of later medieval writers.

Aelfric was not an original thinker. He was concerned with the promotion of a single faith, of one approved doctrine. His sense of the past is conveyed through a catalogue of examples, his credibility rooted in the authority of earlier written material, his knowledge of the world grounded in received opinion. His is an approved exposition of the model of divine purpose and revelation. The written is The Word, timeless, placeless and autonomous. Aelfric was promoting a hybrid philosophy of Mediterranean origin filtered through the medium of Latin which, by definition, drew nothing from the local scene. He writes eloquently about the geography of heaven (Barker 1988),[23] but of the familiar world around him, next to nothing. To know something the authority of the written word was essential; 'layman require that teachers should impart to them the evangelical lore, which they have learned in books that men should not err in ignorance' (Thorpe 1844–6, II, 315).

The hill-figure at Cerne presents a non-Christian image. What of non-Christian, heathen practices alluded to by Aelfric? We hear of such in terms of what puts our souls in danger. He denigrates mindless women passing their children 'through the earth' at crossroads, to divination 'by foolish men ... with great error, after heathen custom' to witches and to wizards and to the casting of runes. Aelfric carefully tells us what not to do, instructing us 'not to take our health from a spring or a well or a stone or a tree, unless the tree is revered as the Holy Rood [Cross]' (Thorpe 1844–6, I, 474 and II, 241). Such references are all found in the context of a sermon or homily, or a saint's life. While suspecting these reflect local practices and were familiar to his audience, we cannot be certain. There is no reference to the practice of anything that suggests the involvement of an idol of curious form, let alone a hill-figure – but hill-figures are not found in biblical and patristic writing.

There are, however, hints of non-Christian practices surviving in boundary surveys of neighbouring manors of Buckland Newton and Hermitage (Barker and Seaward 1990). Both these parishes lie a few miles to the north of Cerne Abbas on the edge of the tenth century Cerne estate at Minterne, on the borders of the clay vale of Blackmore (Figure 39). On the edge of the chalk scarp beside the road (the present A352) leading down into the moor there was, by the fourteenth century, a *crucem de la rode*, 'cross of the rood', which appears as *ad rodem*, 'at rood'; in the Forest bounds of 1299/1300. The site is referred to again variously as Rodehill's Ash (... wheretofore Late did grow great Ash) and again as Redhill, where in a survey of 1616 John More drew a tree on Roode-hill (Barker and Seaward 1990, 15).

Rodehill affords a magnificent view across this part of the Vale and the name suggests that here, overlooking the Forest and on the boundary between the royal estate of Hermitage and the Glastonbury estate of Buckland Newton there once stood a large wayside cross or rood, and a large Ash tree. Buckland Newton parish church is dedicated to the Holy Rood. The Feasts of the Holy Rood played an important part in the hunting season which opened on 3rd May (Feast of the Invention) and 14th September (Feast of the Exaltation) (Cummins 1988, 33 and 56). While there is no evidence the Rood was already standing by the tenth century, it is interesting to note that Aelfric's *Colloquy* includes a conversation with a huntsman:

Huntsman:	I am a huntsman
Pupil:	Whose?
Huntsman:	The King's
Pupil:	How do you carry out your trade?

There then follows a brief description of the methods used and the animals caught (Swanton 1975, 109–111). There is, of course, no indication as to the location of the royal estate where this might have taken place. Blackmore was not designated Forest until Norman times. We might note, however, that it was Woden who led the Wild Hunt of lost and noisy souls across the night sky, and it was Woden who was ancestor of the West Saxon Kings (Yorke 1990, 16) and it was on an Ash Tree, the 'World Ash', *Yggdrasil*, that he hanged himself to receive the power of the runes (Branston 1980, 79 and 114).

Boundaries and early landscape

On the tenth century bounds of Buckland Newton we find a *cristemeleighe*, 'a clearing with a cross' mentioned again in 1317, [land] *atte Crouche*, 'at the cross' (Mills 1989, 255). In a survey of 1615 on the western bounds of the royal manor of Hermitage John Norden records a large tree, *Trimtre Oak*, which may be OE *treo-mael* 'crucifix tree' (for discussion see Barker and Seaward 1990, 11). 'The sign

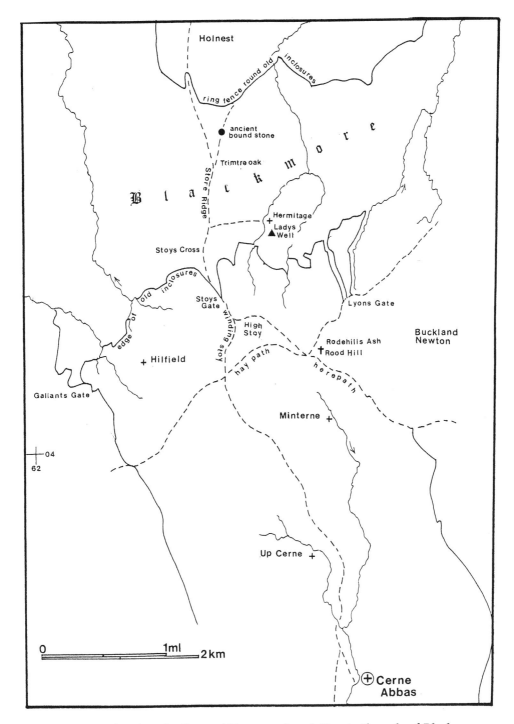

Figure 39. *Map showing the Cerne Abbas area in relation to the vale of Blackmoor.*

of the Holy Rood is our blessing, and to the Rood we pray, though not to the tree, but to Almighty God who for us hung on the Holy Rood' writes Aelfric (Thorpe 1844–6, II, 241). 'The new crucifix was much in evidence during the tenth century reformation ... and the individual had a part to play in his own redemption' (John 1996, 132 and 133). We have no means of telling whether there were crucifix trees within the estate, away from the boundary.

The western edge of the Hermitage boundary that led past *Trimtre Oak* lay along a drove route that made its way down the steep scarp slope below Stoys Hill and out into the moor as far as a large stone, *la Ruweston* (the 'rough stone') of 1299/1300, recorded as a *meere stone* ('boundary stone') *in a pitt* about 1550 and described as an *ancient boundstone* in the Hermitage boundary survey of 1740. The stone marked the meeting place of the Hermitage bounds with those of Holnest and Hilfield; it also marks a hundred boundary. The stone was certainly in place by 1299 when it lay on the bounds of the Royal Forest. From its description it sounds to have been a single, large half-buried stone, perhaps a sarsen. It has since been lost. It may have been the landmark which gave its name to the route that led to it, found in *staneweysfote* of 1299, 'the foot of the stone way'; latterly 'stoys way' (now Stonerush Drove) and to the prominent hill above it – 'stoys hill' in 1569–74, 'High Stoy' of 1888 and of today. (Barker and Seaward 19990, 7).

If this is a not a description of the route itself, a 'stony way' there may be a reference to the stone out in the open moor to which the 'stone way' was directed. If the stone were indeed ancient it could earlier have been an object of veneration involving the kind of practices alluded to by Aelfric in his *Homilies*. The manor of Hermitage – as its name suggests – was by 1315 the site of monastic cell sited immediately below the chalk scarp, lying within the royal forest beside a perennial spring, Lady's Well, and only a little distance off Stoys Way (Barker and Seaward 1990, 21) Anyone setting out for the Moor bent on 'taking their health from a stone or a spring' would – by 1315 – have had the services of a priest close to hand.

Biblical Giants

And what of Aelfric and Giants? Aelfric embraces Giants in his thinking through the words of the Books of the Old Testament in the way he could never embrace the epic traditions of the giants and heroes of the Germanic world. The word 'giant' itself comes from the Latin *gigas*.[24] The Biblical references were (and remain) rather obscure and probably provoked a sense of mystery in the listeners. In *Genesis* 6:4 we learn 'there were giants in the earth in those days ...'. They appear again in *Numbers* 13:33, 'and there we saw the giants, the sons of Anak, which come of giants ...'. These were Pre-adamite Giants who colonized far and wide before the children of Noah. 'These were indeed mighty men of renown and should have had the appropriate stature' (Piggott 1989, 48). As Mankind degenerated, his stature grew less and giants became a thing of the past. Aefric's students also heard about Gog and Magog; Magog innocently enough as Noah's grandson. The same name was also given to the homeland of Gog. Both names appear in *Ezekial* (38:39) where Gog is ruler of the wild hordes of Magog and they appear together again in *Revelation* summoned by Satan at the Apocalypse. But they were not yet Giants of medieval history, nor yet become the composite *Gogmagog*.

Biblical authority has Giants walking the earth both before and after the Flood. 'It happened after Noah's Flood' writes Aelfric (Thorpe 1844–6, I, 319) 'that Giants would raise up a city, and a tower (stypel) so high that its roof should ascend to Heaven. There was then one language among all mankind and the work was begun against the Will of God. So God ... scattered them ... and gave to each of the workman an unknown language.' After the building of the Tower of Babel, 'mankind' he continues 'was deceived by the devil ... and wrought images of gold ... silver ... stone ... wood ... and devised names for them; the names of those men who were giants and evil-doing'.

Aelfric is pre-occupied by evil-doers but he does not develop the theme of the evil-doing giant. The devil, however, is described in vivid terms but of no defined size or form; adjectives include 'swart-black', 'sulphurous', 'feathery', 'sharp-visaged', 'ample-bearded', 'flaming-eyed' and 'burning-mouthed'. This creature may be hideous and set on making trouble, but it is not gigantic and certainly not clavigerous and ithyphallic. There are no echoes here of the Cerne Abbas hill-figure.

The Medieval world turned Gog and Magog into real-live Giants, and found them a British *locus* (Westrem in Tomasch and Gilles 1998, 58). It also provided a site and a *raison d'etre* for giant hill-figure cutting. Aelfric was probably familiar with the tradition, first found in Josephus, that it was Alexander who had made himself personally responsible for confining these wild lost races of Gog and Magog behind a wall to protect the world from them until the coming of the Antichrist (McGinn 1994, 140; Gerritson and van Melle 1998, 20). But by the time of Geoffrey of Monmouth, writing about 150 years later than Aelfric, not only have Gog and Magog become individual giants in their own right but they have a significant part to play in the heritage of the British kingdom. And he uses the composite *Goemagot* – Gogmagog – which has been explained in terms of his Welsh origins (Westwood 1994, 29).

Medieval Giants

From the seventh century on, beginning with the Franks, more and more cities and peoples of western and northern Europe began to claim Trojan ancestry in imitation of Rome (Gerritsen and van Melle 1998, 140). For Geoffrey of Monmouth it was *Brut* or *Brutus* for the Britons. His *Historia Regum Britanniae* ('History of the Kings of Britain') was written about 1135. The appeal of the book was immediate and numerous copies were made, although it drew derogatory criticism from the very beginning from more serious-minded chroniclers (Thorpe 1966, 28–29). Four hundred years later it was still going strong; there were three major printed editions produced in the sixteenth century and poetic versions were produced by both Drayton and Spenser.

The prehistory of Britain begins with Brutus who, accompanied by Corineus after the sack of Troy, fought their way across the continent until they reached the British Isles where they came across a race of giants. Brutus founded London, having personally selected the site, and his dynasty reached its apogee in the reign of King Arthur of the Round Table. In our search for medieval giant hill-figures in the English landscape, the episode in question is probably worth quoting in full:

> Brutus loaded his ships with all the riches he had acquired [in Gaul] ... so with the winds behind him, he sought the promised land, and came ashore at Totnes.
>
> At this time the island of Britain was called Albion. It was uninhabited except for a few giants. It was however, most attractive ... and it filled Brutus and his comrades with a great desire to live there. When they had explored the different districts, they drove the giants whom they had discovered into the caves in the mountains. With the approval of their leader they divided the land among themselves. They began to cultivate the fields and to build houses so that in a short time you would have thought that the land had always been inhabited.
>
> Brutus called the island Britain from his own name ... Corineus, however, following in this the example of his leader, called the region of the kingdom which had fallen to his share Cornwall, after the manner of his own name.
>
> Corineus experienced great pleasure from wrestling with the giants, of whom there were far more there than in any of the districts which had been distributed among his comrades. Among the others there was a particularly repulsive one, called Goemagot, who was twelve feet tall. He was so strong that, once he had given it a shake, he could tear up an oak-tree as though it were a hazel wand. Once, when Brutus was celebrating a day dedicated to the gods in the port where had landed, this creature, along with twenty other giants, attacked him and killed a great number of the Britons. However, the Britons finally gathered together from round and about and overcame the giants and slew them all, except Goemagot.
>
> Brutus ordered that he alone should be kept alive, for he wanted to see a wrestling match between this giant and Corineus, who enjoyed beyond all reason matching himself against such monsters. Corineus was delighted by this. He girded himself up, threw off his armour and challenged Goemagot to a wrestling-match. The contest began. Corineus moved in, so did the giant; each of them caught the other in a hold by twining his arms around him, and the air vibrated with their panting breath. Goemagot gripped Corineus with all his might and broke three of his ribs, two on the right side and one on the left. Corineus then

summoned all his strength, for he was infuriated by what had happened. He heaved Goemagot up on to his shoulders, and running as fast as he could under the weight, he hurried off to the nearby coast. [Totnes is 9 miles up river and Corineus had a long way to run; William Camden (1586), found fault with Geoffrey's work as a whole but nevertheless gives the site of the Leap at Pymouth Hoe]. He clambered up to the top of a mighty cliff, shook himself free and hurled this deadly monster, whom he was carrying on his shoulders, far out into the sea. The giant fell on to a sharp reef of rocks, where he was dashed into a thousand fragments and stained the waters red with his blood. The place took its name from the fact the giant was hurled down there and it is called Goemagot's Leap to this day. (Thorpe 1966, 72–73)

Tangible 'proof' of this story is found in the *Plymouth Corporation Audit Book* in references to the maintenance of a Giant (or Giants) cut in the turf on the Hoe.

The first dates to 1486 and reads: 'Item paid to Cotewyll for ye renewing of ye picture of Gogmagog upon ye howe'. There are two further references to cleaning in 1501 and 1529. In 1541 we find 'It[em] P[ai]d to William Hawkyne, Baker, for cuttyng of Gogmagog, the pycture of the Gyaunt at Hawe 8d'. It is clear there is only one figure involved. By 1602, when Carew published his *Survey of Cornwall*, there are two figures, which he describes as 'the portrayture of two men, the one bigger, the other lesser with clubbes in their hands (whom they terme Gog Magog)' (Marples 1949, 209). In 1630 we hear of 'the portraiture of 2 men of the largest volume, yet the one surpassing the other every way ... these they name to be Corineus and Gogmagog' (Marples 1949, 211–212). The figures were destroyed in the building of the Citadel by Charles II. They were probably cut on the steep west side of the Hoe and not, of course, on chalk. But were the outlines, one wonders, ever picked out in paint for special occasions?

Thus some years before 1486, Geoffrey of Monmouth's account had prompted the cutting of an image to record the momentous events which heralded the beginnings of Britain.[25] It (or they) remained throughout the Tudor period. We have a context which certainly suggests a hill-figure cut as a patriotic 'wonder' – the wondrousness of a negative image – an impression in the ground left behind by Gogmagog after his last desperate struggle. We have here a medieval hill-figure created in response to a written source. These were hill-figures with a name and a location and a pedigree – and the writer had *auctoritas*, authority.

The Middle Ages was an overwhelmingly bookish culture and very credulous of the written word. A large and heterogeneous collection of materials was available (there was no systematic bibliography available until the middle of the sixteenth century), and a well-edited and harmonious exposition on such material was admired (Lewis 1964, 11). And Geoffrey of Monmouth, appropriately enough, re-assures his readers by claiming his *auctoritas* from a lost source. He does not allude to Giants, he tells us about them. His account suggests we may be mistaken seeking oblique references to the Cerne Abbas Giant in medieval writers. If Cerne had ever been seriously involved in an encounter of the gigantic kind, we should surely know about it. Medieval Giant-cutting needed authority. The written source would have come first.

Direct evidence of any traditional name for the Cerne Abbas Giant is confined to a statement by Stukeley in 1764, that 'the people there give the name of Helis' to the figure (Hutchins, see above, and Piggott 1932, 214). It is of note that William of Malmesbury (died *c.*1142), a contemporary of Geoffrey of Monmouth (died 1155), while giving a detailed account of St Augustine's visit to Cerne (bequeathing us a Well – a more permanent feature than a hill-figure) makes no mention of the overthrowing of Helis – although the missionaries did meet with a hostile reception. An oft-quoted statement from Walter of Coventry's thirteenth century version of the story (otherwise *verbatim*, notes Piggott (1932, 330) adds, after reference to Cerne and other Dorset religious houses 'in which country the god Helith was once worshipped.' But there is no Galfridian-style flourish with scenes of the forcible banishment of heathen gods, cleansing and re-dedication of the exciting sort we read about in Aelfric. Walter of Coventry does nothing to give the reputation of medieval Cerne a clear head-start in competition with its neighbours. Helis did not enjoy the same fate – and posthumous reputation – as Gogmagog.

Hercules

Perhaps, on reflection, we should lay less stress on looking for Giants *per se*. Hill-figures are, by definition, very large or no one would see them. There are giant figures, giant horses, giant crosses, giant badges – even a giant panda – where giant is simply an adjective to indicate size (Bergamar 1997). On the hill-side at Cerne we have a giant humanoid image most usually seen, from Stukelely's time on, as a representation of the pagan god and hero Hercules (Piggott 1938, 323–331) It is a scaled-up outline of a figure-type also found represented very small, on coinage, as figurines and on pottery; in AD 191 the emperor Commodus declared himself an incarnation of Hercules and fit for adoration (Piggott 1932, 326). Hercules was the son of Jupiter by a mortal mother and known for his physical size and prowess, *ex pede Hercule*, was a Latin proverb for describing someone of reputation and 'standing.' The idea long-persisted, found in St Augustine (Bettenson 1972, 639), that the offspring of the 'angels of God' and 'daughters of men' grew into giants.

With the advent of Christianity Hercules, along with other classical pagan gods and heroes, does not disappear (Seznec 1953). Hercules is found in a ninth century Carolingian context at both the coronations of Charlemagne, Holy Roman Emperor, and his grandson Charles the Bold, eighty-five years later. Theodolphus, Bishop of Orleans, composed a work for the Carolingian court, *Contra uidices* (to judges) which includes a famous passage describing a silver vessel decorated with scenes from the life of Hercules, a work which draws particularly on that of St Augustine who argued that the gods had prepared man by degrees for Christian wisdom. For Theodolphus, writing at the time of Charlemagne's coronation AD

799–800, Hercules represents Virtue, he stands for 'the proper use of judicial function within the Frankish kingdom' (Nees 1991, 91). But as Nees points out (1991, 32) at one and the same time, Hercules also provides a model for behaviour deeply tainted and imperfect – a warning that rulers needed to distinguish carefully between pagan virtue and justice and Christian virtue and justice.

The Labours of Hercules formed a carved relief around the specially constructed imperial throne, the *Cathedra Petri* presented to Charles the Bald, Charlemagne's grandson in AD 875 (Nees 1991, 148). Whatever the precise iconographic significance there is no doubt that two of the most prestigious of continental Christian events were accompanied by the overt use of pagan classical imagery, and for the second, worked into a sumptuous item of church furniture. Sadly, we shall never know the design of the new fittings for the Benedictine House at Cerne little more than ten years later.

By endowing pagan classical mythology with a lofty spiritual and allegorical significance, Christendom accommodated – indeed imbued – the old gods with new importance. If there had been chalk hills around the Carolingian court at Aachen an image of Hercules would have occasioned no surprise.

Hercules was to retain and to enhance his good name. 'My lord Monk, Cheer up, for it's your turn ... which monastery's yours, in heaven's name?' And so the tonsured monk in Chaucer's *Canterbury Tales* takes his turn at story-telling and the company hear about Hercules. His tales includes lives of Lucifer, Adam, Samson, Zenobia, Nero, Alexander, Julius Caesar and Croesus. 'If I don't tell these stories in due order ... according to the chronological sequence as written in the books ... I beg you excuse my ignorance.' Hercules the sovereign conqueror comes fourth before Nubuchadnezzar (Wright 1985, 181–182). 'There's no one since the beginning of time who killed as many monsters as did he; And throughout all the wide world ran his fame For boundless strength and magnanimity.' And The Monk concludes with some cautionary advice about the Herculean character that echoes that expressed by Nees (1991) for the Carolingian court:

> Whoever knows himself is truly wise
> Watch out: when Fortune wants to play a trick,
> She bides her time before she overthrows
> Her victims in a way they least expect.

A great banquet given by Philip the Good of Burgundy in 1454 took place in a hall hung with tapestries illustrating the life of Hercules, the climax of the feast was the appearance of a huge giant dressed as an armed saracen and leading an elephant (Daston and Park 1998, 107). Godfrey of Bouillon, one of the popular heroes of the Middle Ages, had his deeds of valour published as the labours of Hercules as late as 1688 (Gerritson and van Melle 1998, 127). It was not difficult to find Christian symbolism in a life of dedication and a death which led to immortality.

Mythical history to allegory

It was the publication of Ovid's *Metamorphoses* that played a crucial part in the dissemination of classical stories, and innumerable versions were produced after the introduction of printing. Classical mythology was brought to the attention to anyone who could read (Febre and Martin 1990, 273). It was however, the publication of *Ovide moralis*, in French, in the early fourteenth century, that the work was formerly accommodated within the Christian *milieu* in being given an allegorical Christian meaning (Barkan 1986, 72–3, 107–108, 114–116; Innes 1955, 20; Copeland 1991, 107–130). From the fourteenth century onwards, anyone who had been to school could expound on the *gesta deorum* – the lives and loves of the old gods – among which was numbered Hercules. It was a Christian interpretation which, through a myriad of hidden meanings, was to provide an essential vehicle for the artistic expression of the Renaissance.

The spread of printing hugely increased the demand for book illustration. 'The response was the invention of the emblem, one of the most influential creations of the late Renaissance. The original intention of the inventor, Alciati (1492–1550) was to devise epigrams that were especially enigmatic ... woodcut images were added and ... by mid century the visual image had become an indispensable part of the emblem' (Ashworth in Lindberg and Westman 1990, 310–311) who argues that a veritable 'emblematic world view' was the result. The illustration, device or *impresa*, consisted a visual image, a short motto and a slightly longer epigram, few of which were Christian although they inherited a well-established tradition of iconological meaning. By 1600 there were hundreds of different emblem treatises in print 'an outgrowth of the love for proverbial wisdom' – such works were used for instruction, for insight, for moral improvement – and Hercules duly appears as a child with snakes, or as an adult with a lion skin or a staff or club.

Ethica is the choice made by Hercules; we learn, 'Young man imitate Hercules: leave the left-hand way, turn from Vice ... no way is impassable to Vertue ...' (Freeman 1948, 89–90). Well endowed with allegorical meaning, Hercules stood his ground alongside Giants who also proved rather difficult to give up. John Bale, lapsed priest and author of a biographical catalogue (begun 1548), sought to fill the gap in the early history of the kingdom by explaining how Britain had come to be occupied by the race of giants encountered by Brutus and Corineus (Piggott 1932, 49; Ferguson 1993, 87).

In 1592 Walter Raleigh was granted the Manor of Sherborne by Elizabeth I, a large estate about ten miles north of Cerne Abbas. (Raleigh also claimed the manor of Up Cerne). He was, like Bale, (and clearly unlike Leland) ready to believe that giants existed in history and included an essay on them in his *Historie of the World* (1614). He took sharp issue with Goropius of Antwerp on the matter:

> Of these Giants which Moses calleth mightie men, Goropius Becanus an Antwerpian, (who thought his owne wit more Giganticall than the bodies of Nimrod or Hercules) hath written a large discourse, intitled

Gigantomachia and strained his braines to prove that there were never any such men: his reasons (whoever desires to loose time) he may find them in the Treatises before named. (Raleigh 1614, 1 5 8)

Besides all the Giants found in 'profane histories' argued Raleigh, 'the Scriptures doe clearly and without all allegorical construction avow ... and then he gives a full list of Giants with references, and quotes the height of Goliath, whose size puts us out of doubt and concludes with Samson'. Raleigh is a writer on a 'world' scale; he is no chorographer or collector of local material although on the matter of The Flood, he notes with interest a great inundation in Holland in 1446 and another in Languedoc in 1557 (Raleigh 1614, 1 7 5). (He may have used an examplar; St Augustine also uses personal knowledge of floods to illustrate the significance of Noah's experience). The work of William Camden 'preserver of our antiquities' clearly finds tacit approval but Raleigh makes no use of supporting material for our 'giant' edification, no 'gigantick sepulchres' or bones, and no field monuments.

Goropius argued that the term *giant*, was simply one originally applied to oppressors and tyrants. In mid-century John Twyne had attempted to clarify things by sorting giants into four categories (Ferguson 1993, 108–109). The fourth and last category included 'good giants' who 'tended to be called giants as it were by courtesy (*ex dignitate*) for the beneficent services.' Such were Atlas, Orpheus and Hercules. But within a generation or so the rising conflict between the will to believe and a growing discontent with explanations that failed to square with reason and experience, and the giants of pre-Trojan times – good and bad – were consigned by the new antiquarian scholarship to the Albionic rubbish heap and Hercules was released to the tender mercies of pamphleteers and satirists. That was the age of Thomas Hobbes and his Leviathan 'when Nimrod prov'd the stoutest hunter, and Hercules travelled to tame Monsters or Usurpers, the world was in this subjection ...' (Smith 1994, 182 and 304).

Convenientia

In 1594 an Ecclesiastical Commission of Enquiry met at Cerne Abbas to explore rumours of Walter Raleigh's alleged atheism. The case was heard and Raleigh's name and reputation were publicly cleared. An account of the enquiry (Lloyd 1967, 256–265) includes an interpolated section (pp. 258–261) on the Cerne Abbas Giant. We have an account based on a written source break off part-way through, to make way for a sub-section the subject of which has no demonstrable connection with main text. It is a neat example of *convenientia* a device well-known to medieval scholarship whereby subjects were linked simply by virtue of supposed con-venience or 'coming together', that is, by adjacency (Foucault 1970, 18). Here we have an attested visit by a group of Tudor Church Commissioners to Cerne Abbas sandwiched with a giant hill-figure of unknown origin:

The witnesses arrived, passing beneath the hill where the Giant of Cerne presided, cut in the chalk before Christianity came ... God of Fertility and the Underworld ... another claims he is Hercules ... by then the Vegetation God with fertility associations. The actors arrived, some coming over the hill known as Black Down, some up Yelcombe, others past Elwood, names given in honour of the Giant. The voices of the interrogators begin ... A chuckle seemed to come from the Giant on the hill.

The problem is of the same order as that faced by John Hutchins. It is the question of how an image is to be read; and whether such an image can safely be dated on appearance alone; whether a hill-figure which looks ancient must necessarily be so. Here Hutchins desists whilst others continue, immoderately. Working on the premise that the hill-figure is ancient then it can only have survived at variance – if not in direct conflict – with whatever the prevailing view of the day was deemed to have been. And for the Lloyd account it has therefore to be both pre-Christian and anti-Christian, (Puritan and Catholic) and thus the image of a pagan god. It follows that it is primitive and 'cult' and atheistical and stands to mock mindless country people (we must understand) who climb the hill with mattock and hoe to clean and maintain the figure every few years over countless centuries.

Such an approach is hard to defend for the end of the sixteenth century. Raleigh's thinking happily accommodated Giants. Raleigh had read his Ovid and was well content with the symbolic and allegorical content presented by the lives of the profane gods:

> ... the prophecies that Christ should break the Serpents Head and conquer the power of Hell, occasioned the fables of Hercules killing the Serpent of the Hesperides and descending into Hell ... so was borrowed ... the conversion of their Heroes ... (Raleigh 1614, 1 6 4).

Wherever his atheism lay it was surely outside the highly sophisticated artificial world of the emblem, the device, the impresa representing arcane, ancient and eternal truths. The hill-figure image of Hercules, had we any evidence for its existence at Cerne in 1594, would have been known and understood by anyone who could read.

Giants and other hill-figures

But what did workaday medieval giants look like? They processed in festival and burlesque, and doubtless got up to mischief (Newman 1997, 105–111; Shortt 1988). Gogmagog at Plymouth is described as club bearing although the club belongs to Hercules, a good giant, and Gogmagog was a bad one. And if the second 'giant' was intended to represent Corineus why does he have a club at all? The question is posed by Marples (1949, 212). The contest was essentially a wrestling match. Gogmagog was often shown with an oak tree he was wont to brandish[25] but Corineus should have been unarmed. The question remains unanswered.

There are three other Giant humanoid hill-figures on record, another seemingly known by the name of Gogmagog was said to have been cut on the ramparts of Wandelbury Rings on the Gogmagog Hills north of Cambridge first mentioned about 1605 (Marples 1949, 204–209). This figure was the subject of lengthy investigation by Tom Lethbridge in the 1950s; the rather bizarre images he published were probably a reading of surface and sub-surface features of mostly natural origin (Lethbridge 1957; Clark 1997). Nothing remains of the Giant – or its name – said to have been cut on Shotover Hill north of Oxford first recorded by John Aubrey (see Hutchins, above) and which had disappeared by 1763. Both these hill-figures appear to be post-medieval in date and an association with the universities of Oxford and Cambridge has been noted by other writers (Lethbridge 1957, 64).[26]

The Long Man of Wilmington in Sussex is first recorded in 1710 in an estate survey (Sussex Archaeological Society 1995) and as for both the Cambridge and Cerne figures there have been a number of attempts to establish a much earlier origin (Newman 1997, 126–150). The Wilmington figure was restored and lined with brick in 1874. The pair of staffs he holds may formerly have been a rake and a long-handled scythe. He has been identified as a whole range of figures from that of a Roman standard-bearer, to the figure of the god Thor, or even a Saxon haymaker (Marples 1949, 180–203). The matter remains wholly unresolved.

Hill-figures are not difficult to set out (Barker 1997 and 1998), and the cutting on shallow hillside soils is a relatively straight-forward matter for pick and spade. The exercise is not time-consuming and needs no special skills, and a hill-figure will quickly grow over if – for whatever reason – the interest is lost. But at the outset such an activity needs both approval from the landholder and *auctoritas*, – an author and an authority – to carry it out on the required scale to the appropriate design. A hill-figure is emblematic and even on the most mundane level it needs to 'say' or represent something. Such has been made plain by informal discussion on the possibility of cutting a new hill-figure in a suitable location to mark the coming millennium.

Hercules is an interesting example of a stock character-image which, over time and with adjustments, has been able to fulfill a variety of purposes, from the wholly serious-minded to the frankly ridiculous, from quasi-god to lampoon – with ready potential for *double entendre*. It is an image which is capable of demonstrating a continuum of meaning which, paradoxically, makes the hill-figure more difficult to date on stylistic grounds, not less. Select your period and aprioristic argument becomes tempting; the loop of reasoning closes just too easily.

As a symbol of power, of justice, of fidelity, of *Vertue*, of virility, even the most cursory of explorations into the Medieval and Renaissance *corpus* presents a rich matrix of classical and allegorical allusion which can provide a moral context for the figure anywhere from the ninth century to the seventeenth. Aelfric was well-acquainted with Biblical giants, his contemporaries with their mythical – or other – responsibility with regard to large and rather mysterious structures. His peers in the Carolingian world were using Herculean imagery in high places.

By the twelfth century, we have exampled the cutting of hill-figures to illustrate a great event in proto-history. Chaucer has a monk in Holy Orders tell us about Hercules. Following periods of enthusiastic copying of the classics, their allegorical use is further enhanced with the coming of Printing and Protestantism and is found in Ralegh's great work, interleaved with Biblical, Ancient Egyptian, and other sources.

Medieval Christian iconology was complex but regulated, and fear of both Idolatory and of Blasphemy was real (Camille 1989). The availability of other human forms from the classical canon was to give expression to a whole variety of sentiments (not always praiseworthy) which were accommodated in aristocratic, patriotic and religious contexts from the tenth century onwards – if not before.

If Hercules 'sovereign conqueror' was well-known to Chaucer's monk, we might pause in conclusion to consider what category of human image did not have *auctoritas*. What image might have given real offence on a medieval hillside? Returning to Aelfric we are directed towards those which are non-Biblical, Norse or Germanic images, or those too sacred for unregulated use, that is, images of Christ, of the Devil and of the Saints. There are, for example, clear parallels between the style of Woden's death on a tree and the Crucifixion, but Woden and his company (unlike their classical counterparts) are wholly excluded from the Christian canon.

'To see is to have seen ...'

Field archaeologists define themselves by looking at things, but what they are able to recognise will often depend on what they have seen before (Bradley 1997, 71). The image of the Cerne Abbas hill-figure was first 'seen' by the antiquarian-minded who immediately saw it as belonging to the pre-Christian English, the 'Antient Britons.' It is Iron Age and/or Romano-British to those whose period of research that is. Archaeologists have tended to follow an *a priori* assumption that it is of this date, to seek out supporting material and develop the whole as a coherent thesis. Later folklorists fleshed out the picture and supplied the human – and mystical – fertility touch. A medieval origin has scarcely been considered – mistakenly – given the presence of a religious house. The image has changed a little (Grinsell 1980, 118–121) while interpretation continues to change with the times.

It is impossible to set out freehand a figure the size of the Cerne Abbas Giant on a slope as steep as that presented by the Cerne Abbas hillside (Barker 1998). The Giant started life as a prepared drawing by 'persons who were not quite unacquainted with the rules of proportion observed by statuaries and painters ...' says John Hutchins, an observation duly noted by those who measured and set out a second figure in the summer of 1997. It was Hutchins, in the steps of Stukeley, who set us off on the right course of inquiry. And the Cerne Abbas Giant almost fooled him.

* * * * * * * *

Cultural contexts

RH: Once again the conclusion to be drawn from a review of this major early source is wholly negative. It leaves a big question mark hanging over what we see. Could a major Benedictine abbey have tolerated the existence of a blatantly erotic obviously pagan, figure upon its very doorstep, for a period of almost a thousand years in which it was governed by abbots who included individuals of notable rigour and piety, and visited regularly by ecclesiastical authorities? In his influential essay in 1981, Joe Bettey was still prepared to admit that it might have done, given the existence of carvings in medieval English churches which twentieth-century scholarship has customarily taken as representation of formerly beloved pagan deities (Bettey 1981, 119). They consist of figures of men with large erections, (more commonly) of naked women squatting facing the onlooker in such a way as to display their vulvae, and (most common of all) of human heads set among foliage and with leaves gushing from their nostrils and mouths. The first sort is too rare to have been given a generic name by scholars, but the second has become known by the Irish colloquial term of sheela-na-gig, and the third as Green Men.

In his evidence set about above, however, Dr Bettey decisively rejects this parallel, and it is important to expand upon his reasons for doing so. In 1978 Kathleen Basford published the first detailed study of the foliate heads, and concluded that there was absolutely no evidence that they had been intended to represent pre-Christian deities or nature spirits. Eight years later, Anthony Weir and James Jerman brought out an equivalent study of the erotic images, and demonstrated that they were misfits in a specific style of Romanesque art, which had commenced in pilgrimage churches in central France and spread west and south from there. They were clearly designed to be objects of disgust and not of reverence, illustrating the horrors of lust (Weir and Jerman 1986). All these kinds of carvings tended to appear not in churches where the influence of the parishioners was strong, but in those which were patronized by wealthy churchmen or laity who were prepared to spend extra money upon didactic or decorative representations. They were not, moreover, part of a single movement, for the heyday of the erotic figures was in the twelfth century, and that of the foliate heads in the fifteenth. These changes in expert opinion remove the cultural context which had formerly been presumed to underlie the survival of an ancient phallic figure next to a medieval monastery.

After the destruction of the abbey local opinion became for a time if anything even less favourable to the preservation of heathen images. During the early Stuart period, Dorchester developed into the very model of a Puritan community, dedicated to complete moral and religious reformation designed to create a godly local commonwealth purified of all associations with paganism or Popery. This episode in the town's history had left an exceptionally large number of records of many kinds, which have recently been used as the basis for a celebrated monograph upon it (Underdown 1992). The evangelical reformers of Dorchester worried about a great many local matters, from the lighting of a Midsummer bonfire at the town's end to whether musicians should be allowed to perform within its precincts, and also vexed their consciences over national political and ecclesiastical policies. It seems extraordinary that none of them, either in the public or private records from the time, should have commented upon the presence of a rampant pagan figure, of colossal proportions, carved only a few miles away.

On the other hand, the cultural context for the making of a new Giant, even a rude one, in seventeenth-century England, is reasonably good. The Cerne carving and the equally enigmatic and undated Long Man at Wilmington, Sussex, are the sole survivors of a number of huge male figures carved into slopes which existed in the Tudor and Stuart periods. Katherine Barker mentioned those on Plymouth Hoe in her contribution above, and one can add others on Shotover Hill, Oxford, and the Gogmagog Hills near Cambridge (Crawford 1929). Some of these may, of course, be laid open to the same possibility that hovers over the Cerne one, of having survived from remote antiquity, but it should be noted that the Gog-Magog example was described by a writer in about 1640, quite specifically, as having been cut by 'the scholars of Cambridge' (Scott 1937, 104).

All this is hardly surprising, given the popularity of tales about Giants, and pictures of them, in the chapbook literature of the Tudor and Stuart ages, Those same stories and ballads, preserved in such collections as that of Samuel Pepys at Magdalene College, Cambridge, display abundantly at times the sort of earthy vulgarity manifested so plainly by the Giant of Cerne, and are illustrated by woodcuts sometimes as crude in their form as that figure. Model giants were, moreover, stock figures in urban processions and shows; during the sixteenth century they are recorded as being hauled along in such entertainments at Coventry, Chester, Salisbury, and London (Hutton 1996, 314; Phythian-Adams 1976, 110–17). The Salisbury Giant is preserved in the city museum. In his present form he makes a demure figure, but not all of his brethren may have looked so respectable. In 1599 the first Puritan mayor of Chester, Henry Hardware, suppressed three features of the customary Midsummer Show, the Giants, the 'feathered devil', and the 'naked boys', as offensive to public morality (Clopper 1979, 197–9).

The Cerne Giant as Hercules

The Cerne figure, however, is not just any Giant, or even any priapic Giant. He is, almost certainly, intended to represent Hercules; and here the evidence of the former existence of a cloak hanging from one arm reinforces the impression of this identification, made long ago by Stuart Piggott (Piggott 1938). Here again, the revival of classical forms which is a feature of Tudor and Stuart culture would provide an appropriate context. Dr Bettey, however, goes much further than this, and in his evidence above suggests a specific moment and motive for the making of that particular image in that particular place, which I personally find convincing.

Seventeenth-century society and the birth of the Giant

It remains true, however, that nobody has yet discovered a birth certificate for the Giant, a seventeenth-century document which records its creation. Is this very significant? The answer must be an emphatic negative. After 1640 the hitherto profuse local estate records for Cerne dwindle away almost to nothing, while the documents for nearby communities such as Dorchester also fall off sharply. The Giant, appears, effectively, in a gap in the evidence. Would it have been possible for such a colossal undertaking to have been carried out without some contemporary reference to the event having survived? Clearly it could have been, if the story of the other Wessex chalkland carvings is taken into account. Nine 'white horses' are known to have existed upon Wiltshire and Dorset hill-sides during the eighteenth and nineteenth centuries, and have always been recognized as belonging to that period. When the records for them are considered, however, it becomes apparent that in six cases there is no contemporary note of their creation. We are fairly certain of the approximate date of each only because of later oral testimony which identified the time and the people concerned. The latter represented quite a variety, including gentry, an urban corporation and (mostly) local farmers (Marples 1949, 67–127).

This is the pattern which we find at Cerne, except that more time had elapsed before the first enquiries were made; perhaps over a hundred years. It is not surprising that when the antiquarian John Hutchins recorded replies to them, in the 1750s, he found quite a variety of response. Some people told a story about an actual Giant who had terrorized the locality by eating its sheep, and been killed while sleeping on the spot where his outline was preserved. Others said that it had been cut in derision of the last abbot, a lecher, with the club upraised in anger at the dissolution of the abbey. It was the most sophisticated witness to whom Hutchins spoke, the steward of the manor, who confidently provided the information, quoted below by Joseph Bettey, that it had been made in the time of Denzil Holles. Hutchins, however, took care to counter this by adding immediately that old people whom he had met upon his visits claimed that it had existed since time immemorial (Hutchins 1774, II, 35–7; British Library, Stowe MSS 753, ff. 170–3, and 754, ff. 118–19).

The canard about the last abbot is a ripe piece of Protestant myth-making; Dr Bettey sets out the known facts concerning that unfortunate individual. He also comments, accurately, upon the wild tales which folklore could develop around events and monuments in a relatively short period. It should be noted, furthermore, how telescoped a sense of time ordinary people in early modern England generally had. To illustrate this quickly from one fairly local example, we need only look at the parish accounts of Mere, another chalkland village a short distance to the north across the Wiltshire border. In 1565 it instituted the custom of holding a parish feast each May, presided over by a 'cuckoo king' and a 'cuckoo prince'. This lapsed in 1573 and was revived in 1576. In 1577 it was described as being held according to 'old custom'. In other words, a dozen years were sufficient to consign something to a generalized antiquity (Baker 1980). By

Hutchin's day, the Giant of Cerne had been in existence for a great deal longer than that.

What is very noticeable from John Hutchin's writings, both in his published history and his private letters, is that he himself instinctually wished to believe that the figure was ancient, and so took some pains to lay out the evidence, however honestly, in such a way as to favour this view. It is precisely this approach which has been taken by antiquarians and archaeologists ever since. The role of the early antiquarians in the story is an important one, and to examine the first published accounts, drawings and discussions of the Giant in the mid-eighteenth century I would like to call on my next witness, David Morgan Evans. Mr Morgan Evans is the General Secretary of the Society of Antiquaries of London which was founded in 1707; he has investigated the Society's records relating to the Giant and early discussions of it.

* * * * * * * *

Eighteenth-century descriptions of the Cerne Abbas Giant

David Morgan Evans

The earliest depiction that we have of the Cerne Abbas Giant, inserted in the Minute Book of the Society of Antiquaries of London, has never been published. This can now be remedied, and the background examined. The eighteenth-century 'discovery' of the Giant has been described (Castleden 1996), but the process was a more complex affair than has been realized.[27]

There appear to be two lines of enquiry about the Giant during the eighteenth century. One involves publication in the magazines of the period. While it has been assumed that the *Gentleman's Magazine* account of the Giant is the earliest, it is actually derived from the *St. James's Chronicle* for October 1763, which in its turn is derived from the *Royal Magazine* for September 1763. The other line of enquiry started with the Bishop of Bristol's visitation to Cerne Abbas in the 1730s, and can be traced through to the discussion of the Giant at the Society of Antiquaries meetings in early 1764. The two lines finally come together in Hutchins's 1774 *History of Dorset* with a final addition in the third edition published between 1861 and 1870.

The account in the *Royal Magazine* of September 1763 is in the form of an anonymous letter (Anon. 1763a):[28]

To the Author of the Royal Magazine.

SIR

I have been a subscriber to your useful and entertaining Miscellany ever since its commencement and I have for a long time intended to communicate to you some curious observations of my own in natural history and philosophy; but at present I shall only trouble you with an exact account of the Dimensions of the Giant cut out on the side of a very steep Hill, near Cerne in Dorsetshire. This monstrous figure, viewed from the opposite Hill, appears almost erect, with a huge Crab-tree Club in his Hand, raised over his Head, just going to strike a Blow, which seems sufficient, as it were , to overturn a Mountain. As I send you the Dimensions of this figure, which I took myself, I hope some of your ingenious Correspondents will favour us with an Account of its Origins and Use; it is supposed to be above a thousand years standing, as there is a Date between its Legs, and the Figures are not legible. It is plain there were but three Figures; so that, supposing the first to be a 9, it must have been formed a long time ago. Some think that it was cut by the Ancient Britons, and that they worshipped it; others believe it to be the Work of the Papists, as here was formerly an Abbey &c.,&c. But, however that may be, the Dimensions are as follow

There then follows a list of twenty-nine dimensions but no drawing. The correlation of the measurements between the various magazine articles is discussed below.

In October 1763 a similar letter appeared in the *St James's Chronicle* (Anon. 1763b).[29] This letter also has no identifying marks. The article is addressed 'TO THE PRINTER'. This version cuts out the preliminary compliments and begins 'SIR, I have sent you an exact account of the Dimensions of the Giant cut out on the side of a very steep Hill, near Cerne in Dorsetshire.' The text is then exactly the same as the previous letter, as are the measurements. The derivation of this letter from the *Royal Magazine* is clearly acknowledged at the foot of the piece. The *St James's Chronicle* version is of interest because it was through reading it that Stukeley first enquired about the Giant of John Hutchins (Lukis 1883, 129).

In July 1764 exactly the same anonymous version of the *St James's Chronicle* letter occurs in the *Gentleman's Magazine*, but addressed to 'Mr URBAN' (Anon. 1764). The source of the letter is not acknowledged. The text is the same but there are two significant differences. The dimensions listed at the end of the letter are different and it is illustrated with a drawing of the Giant, complete with some measurements.

The order and descriptions of the twenty-nine measurements of the Giant is the same for all three publications. They begin with the 'Length of his foot' and progress to the thickness of the club. The detailed figures for the measurements in the *Royal Magazine* and the *St James's Chronicle* are both the same. However they differ in significant detail and in their lack of association with a drawing from those given in the *Gentleman's Magazine.*[30] The importance of these differences in detail lies in the survey work that must have taken place on the Giant, including the provision of the drawing. It is interesting that the *Gentleman's Magazine* could have access to new measurements and a drawing but still had to depend upon an earlier text with its theories of origins.

We can now turn to look at the notices of the Giant which took place in a rather less public fashion. The earliest occasion occurs sometime between 1733 and 1737. This is derived from the contents of the letter from the Reverend John Hutchins to the Bishop of Carlisle (Bettey 1981, 121) and which the Bishop laid before the Society of Antiquaries on 9th February 1764.[31] While there is gap of almost 30 years between the visitation and the Society meeting this would nonetheless be the earliest record that we have of notice being taken of the Giant by those outside Cerne Abbas.

The entry in the minute book for 9th February 1764 reads:

> With regard to the Draught of the Giant at Cerne Abbas, Mr. Hutchins mentions a wild fanciful Story, broached by the Inhabitants thereabouts, concerning the *Origin of the Figure. [note in the margin in the same hand: * Mr. Hutchins himself thinks it was without doubt, intended for a memorial of the Saxon God Heil]* Many ancient People have it handed down to them, by Tradition, for several Generations, that this figure has been there in a remote Age. He relates, that being present at his * Grace *[note in margin * Dr. Secker]* of Canterbury's primary and only Visitation, when he was Bishop of the Diocese, after Dinner his Lordship enquired concerning this Figure, of the Minister of the Town (a plain, but very honest Man) who gave a very tedious & circumstantial but most diverting Relation of what he had heard from his Parishioners. The Particulars Mr. Hutchins has forgot, but the substance was, That anciently a Giant fixt his Quarters at, or near, this Town, & was a very troublesome Neighbour: That one Morning he took a Walk into the Vale of Blakemore, on the other side of the Hill, &, lighting on a Flock of Sheep, he devoured a Score or two. On his return home, finding himself tired with his Walk & Breakfast, he lay down on the side of the this Hill to take a Nap. The Inhabitants seized the Opportunity, pinioned him down, killed him, marked out his Figure, & left the Birds to pick his Bones. Thus far goes the tradition concerning the Giant.

Mr. Hutchins then related the tradition of St Augustine punishing the inhabitants of Cerne Abbas for cutting off his horse's tail or attaching fish tails to his robes. A marginal note in the minute book notes the similarity of this tradition with that concerning Thomas a Becket punishing a knight for a similar offence (*cf.* Hutchins 1774, II, 287).

The importance of this account, if Hutchins's memory is to be trusted, is that it gives us the earliest reference to the Giant in broadly its current form. The circumstantial details can all be confirmed as correct.[32] John Hutchins would have been present at the telling of the story, as the rector of Melcombe Horsey;[33] Dr Secker went on to become Bishop of Oxford from 1737 to 1758, before becoming Archbishop of Canterbury (Stephen and Lee 1998, 368–9), and could be a source of information for Oxford antiquarians. We cannot be sure who the 'plain, but very honest' Minister of the town was. There are two candidates. John Derby, vicar from 1710 until 1736 and his successor John Veneer. The description of the Minister present at the visitation seems best to fit John Derby (Hutchins 1774, II, 296; Foster 1891, 396–7) and this can be confirmed.[34]

From this account we can conclude that in the 1730s 'the parishioners' told a folk-tale about the origin of the Giant, and that 'people' said that the figure had been there 'in a remote age'. As the Minister concerned is John Derby, it would take an awareness of the Giant back to within sixteen years of the first notice of it, the cleaning of 1694 (Castleden 1996, 17 and see above). The reliance that can be put on dating from local memory is, of course, another matter (*cf.* Thomas 1996).

The next notice of the Giant that we have is in 1742, in a pamphlet published by the Reverend Francis Wise (Wise 1742). The text has been published and the controversial circumstances of its appearance considered (Castleden 1996, 18).[35] For our purposes it is worth noting that Wise was aware of the existence of Hutchins and his proposed county history, that he preferred to live in Oxford, and that he was elected a Fellow of the Society of Antiquaries in April, 1749.[36] His account appears to be based on hearsay. It shows however an awareness of the Giant in antiquarian circles.

Interest in the Giant in the 1750s involved a number of inter-connected antiquarians and two in particular. Dr Charles Lyttelton, a member of the Grenville family, was Dean of Exeter, 1748 to 1762, then Bishop of Carlisle 1762 to 1768. He was President of the Society of Antiquaries from 1765 to 1768 (Society of Antiquaries 1945, 7; Stephen and Lee 1998, 368–9). Jeremiah Milles followed Dr Lyttelton, first as Dean of Exeter in 1762 and second as President of the Society from 1768 to 1784 (Society of Antiquaries 1945, 8). In 1751 John Hutchins gave details of the Giant to Charles Lyttelton at his request (Bettey 1981, 121). Hutchins first mentions that the Steward of the Manor says that the Giant is 'a modern thing' cut by Lord Hollis (which would make it mid-seventeenth century) but in a subsequent letter postulates that it is Saxon. In 1756 Lyttleton also asks Francis Wise, by this time a Fellow of the Society of Antiquaries, for his views, which are summarized that the Giant was 'only an humble imitation of the Saxon manner' thus confirming his view in 1742 that it was not of a great antiquity. Moreover, he had by this time seen the Giant for himself.

In 1754 Richard Pococke FSA, on one of his many tours visited the Giant. Richard Pococke was a cousin of Jeremiah Milles, who had toured with him (Cartwright 1889, 143–4; Stephen and Lee 1998, 12–14). Pococke visited Hutchins in Wareham in September 1750 (Cartwright 1888, 91) before returning to Dorset in October 1754 and including the Giant on his travels. Pococke had at this stage gained the information, perhaps from Hutchins, that a name for the Giant could be 'Hele', he thought it to be about 150 feet long and after describing it he makes the first noted classical identifications of 'Hercules' or 'Priapus'. He also mentions the Lord of the Manor contributing to its regular cleaning.[37]

Nine years later the Giant became again the subject of antiquarian interest. There appear to be two strands of enquiry. The first is started by William Stukeley in October 1763, having seen the St James's Chronicle copy letter. He writes to Hutchins and we have Hutchins's reply of 22nd October 1763 (Lukis 1883, 129–31).[38] Hutchins says that he has not seen the St James's Chronicle letter but will give his 'best account'. He gives a limited number of measurements (eight lengths and four breadths including the trenches), repeats the tradition of the sheep-eating Giant and postulates that 'if, as some have said, the god Heil was worshipped here, it may be a memorial of him, and work of the Saxon age'. Later in the same letter Hutchins writes that he has never heard the Giant called Hercules and 'I wish I could oblige you with the draught, but I am a bad draughtsman, and it is near 20 miles from me, and the fear of the gout confines me at home'.

There is a little more detail in the letter of 29th Nov 1763 (Lukis 1883, 132–3):

> Revd. Sir, I had the favour of yours, and immediately applied to a friend to get me a sketch of the Giant at Cerne, and procured a person to take a draught and make proper measurements at Aggleston. I did not receive the Giant till yesterday, and deferred writing till I could send both draughts together. I have nothing more to add concerning the Giant, but to ask pardon for an inaccurate description of a thing that I had not seen for a great many years.[39]

It is possible that Hutchins had not visited the Giant since his move to Wareham in 1743. It is also worth mentioning that Hutchins had been warned about Stukeley and his opinions. His great friend, Charles Godwyn, Fellow of Balliol College (Hutchins 1774, I, iii) wrote to him on 23rd December 1763:

> I find you correspond with Dr. Stukeley. You must be very cautious there. He is extremely injudicious, and whimsical to the last degree. His 'Carausius' is one of the wildest books that were written; and he is going to publish another as wild upon British Coins. He sometimes tires the patience of the Antiquarian Society with a dissertation, which never fails of exciting laughter. (Nichols 1814, 240)

Shortly after this exchange with Stukeley, Hutchins was back in correspondence with Charles Lyttleton, by now Bishop of Carlisle and sent him on 16th January 1764, a letter and a drawing of the Giant (Bettey 1981, 121).[40]

This account of the Giant was given before the Society on 9th February 1764, the Lord Bishop of Carlisle being in the chair:

> ...was pleased also to communicate Extracts of two letters from the Revd. Mr. Hutchins, Minister of Wareham in Dorsetshire; the one inclosing a

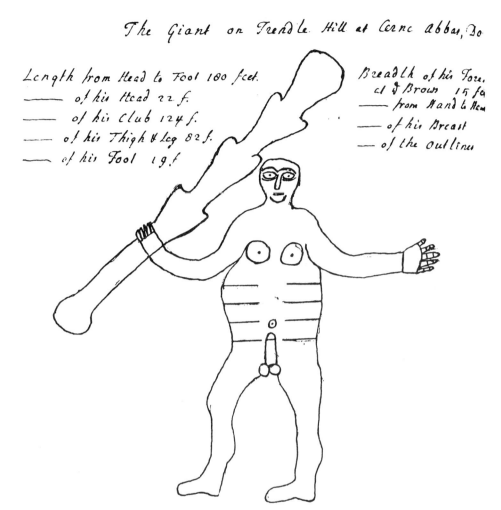

The Giant on Trendle Hill at Cerne abbas, Do.

Length from Head to Foot 180 feet.
——— of his Head 22 f.
——— of his Club 124 f.
——— of his Thigh & leg 82 f.
——— of his Foot 19 f.

Breadth of his Fore,
cl & Brow   15 fa
——— from Hand to Hem
——— of his Breast
——— of the Outlines

Figure 40. *Sketch of the Cerne Abbas Giant, November 1763. From the Minute book of the Society of Antiquaries of London, IX (July 1762-April 1765), between pages 199 and 200. (Illustration courtesy of the Society of Antiquaries of London. Copyright reserved)*

Draught & Admeasurement of Aggleston, the greatest piece of Antiquity in that County, the other inclosing a Draught of the Giant at Cerne Abbas, in the same County also.

Stukeley was not present at this meeting. It might be possible that there was a move to pre-empt Stukeley although a more probable explanation is Stukeley's unwillingness to stay late for Antiquaries' meetings, which followed those of the Royal Society.[41] However at the meeting of the Antiquarian Society on 16th February 1764 'Dr Stukeley read some observations on Mr. Hutchin's Account of the Giant at Cerne Abbas in Dorsetshire, communicated to the Society at their last meeting, & promised to favour them with a minute thereof at some other

Opportunity: for which thanks were returned to him'. This duly happened at the Meeting on 15th March 1764 when 'Dr Stukeley read, & delivered in a Minute of the Observations made by him on the Giant of Cerne Abbas in Dorsetshire read to the Society the 16th of Febry last'.[42] The rest of the text contains Stukeley's conjectures and identifications, including his ideas about Hercules. The text of Stukeley's paper is printed from his own minute in the third edition of Hutchins's History of Dorset (Hutchins 1861–70, I, 35–6).

Bound in with the minute book entries is the 'draught' of the Giant together with measurements (Figure 40).[43] The size of the paper and the handwriting is different from the main minute book and it must be the draught sent by Hutchins to either the Bishop of Carlisle or to Stukeley. Given its location in the minute book and the reference to it by the Bishop the former is the more likely. The details of the measurements of the Giant are exactly those contained in the letter sent to Stukeley on 22nd October 1763. These measurements are fewer in number and different in detail from either the *Royal Magazine/St James's Chronicle* or the *Gentleman's Magazine*/Hutchins 1774 sets. The letter to the Bishop, read at the Society, although following the same lines, contains more detail than that sent to Stukeley. This 'draught' must stand as the earliest representation of the Giant, its source being the 'friend' that Hutchins sent to draw it in October 1793. The measurements, however, are probably those taken by Hutchins himself but, at his own admission, some considerable time earlier. This sketch was not to stay for long as the best representation of the Giant.

The *Gentleman's Magazine* for July 1764 (Anon. 1764, 336) contains, as item XXV, 'Dimensions of a gigantic figure at Cerne, in Dorsetshire'. The text of this letter and its origins have already been discussed. The dimensions, coming from a new source, were then given and are accompanied by a picture of the Giant (dated August 1764) with the dimensions on it. The new measurements in the *Gentleman's Magazine* are listed in the order followed by the *Royal Magazine*. Unfortunately there is no source or reference for this survey and drawing. There are no initials or name, only the date.

Finally, we come to the drawing and the measurements that are published in Hutchins's *History of Dorset* (1774, II, 293). This picture of the Giant follows the *Gentleman's Magazine* illustration but is famously devoid of genital detail and while the measurements are listed in a different order they are the same as those in the *Gentleman's Magazine* including the mistake over the transcription of the breadth of the knots on the club. Where the Hutchins publication differs is in the letters and figures between the legs. The *Gentleman's Magazine* description is of only three figures, the first being a '9'. Hutchins mentions 'certain rude letters scarce legible, which are given here as copied Aug. 1772. It is plain that there were no more than three. Some affirm them to be proof of the great antiquity of this figure, which they refer to Saxon times. Over these are three more figures, probably modern. If these are intended for a date, we may read it as 748'. He then wonders if they reflect a 1748 repair and he goes in for various conjectures. While his account reflects caution about Stukeley he was not followed by the editors of the third edition (Hutchins 1861–70).

Besides clarifying some of the eighteenth-century sources for the Giant some conclusions might be drawn. Stukeley can be ruled out as a source for the letters in the magazines about the Giant, and as any sort of original source for its discovery or study. As the publication of the magazine letters is before the Antiquaries meeting in 1764 this again was not directly the source. The magazine letter is different from the views expressed by any of our known commentators and this suggests a different person. The source of the *Gentleman's Magazine* drawing and measurements remains a problem. Its association with an earlier text suggests that the editor obtained the drawing, by whatever means, and then revived the letter. It could be that Hutchins had commissioned a measured drawing after the Antiquaries meeting, but against that we have his evidence for having detail added in 1772.

While these accounts do not help greatly with the question of date it does seem that Hutchins's local knowledge of the Giant was limited. Before 1764 he has two known contacts and one unknown. The known ones are the local Minister, John Derby, who tells a folktale for after-dinner entertainment and the Steward of the Manor who says that the Giant was made by Lord Hollis. The unknown source provides the name for the Giant of 'Hele' or 'Heil'. Given that the resident Manorial Steward would be responsible for the cleaning of the Giant, greater weight might be put on his evidence than on Hutchins's 'ancient people'.

* * * * * * * *

Recent approaches to the history of the Giant

RH: With more audacity, I would like also to consider the work of more recent, post eighteenth century, scholars. In doing so I do not wish to give an impression of dancing upon the grave of the notion that the Giant may be a relic of pre-Christian religion; it may yet be proven to be so. What I wish to address instead is the not unimportant question of why, since the birth of professional archaeology about a century ago, its practitioners should have inclined to this idea so markedly when, as has surely been indicated, it was no foregone conclusion to do so.

The answer must surely take account of the fact that in the first few decades of this century, the infant disciplines of archaeology and folklore studies overlapped heavily with each other, both in subject matter and in personnel, and shaded in turn into a romantic mysticism. The union of all three is illustrated perfectly by the person who launched the twentieth-century sequence of scholarly enquiries into the age of the Cerne figure: Sir Flinders Petrie. He decided that its date was Bronze Age, on the strength of an arbitrary identification of some pits nearby as prehistoric flint mines and the alignment of some early boundaries. He then went on to quote the testimony of the village sexton, that a maypole had formerly been put up every year in the earthwork above the Giant's head, and danced around; this he proposed to throw some light upon the original purpose of the carving, as an ancient god of fertility (Petrie 1926, 10). The impression was thus powerfully conveyed of an unbroken tradition of religious observance devolving into folk practices, preserved in the English countryside ever since the end of the Stone Age.

This impression embodied a set of attitudes which Petrie shared with most of his generation, best expressed in, and reinforced by, Sir James Frazer's classic text *The Golden Bough*, rural England was viewed as an essentially unchanging society, full of ancient secrets with which urbanized and industrialized society had lost contact and which it now needed to rediscover. In particular, its seasonal rituals and its superstitions faithfully preserved remnants of pre-Christian religions, belief-systems which the modern English imagination found increasingly fascinating as allegiance to Christian tenets weakened. It was not, however, supposed that the 'folk' themselves had any understanding of the true significance of their folklore; rather, they carried on immemorial practices blindly, propelled by custom, and it was educated elite to determine the genuine origins and purpose of the traditions in order that the whole society, including the practitioners, might be instructed and educated about them (Hutton 1996, esp. vii–xi and 295–303). This was only a reinforcement of an attitude built into scholarly perceptions of the Giant since they were first formed; back in the mid-eighteenth century, nobody in Cerne seems to have thought that the carving was a relic of ancient pagan religion. It was Hutchins and his successors who were inclined to the view that it should be, and that this view should be shared by everybody else.

A potent symbol of the modern combination of archaeology, folklore studies and romance consists of that maypole which Petrie suggested had traditionally been erected above the figure, apparently connecting the recent past with remote antiquity. To O G S Crawford, writing three years later, the earthwork in which it had apparently been set was already 'the maypole enclosure' (Crawford 1929, 280). Half a decade after that the meticulous F H L Darton examined local records and traditions carefully and found that there was absolutely no evidence that maypoles had ever been set up anywhere near the Giant (Darton 1935, 320–30). This view has been reinforced recently in the most detailed study of Dorset folk customs yet made (Robson 1988, 56–64). It has not, however, made any impact upon the world of professional archaeology. As late as 1992, one of the members of that world who has written with the most perception and popularity upon the nature of prehistoric British religions, Aubrey Burl, thought it sufficient to see off any challenge to an ancient dating for the Giant by citing a reference to a maypole which had existed at Cerne (in an unspecified place) in 1635 (Burl 1992). Behind this piece of academic mythology lies the work of a local Victorian antiquary, Colley March, who was fascinated by the notion of maypole customs as relics of primitive 'Aryan' solar worship. It was he who recorded the information from the sexton which was quoted by Petrie and which seems to have been, simply, wrong (March 1901).

Petrie and Crawford were two of the leading figures in early twentieth-century archaeology who contributed to the debate over the age of the Giant. A third was Stuart Piggott, and in his best-known essay upon the subject, in the journal *Antiquity*, he immediately evoked a sense of rural mystery and wonder. Cerne, he told his readers, is 'remote in a lonely valley of the Dorset hills' (Piggott 1938, 327). Even in his time, when it was much declined from its former importance, it was actually situated upon a busy arterial road linking two local capitals; but this reality was at odds with his purpose, which was represent the place as a secluded traditional community in which the cult of a pagan deity might long have been kept alive. He addressed this theme in a different fashion in a parallel essay in the journal of the Folk-Lore Society. Here he drew attention to the fact that in recent times the earthwork above the Giant had been called 'The Frying Pan'. He pointed out that in the southern English Mummer's Play, performed by groups of working-class people touring pubs and private homes in the Christmas season, there appears a character usually called Beelzebub, who is equipped with a club and a frying pan. At the time at which Piggott was writing, scholars supposed the play to be itself a survival of ancient pagan religion, representing a prehistoric ritual of death and rebirth. He suggested that both 'Beelzebub' and the Cerne Giant might represent the same archaic god (Piggott 1929).

He had indeed made a correct connection, but from the wrong end. Since the 1970s experts have realized that there are in fact no certain records of the Mummers' Play before the early-eighteenth century, and that far from being a relic of pagan ritual it is a piece of knockout comedy put together between 1650 and 1740 and reaching a height of popularity a century later (Hutton 1996, 70–80). These seems to be no connection between the Cerne figure and Beelzebub except that they both carry clubs; but at some time in the nineteenth century that was sufficient for the identification to be made. As a result the earthwork above the carving, The Trendle, had its name altered in popular parlance to The Frying Pan, an indication of local enthusiasm for the play at that time.

In both cases, of the entertainment and of the Giant, a systematic study of medieval or early modern records would have raised similar doubts concerning an early dating, but this was exactly the sort of investigation which archaeologists and folklorists in the early twentieth century never troubled to undertake. Instead they preferred to look at folk customs as they looked at the Giant, set in the context of the present and of the recent past, and project their imaginations backward into a timeless antiquity to create pictures of a colourful primeval religion which somehow lived on concealed within the familiar contours of the English countryside. It is not surprising that Piggott's suggestion was immediately hailed as a great discovery by one of the leading folklorists of the time, Alice, Lady Gomme (Gomme 1929).

How powerful, and adaptable, that imaginative projection could be is demonstrated by the examples of Harold Massingham and Jacquetta Hawkes. The former was a very popular writer upon rural England, which he invested with an intense romantic affection proportionate to his hatred of modern urban and industrial societies. To give his vision a prehistoric dimensions, he leaned heavily upon the work of archaeologists such as Crawford and Piggott. In his memoirs, he explained why it was vitally necessary for readers to ignore the doubts raised by Darton and to continue to believe that the Cerne Giant was a pagan figure, which had survived the Middle Ages with the tolerance, indeed the blessing, of the abbey just beneath it. The two represented the reconciliation of the two vital forces in the English soul; the figure standing for the sleeping power of the earth, which the modern age needed to venerate anew, and the monastery for a religion which had purged society of the grossness and cruelty of paganism while retaining an awe of the natural world. With both, he believed, the English might yet be spiritually redeemed (Massingham 1944, 95–6).

Jacquetta Hawkes had in common with Massingham an immense popularity as a writer and an affection for the English countryside accompanied by a detestation of most aspects of modernity. She had herself been a archaeologist, and after her retirement to become a full-time author she acted very much as a mouthpiece of professional archaeology to the general public. When considering the Cerne Abbas Giant, she assumed automatically that it was an image from the pagan past, but whereas Massingham's vision had caused the monks to honour and so preserve the figure, in Hawkes's it was the country people themselves who had defied the power of the Church to preserve their beloved old deity. The myth of the maypole dancers in the earthwork was summoned up again to represent this spirit of resistance which, in the ideology with which Hawkes infused her books, might yet provide the force necessary to oppose the iniquities of modern culture (Hawkes 1954, 143–4).

Summing up

It can be seen from all that has been set out here for this case that the Giant provokes a strong set of emotions. Even among an ostensibly scholarly and objective community these have worked in favour of a belief in an ancient date for the figure. No wonder such a belief has by now been implanted so firmly in the popular imagination. I would suggest instead that whatever the resolution of the mystery of the figure's age, the implications are going to be important and exciting. If it really does turn out to be prehistoric or Romano-British, then historians will have to ask some hard and fascinating questions about the way in which medieval and early modern writers, at all levels. chose to record or to ignore information. If I and my colleagues here are correct, and it was actually first cut in the seventeenth century, then our appreciation of that period will be greatly increased. The Giant will not be revealed as a 'fraud' or a 'fake', but remain a virile and audacious figure, representing a pagan god or hero within a different context. It will merely shift its focus, from being associated with Dorset's prehistoric barrows and hillforts to being grouped with monuments such as the castles at Corfe and Sherborne, with their dramatic memories of the Civil War. The imagination of the twenty-first century should be creative, and elastic, enough to provide it with new poetic and political redolences to replace any that it may lose.

Notes

1. See *Daily Mail*, 22nd August 1905
2. Public Records Office, SP1/89/123–5; *Letters and Papers of Henry VIII*, VIII, 148; IX, 256; XIII(2), 1090.
3. Betty 1989, 86; *Letter and Papers Henry VIII*, XIII(2), 1092.
4. Public Records Office, E315/397; SC6/Hen VIII/655(106).
5. Public Records Office, E318/21/1138; SC6/Hen.VIII/662; Dorset Record Office, 396/E249; D396/T113, T114.
6. Public Records Office, E134/27 Eliz. T9; C3/184/75; C22/631/17.
7. Dorset Record Office, D396/E249.
8. Public Records Office, E36/157; British Library, Add. MSS. 6027.
9. Dorset Record Office, PE/CEA/CW 2, Cerne Abbas Churchwardens Accounts', 1686–1758.
10. Underdown 1979; *Notes and Queries for Somerset & Dorset*, VIII, 347–9; XII, 52–5; XIV, 1–3; XVIII, 157–9, 169–72.
11. Public Records Office, SP Dom., 1638, 393/54, 54; *Ibid.* 1638–9, 400/2.
12. Betty 1981, iii; For legal suits which Holles was involved see Public Records Office, C5/21/52; C5/22/66; C5/26/88; Plea Roll 2578/252; Court of Requests. Charles I/Bundle 27.
13. British Library, Add. MSS, 32697 ff 4–9. A. Collins, *Historical Collections of Noble Families*, 1752, 100–62.
14. I am grateful to James Russell for providing this reference.
15. Public Records Office, C5/21/52; C5/26/88; C22/258/19; Crawford 1979, 182–3.
16. Public Records Office, Sp 78/122.
17. Dorset Record Office, PE/CEA/CW2.
18. For brief details of Hutchins and his career see Betty 1994, 125–31.
19. British Library, Stowe MSS 753 ff 170–3, Letter from John Hutchins to Dr Charles Lyttleton, Dean of Exeter, 28 August 1751.
20. British Library, Stowe MSS 753 f 294.
21. The unreliability of local memory is illustrated by the incredible fables told to the archaeologist William Stukeley when he visited Dorset in 1723 (Stukeley 1724) and by Thomas Hardy in *The Mayor of Casterbridge* (Hardy 1886).
22. The role of poets and story-tellers in the myth-making process is something explored by Ferguson (1993, 114–133) for the Medieval world in his chapter 'Poesie Historical.' An interesting case is cited by Lummis (1999, 35) as late as the end of the eighteenth century. The log of the ill-fated *Bounty* records the crew catching and eating both Brown and White Albatrosses along with *Pintada* and other sea birds in March 1788. It was ten years later that Samuel Taylor Coleridge's poem *The Rime of the Ancient Mariner* was first published, where the albatross is a bird of good omen and to kill it brings certain disaster. Perhaps the subsequent superstition about albatrosses is a case of nature imitating art, of a poet creating a belief rather than recording its existence, notes Lummis.
23. The Domesday assessment of the Cerne Valley estates, like that for the early ecclesiastical estate of Sherborne, seems to reflect a 9-fold unit for which there may be some evidence in the historic landscape (Barker 1988, 30–31). The number 9 was reserved for God's Kingdom. At the Second Coming, Aelfric felt the Religious would be well-placed for re-admittance to Heaven as the Tenth Company (a place lost by Lucifer/the Devil) and everyone else would be entitled, according to his deserts, to join one of the other 9 which were graded in excellence. Was this just possibly a Dorset

valley administered according to the biblical geography of Heaven? Was this the model? The comment made by John (1996, 127) about the work of an American scholar, Dr Milton McGatch is interesting here. McGatch, notes John, 'sees Aelfric not as an intellectual but as a man who wished to make himself an efficient ecclesiastical administrator.'

24. The tumbled remains of what are probably the baths of Roman Bath are described in an Old English poem, *The Ruin*, as 'the work of the Giants'. Exactly what the writer may have meant by 'Giants' is difficult to know (Alexander 1966, 30).

25. We note that Gog and Magog were also guardians of London which, according to Geoffrey of Monmouth, was founded by Brutus. Two giant figures destroyed in 1940 were re-created in 1953 and stand 3m tall. A pair of much earlier giants were destroyed in the Great Fire of 1666 London's first recorded giant is 1413. A century later, in 1522, the giant figures of Hercules and Samson greeted Charles V in 1522 (Newman 1997, 106–107)

26. Two large oak trees either side of the road on the edge of the Up Cerne / Hermitage parish boundary are poetically named Gog and Magog on the first edition of the OS 1:2500. The trees have been felled and only the stumps remain.

27. This article first appeared in *The Antiquaries Journal* Volume 78 (1998) and is reproduced by kind permission of the Society. Some changes have been made on the basis of advice kindly given by Mr J H Bettey. While still unsure about the date of the Giant a personal preference for a mid-seventeenth century origin is declared.

28. The *Royal Magazine* or *Gentleman's Monthly Companion* was published from July 1754 until December 1771. I am grateful to Richard Meager for assisting me with obtaining this article.

29. The St James's Chronicle or British Evening Post was published twice weekly from March 1761 until August 1866.

30. While the overall length of the Giant agrees at 180 feet only another five dimensions exactly correspond, that is the measurements of the feet, the mouth, the breadth of the elbow and the diameter of the eye. The breadth of the thigh and the nose varies by six inches and five of the others are within two feet. Some figures appear to be wildly out, for example the *Royal Magazine* gives the breadth of the knots on the club as 22 feet, the *Gentleman's Magazine* as 4 feet, but examination of the measurements on the drawing show that this is a transcription error and that this should be 24 feet. This error is repeated by Hutchins. There appears to be no patterns in the differences that can be distinguished and the conclusion is that they are original survey errors.

31. Minute Book of the Society of Antiquaries of London IX (July 1762 – April 1765), 1764, 200.

32. Cerne Abbas was in the Diocese of Bristol at the time (Hutchins 1774, I, xxxiii) and was the centre for visitations (Hutchins 1774, II, 286).

33. He was the rector of Melcombe Horsey from 1733 until 1743 when he went to Wareham.

34. There is a problem in that Derby's death is recorded as 8th September 1736 but Veneer's installation is given as 11th February 1736. Since the publication of the original article in December 1998 Dr J H Bettey has kindly informed me that the diaries of the Bishop of Bristol show that the visitation took place in 1735. Mr Derby is therefore the after-dinner speaker.

35. Further references can be found in the appropriate entries in the *Dictionary of National Biography*.

36. Minute Book of the Society of Antiquaries of London V (March 1745 – September 1749), 1749, 226.
37. This confirms the Manorial link mentioned by Hutchins.
38. It should be noted that the letter which is dated 13th February and attributed by the editors to 1763 (Lukis 1883, 128–129) fits 1764 better, as Hutchins refers to the 'draughts' of the Gyant of Cerne and Aggleston which were not in existence until the late autumn of 1763.
39. Agglestone 'barrow' on Studland Common caused much excitement at the time but is a natural feature.
40. And see Minute Book of the Society of Antiquaries of London IX (July 1762 – April 1765), 1764, 197–201.
41. This can be supported by his opposition to the proposal, in May 1764, for the Royal Society to change the time of its meeting to 6 o'clock, as the Antiquarians meeting after them, Stukeley stated 'in winter time especially, I can be present there but seldom'. This is because he wished to avoid 'the damps, the dews of the night, the rains and other inconveniences according to the laudable customs of our ancestors' (Lukis 1883, 384–5).
42. Minute Book of the Society of Antiquaries of London IX (July 1762 – April 1765), 1764, 204 and 233–5.
43. Minute Book of the Society of Antiquaries of London IX (July 1762 – April 1765), 1764, between pages 199 & 200. The measurements on the right side have been obscured due to later binding.

Bibliography

Alexander, M, (translator) 1966, *The earliest English poems*. Harmondsworth. Penguin

Anon., 1763a, [Anonymous letter]. *Royal Magazine*, 9, 140–1

Anon., 1763b, [Anonymous letter]. *St James's Chronicle*, 404 (Tuesday, 4th October to Thursday 6th October 1763)

Anon., 1764, Description of a gigantic figure. *Gentleman's Magazine*, 34, 335–6

Ashworth, W B, 1990, Natural History and the Emblematic World View. In D Lindberg and R Westman (eds), *Reappraisals of the Scientific Revolution*. Cambridge. Cambridge University Press. 303–332

Baker, T, 1908, The Churchwarden's Accounts of Mere. *Wiltshire Archaeological and Natural History Society Magazine*, 35, 37–55

Barkan, L, 1986, *The Gods made flesh, metamorphosis and the pursuit of paganism*. London and New Haven. Yale University Press

Barker, K, and Seaward, D, 1990, Boundaries and landscape: the Tudor Manors of Holnest, Hilfield and Hermitage. *Proceedings of the Dorset Natural History and Archaeological Society*, 112, 5–22

Barker, K, 1998a, Brief Encounter: the Cerne Abbas Giantess Project, Summer 1997; an exercise in experimental archaeology. *Proceedings of the Dorset Natural History and Archaeological Society*, 119, 179–182

Barker, K, 1988b, Aelfric the Mass-priest and the Anglo-Saxon Estates of Cerne Abbey. In K Barker (ed), *The Cerne Abbey Millennium Lectures*. Cerne Abbas. Cerne Abbas Millennium Committee. 27–42

Basford, K, 1978, *The Green Man*. Ipswich. Brewer

Bayley, A R, 1910, *The Great Civil War in Dorset, 1642–1660*. Taunton. Wessex Press

Bergamar, K, 1997, *Discovering hill figures* (4th Edition; first published 1968). Princes Risborough. Shire Publications

Bettenson, H, 1972, *Augustine, City of God*. Harmondsworth. Penguin

Bettey, J H, 1981, The Cerne Abbas Giant; the documentary evidence. *Antiquity*, 55, 118–21

Bettey, J H, (ed), 1981, The casebook of Sir Francis Ashley. *Dorset Record Society*, 7

Bettey, J H, 1989, *The suppression of the monasteries in the west country*. Gloucester. Alan Sutton

Bettey, J H, 1994, Dorset. In C R J Currie and C P Lewis (eds), *A guide to English county histories*. Stroud. Alan Sutton. 125–31

Bradley, R, 1997, To See is to Have Seen: craft traditions in British field archaeology. In B L Molyneaux (ed), *The cultural life of images: visual representation in archaeology*. London. Routledge

Branston, B, 1980, *Gods of the North*. London. Thames and Hudson

Burl, A, 1992, Cultic Twilight. *The Times Literary Supplement*, 21st August

Burnet, G, 1833, *History of his own times* (2nd Edition). Oxford

Camille, M, 1989, *The Gothic idol, ideology and image-making in medieval Art*. Cambridge. Cambridge University Press

Cartwright, J J, 1888, *The travels through England of Dr Richard Pococke, volume I* (= Camden Society (NS) 42). London. Camden Society

Cartwright, J J, 1889, *The travels through England of Dr Richard Pococke, volume II* (= Camden Society (NS) 44). London. Camden Society

Castleden, R, 1996, *The Cerne Giant*. Wincanton. Dorset Publishing Company

Chandler, J, (ed), 1993, *Leland's Itinerary: travels in Tudor England*. Stroud. Alan Sutton

Clark, W A, 1997, Dowsing Gogmagog. *3rd Stone*, 27, 8–10 and 20

Clopper, L, 1979, *Records of early English drama*. Chester. Manchester

Copeland, R, 1991, *Rhetoric hermeneutics and translation in the Middle Ages: academic traditions and vernacular texts*. Cambridge. Cambridge University Press

Crawford, O G S, 1929, The Giant of Cerne and other hill-figures. *Antiquity*, 3, 277–83

Crawford, P, 1979, *Denzil Holles, 1598–1680: a study of his political career* (= Royal Historical Society Studies in History 16). London. Royal Historical Society

Cummins, 1988, *The hound and the hawk the art of medieval hunting*. London. Weidenfeld and Nicolson

Darton, F J H, 1935, *English fabric: a study of village life*. London. G Newnes

Daston, L and Park, K, 1998, *Wonders and the Order of Nature, 1150–1750*. New York. Zone Books

Dugdale, W, 1846, *Monasticon anglicanum*. London. Bohn. (Six volumes)

Febre, L, and Martin, H-J, 1976, *The coming of the book*. London. Verso Books

Ferguson, A B, 1993, *Utter antiquity: perceptions of prehistory in Renaissance England*. Durham and London. Duke University Press

Foster, J, 1891, *Alumni Oxonienses, AD 1500–1714*. Oxford. Oxford University Press

Foucault, M, 1970, *The order of things: an archaeology of the human sciences*. London. Tavistock

Freeman, R, 1967, *English emblem books*. London.

Fry, E A, 1916–23, Dorset Inquisitions Post Mortem 1216–1485. *Notes and Queries for Somerset and Dorset*, XV-XVII

Gerard, T, (ed R Legg), 1980, *Coker's survey of Dorsetshire*. Milborne Port. Dorset Publishing Company

Gerritson, W, and van Melle, A, 1998, *A dictionary of medieval heroes*. London. Boydell Press

Gomme, A B, 1929, The character of Beelzebub in the Mummers' Play. *Folk-Lore*, 40, 292–3

Grinsell, L, 1980, The Cerne Abbas Giant, 1764–1980. *Antiquity*, 54, 29–33

Hardy, T, 1886, *The Mayor of Casterbridge: the life and death of a man of character*. London. Smith, Elder and Co

Hawkes, J, 1954, *A guide to the prehistoric and Roman monuments of England and Wales*. London. Chatto and Windus

Holles, D, 1699, *Memoirs 1641–1648 [written at St Mere Eglise, Normandy in 1648]*. London. T Godwin

Horn, J M, (ed), 1982, The Register of Robert Hallum, Bishop of Salisbury 1407–17, *Canterbury and York Society*, 72

Hutchins, J, 1774, *History of the county of Dorset* (1st Edition. Two volumes). London. W Bowyer and J Nichols

Hutchins, J, 1861–70, *History of the county of Dorset* (3rd Edition. Four volumes). London. J B Nichols and Sons

Hutton, R, 1996, *The stations of the sun: a history of ritual year in Britain*. Oxford. Oxford University Press

Innes, M (translator), 1955, *Ovid, The Metamorphoses*. Harmondsworth. Penguin

John, E, 1996, *Reassessing Anglo-Saxon England*. Manchester. Manchester University Press

Lethbridge, T C, 1957, *Gogmagog*. London. Routledge and Kegan Paul

Lewis, C S, 1964, *The discarded image*. Cambridge. Cambridge University Press

Lloyd, R, 1967, *Dorset Elizabethans at home and abroad*. London. J Murray

Lukis, W C, 1883, *Stukeley's diaries and letters* (= Publications of the Surtees Society 76). London. Surtees Society

Lummis, T, 1999, *Life and Death in Eden*. London. Gollancz

McGinn, B, 1994, *Antichrist: two thousand years of the human fascination with evil*. San Francisco. Harper

March, H C, 1901, The Giant and maypole of Cerne. *Proceedings of the Dorset Natural History and Archaeological Society*, 22, 101–18

Marples, M, 1949, *White horses and other hill-figures*. London. Country Life Books. [Reprinted 1981. Gloucester. Alan Sutton]

Massingham, H J, 1944, *Remembrance: an autobiography*. London. Batsford

Mayo, C H, (ed), 1902, *The minute books of the Dorset Standing Committee 1646–50*. Exeter. William Pollard

Mills, A D, 1989, *The place-names of Dorset. Part 3* (= English Place-name Society Volume 59/60). Cambridge. English Place-name Society

Mowl, T, and Earnshaw, B, 1995, *Architecture without Kings: the rise of Puritan classicism under Cromwell*. Manchester. Manchester University Press

Nees, L, 1991, *A tainted mantle: Hercules and the classical tradition at the Carolingian Court*. Philadelphia. University of Pennsylvania Press

Newman, P, 1997, *Lost Gods of Albion, the chalk hill-figures of Britain*. Stroud. Sutton

Nichols, J, 1814, *Literary anecdotes of the eighteenth century, VIII*. London. Nichols and Bentley

Petrie, Sir F, 1926, *The hill-figures of England* (Royal Anthropological Institute Occasional Paper 7). London. Royal Archaeological Institute

Phythian-Adams, C, 1976, Ceremony and the citizen. In P Clark (ed), *The early modern town: a reader*. London. Longman

Piggott, S, 1929, The character of Beelzebub in the Mummers' Play. *Folk-Lore*, 40, 193–5

Piggott, S, 1932, The name of the Giant of Cerne. *Antiquity*, 6, 214–16

Piggott, S, 1938, The Hercules Myth. *Antiquity*, 12, 327–8

Piggott, S, 1989, *Ancient Britons and the antiquarian imagination, ideas from the Renaissance to the Regency*. London. Thames and Hudson

Raleigh, W, 1614, *The historie of the world*. [Note: references by book, chapter and section]

RCHM, 1952, *An inventory of the historical monuments in the County of Dorset. Volume I. West Dorset*. London. HMSO. (Reprinted with amendments 1974)

Record Commission, 1810–34, *Valor Ecclesiasticus temp. Henr. VIII: auctoritate regia institutus*. London. Record Commission. (Six volumes)

Robson, P, 1988, *Calender customs in nineteenth and twentieth- century Dorset*. Sheffield. Sheffield University. Unpublished M.Phil thesis

Scott, W L, 1937, The Chiltern white crosses. *Antiquity*, 11, 104

Seznec, J, 1953, *The survival of the Pagan Gods: the mythological tradition and its place in Renaissance humanism and art*. Princetown. Princeton University Press

Shortt, H (Revised by Chandler J), 1988, *The Giant and Hob-nob*. Salisbury. Salisbury and South Wiltshire Museum

Smith, L Toulmin, (ed), 1906–8, *The itinerary of John Leland in or about the years 1535–1543*. London. George Bell. (Five parts)

Society of Antiquaries, 1945, *The presidents of the Society of Antiquaries of London* (= Society of Antiquaries of London Occasional Paper 2). London. Society of Antiquaries of London

Smith, N, 1994, *Literature and revolution in England, 1640–1660*. London and New Haven. Yale University Press

Stephen, L and Lee, S, (eds), 1998, *Dictionary of national biography: from the earliest times to 1900*. London. Oxford University Press. (Twenty-two volumes)

Stukeley, W, 1724, *Itinerarium curiosum*. London. Privately printed

Sussex Archaeological Society, c.1995, *The Long Man of Wilmington*. Lewes. Leaflet published by Sussex Past in association with Merrydown Cider

Swanton, M (ed), 1975, *Anglo-Saxon Prose*. London. Dent

Timmins, T C B, (ed), 1994, The register of John Waltham, Bishop of Salisbury 1385–95. *Canterbury and York Society*, 80

Thomas, J, 1996, *Time, culture and identity*. London. Routledge

Thorpe, L, 1966, *Geoffrey of Monmouth, The History of the Kings of Britain*. Harmondsworth. Penguin

Thorpe, B, 1844–6, *The Homilies of the Anglo-Saxon Church*. London. The Aelfric Society. (Two volumes)

Underdown, D, 1979, The chalk and the cheese. *Past and Present*, 85, 25–48

VCH, 1908, *Victoria County History of Dorset – II*. London. Institute of Historical Research/ Oxford University Press

Weir, A, and Jerman, J, 1986, *Images of lust*. London. Batsford

Westrem, S D, 1998, Against Gog and Magog. In S Tomasch and S Gilles (eds), *Text and territory, geographical imagination in the European Middle Ages*. Birmingham. University of Pennslyvania

Westwood, J, 1994, *Albion: a guide to legendary Britain*. London. Harper Collins

Wise, F, 1742, *Further observations upon the White Horse and other antiquities in Berkshire*. Oxford. [Printed pamphlet]

Wright, D P (ed), 1985, The Register of Thomas Langton, Bishop of Salisbury 1485–93. *Canterbury and York Society*, 74

Wright, D (Translator), 1985, *Geoffrey Chaucer, The Canterbury Tales*. Oxford. Oxford University Press

Yorke, B, 1990, *Kings and kingdoms of early Anglo-Saxon England*. London. Seaby and Batsford

PART IV

The case for a living Giant

A living Giant

Barbara Bender

Me lud, gentlemen assessors, ladies and gentlemen of the jury. I and the witnesses I shall introduce have come to rescue the Giant from the dead hand of history. Or rather the dead hand of a particular sort of history.[1]

Professor Darvill tells us most convincingly that the Giant is two thousand years old. He may be right. Professor Hutton tells us that the Giant is two or three hundred years old. And perhaps he is right. Both focus on the origin of the Giant. But that is only one small part of his story, and perhaps not the most important part.

I would suggest that Professors Darvill and Hutton are trailing a rather out-moded notion of history. A history that focuses on origins and events. We Europeans have a strange notion of history (Figure 41). We are obsessed with origins. Our histories are linear, progressive, and divided into stages. Each stage has a label pinned to it. And objects and monuments are popped into these labelled boxes. The Giant, quite rightly, refuses to be pinned down (Figure 42). Typically, the labels on these boxed objects and monuments read: 'Stone axe, third millennium BC'; 'Bronze axe, second millennium BC'; 'Castle, tenth century AD'; 'Field-system, seventeenth century AD'; and so on ... they are frozen into place! And then, since the nineteenth century, we conserve

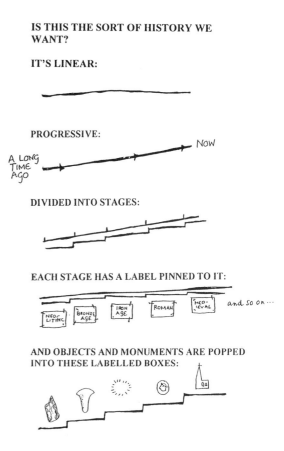

IS THIS THE SORT OF HISTORY WE WANT?

IT'S LINEAR:

PROGRESSIVE:

DIVIDED INTO STAGES:

EACH STAGE HAS A LABEL PINNED TO IT:

AND OBJECTS AND MONUMENTS ARE POPPED INTO THESE LABELLED BOXES:

Figure 41. Is this the sort of history we want?

them. And we tiptoe among these fragments of the past (Figure 43).

In this sort of history, the past is behind us. We carry it like a heavy sack. And because we are nervous of the present and future, we look back over our shoulder to a golden age that never was.

There is an alternative way of thinking about the past, and an alternative sort of Giant.

The Cumbales, a group of South American Indians who live in the high Andes, say: 'The past is in front of us, because we live the consequences today and can change them ..' (Rappaport 1988). In the old days, before the Spaniards came, the Cumbales had communal lands which were divided up by ditches. They also had open grazing land which was not divided. The Spaniards came and took away their land. Then, one of those rare bright moments in colonial history, they were given some of their land back. The land was grazing land. No ditches. But now the Indians divided it with ditches. They were putting down an historical marker; they were, they said, 'correcting history'.

My argument today is that the past is not over and done with. Things do not stop at the point that they are made and first used. The Giant is not second century AD or seventeenth century ... it is second, third, fourth, tenth, nineteenth, and twentieth century. Maybe he was 'born' in the second or the seventeenth century, but he lived – he lives – right through to today. My case is that biography is as important as date of birth.

THE GIANT, QUITE RIGHTLY, REFUSES TO BE PINNED DOWN:

ALL THE OBJECTS AND MONUMENTS - EXCEPT THE GIANT - ARE LABELLED: This stone axe, we say, is third millennium B.C., this bronze axe is second millennium B.C., this castle is tenth century, this field-system is seventeenth century ...

AND SO THEY ARE FROZEN INTO PLACE ...

AND THEN, SINCE THE NINETEENTH CENTURY, WE CONSERVE THEM:

Figure 42. The Giant refuses to be pinned down.

AND WE TIPTOE AMONG THE FRAGMENTS OF THE PAST.

IN THIS SORT OF HISTORY, THE PAST IS <u>BEHIND US</u>. WE CARRY IT LIKE A HEAVY SACK. AND, OFTEN, BECAUSE WE ARE NERVOUS OF THE PRESENT AND FUTURE, WE LOOK BACKWARDS OVER OUR SHOULDER:

Figure 43. We tiptoe among the fragments of the Past.

He lives because he goes on being meaningful. Because people have incorporated him into their lives, their activities, their stories and songs. He is part of their world, sometimes fleetingly – the tourist who stops and guffaws or wonders – sometimes more enduringly, those who see him everyday, walk him, clean him, ask favours of him.

He is, and always has been, part of the identity of the village and the villagers. Sometimes he has been neglected, sometimes, or at some times of the year, he comes to life again.

At all time, through the ages, and today, he has meant different things to different people. Perhaps some of you are here in the village hall today because he is part of your livelihood, he brings people to the village, and because tourists like 'old' things, you want him to be old. Apparently some local people are quite angry that Professor Hutton is suggesting that he's not so old. If you are upset it is because the Giant is important to you in a very particular, twentieth century kind of way.

If we want to understand why the Giant is important to some people and not to others, at some times and not at others; if we want to understand why people have related to him in different ways, we need to look not just at the Giant, but at the lives of the people involved. We need to think what it was like to be a commoner living around and about in the seventh, tenth, eighteenth century. Or to be a monk, an antiquarian, a landowner, a tourist, or a shopkeeper. To be a woman, or a man, or a child. We need to think about changing working conditions, social relationships, changing ideas about the world. We need to explore the changing conditions of existence, and the changing landscape.

Most of the articles that I have read about the Giant treat him as though he was an object, and they compare him to other objects. He's not an object, he is a figure in a working landscape.

Until recently, whenever the National Trust was given a fine country house, they tried to strip it back to its original form, original decoration, furniture and fittings. In so doing, they negated all the life of the house, all the lives, all the changes in fashion and perception. They froze the action. Now they are beginning to realise that this is a terrible negation. The past – whether it is a house or a giant – is always reworked in the present. That is what gives it meaning. We, all the different we's, past and present, give it meaning, and it gives us meaning. Accepting that the Past is always Present, we take it into the future. And it is no longer a millstone.

I have many witnesses to introduce. They are here to celebrate the changing, varied, and ongoing meaningfulness of the great Giant. The first is Rodney Legg. He has written more than fifty books on almost every aspect of Dorset, past and present, including *Cerne's Giant and Village Guide* (Dorset Publishing Company, 1986). His archaeological work includes *Romans in Britain* (Heinemann, 1982), the transcription and annotation of John Aubrey's *Monumenta Britannica* (Dorset Publishing Company, 1980–2) and *Stonehenge Antiquarians* (Dorset Publishing Company, 1986). He is Chairman of the Open Spaces Society and a former member of the Council of the National Trust. Rodney Legg's brief is to comment on the making and re-making of the Giant.

* * * * * * * *

Making and re-making the Cerne Giant

Rodney Legg

BB: The Giant, despite his virility and longevity, is fragile. He lasts as long as people care about him. If he's not scoured and re-chalked at regular intervals, he would disappear. So my first questions are: what's involved in scouring the Giant? how long would it take? How often would it have to be done? And how soon would it be before the Giant disappeared from sight if no-one cared about him?

RL: I suppose that it's an engineering operation of some complexity, involving the entire community, probably combined with celebration and drinking. Ideally, it would have had to take place at least once in a generation of thirty years, and preferably more frequently than that. At the end of thirty years you've probably got a green man, but he'd still be visible. Sixty years – and you'd have lost him completely.

BB: So you think that the idea that's been mooted, that there might have been a very faint trace left, even if he'd been abandoned throughout the medieval period, is nonsense? That it's not possible that Holles, in the seventeenth century, could have picked up on an outline that had been neglected for perhaps a millennium?

RL: Totally impossible. The Giant would have sunk back into the hill-side and disappeared for ever. There are examples of trenches cut into ancient monuments – for example, in 1936 at Maiden Castle – and people have said that the lines cut in the chalk were clearly visible for some time afterwards and then suddenly they were gone. And think of the great scars that were cut across the chalk with the building of the railways: you can see them in Victorian photographs, and then they disappear back into the landscape.

BB: How deep are the trenches of the Cerne Abbas Giant?

RL: At least six inches ...

BB: So would the celebratory cleansing have just been a re-capping of chalk on the upper surface of the cut?

RL: I think that part of the evidence of the antiquity of the Giant is that from aerial photographs you can see shadow lines which show that, rather than clear out the dirty trenches, it was a far cleaner job to dig a fresh trench immediately beside the existing one. This has the effect of moving the figure backwards and forwards ... and also has the effect of thickening some of the members – not necessarily just the penis! – the legs and so on (Figure 44). You tend to get a slightly less athletic figure, although basically he's held together very well. The very fact that you've got these shadow trenches shows that he's not a new being – he's more likely to be many centuries, if not millennia, old.

BB: You're saying he had to be cleaned every thirty years. If, for the sake of argument, we say he was created in late prehistoric times, how many generations are we talking about?

RL: Something like 66 generations. So every 30 to 33 years they'd get round to having major ceremonies and re-cuttings, with a bit of remedial care between times – you've got to remember that the scrub would have tended to regenerate. Sixty to sixty-five years would be the outside limit – not only would they have lost him on the ground but they'd have lost the memory of him ...

He wasn't ever lost. All that happened was that bits of him that didn't mean very much were abandoned. There's the debate about what lies within the knoll which lies beneath his outstretched arm, and the fact that the cloak was found by resistivity tests (see Newman in Part II above), which shows that the less obvious features of the Giant were allowed to grass over because they became meaningless. This is why I was seeing – or imagining that I was seeing – the lines of a dog in the drought years of 1975–6, as a companion to him, to the left further along the hillside.

BB: What do you think of that idea now?

RL: I still think that there are other figures there. He can't just be a one off, although he can be unique in terms of an actual survival. All the odds have been stacked against him for so long that for him to survive as he does in pure Celtic and ancient style means that there must originally have been hundreds, if not thousands, of such figures. And that they were, if not gods, then badges of peoples and tribes or perhaps had religious connotations. Or maybe a mixture of everything – religious, ceremonial, a gathering point ...

BB: Do you think the National Trust should restore the Giant to something closer to the original form? If there was a cloak, or if the penis has got longer, what do we do about the changes that have occurred through time?

RL: I think that where there's been change, where people have done it to the figure itself, the shape of him shifting a little over the years, or, as Gerald Pitman showed in his letter to the *Dorset Magazine* (Figure 45), the navel having been incorporated into the phallus, these are part of the evolution of the figure and they therefore have to be respected. He isn't just a Giant of the prehistoric period, he's a continuing Giant of the people of Dorset, and if they saw fit to re-interpret him, then we have to respect that. That's part of his living history – he's a continuing, living, presence. All I'd add as a caveat to that – if other figures were found, and if other attributes of the Giant – if, for example, it was proved that he was holding, dangling and swinging in his outstretched hand, a severed head, or some other object – then they should be restored (see Part II, Figure 25). Ditto the cloak. Because that's simply revealing trenches that have been allowed to grass over. We have a Giant that has evolved, and also a Giant that is being rediscovered through our own technology and knowledge to something that is more or less complete again.

BB: It's tricky. Things are altered, and we accept the alterations as part of a living history. Things go out of use, which is also part of history, and we want to restore them?

Figure 44. *The Cerne Giant, drawn by Rodney Legg from aerial photographs, in 1986. The present outline is shown in dots. Original trenches which are not grassed over are shown with a continuous line. Broken lines depict indistinct trenching of one leg and the cloak. (Reproduced courtesy of Rodney Legg)*

RL: I live in hopes that we may find something else further along the hillside and that he wasn't alone. On the other hand, a lone god is perhaps more potent as a symbol, rather than one of a frieze of figures.

BB: *Of course there's also the possibility that he's relating to features in the landscape: that he talks to the combe or the rounded hill, or to something on the other side of the valley. That he's in a dialogue with what lies around him.*

RL: He's in an obvious dialogue with other features in the landscape. Above him, there's the Trendle earthwork which might be a Celtic temple, and there's the obvious pagan spring that the Christians adopted, and you've got these large and ancient earthworks which apparently pre-date the Abbey inside the field just below the Giant. And you've also got a very conspicuous corner of the hillside on which there appears to be nothing. Perhaps the least we owe him, and given the obvious interest this hillside had for ancient man, is to do proper resistivity tests and then if anything is found, a sensible archaeological dig – you can prove a hill-figure by one cross trench, you don't have to dig the entire hillside.

BB: *I was thinking less of features made by people, as of the Giant in relation to the land itself. We find it hard to think of that, because we've lost that sense of a land embued with ancestral spirits, or as in some way gendered. Maybe the Giant talks to the land and to the land-forms.*

RL: I certainly like that: after all, on the other side of the valley there's a superb standing stone which the Ordinance Survey never recorded. It's a great big sarsen boulder tucked into the hedge of the prehistoric ridgeway which separates the two valleys – the valley of Cerne and the valley of Sydling. That's the path that the prehistoric and medieval people, took, and that is the point to which the Giant is looking. The stone seems to be a viewing point for the people who are on the road. A wayside stopping place for paying your respects to the Giant. He also looks across at extensive ancient settlement. It's difficult to appreciate that now because we've depopulated our uplands and brought everyone down into the valley.

* * * * * * * *

BB: We must stop, we're moving beyond our brief! But what we are touching on here is very important, and we shall return to it briefly later with Sue Clifford's piece and in Jan Farquharson's poem. Both depict that sense of a larger landscape of people, places and ancestral beings, of a larger gendered landscape. In the meantime, my second witness is Tom Williamson. Tom is a lecturer in Landscape Archaeology at the Centre for East Anglian Studies, University of East Anglia. He specializes in the medieval period, and his recent books include *The origins of Norfolk* (Manchester University Press, 1993).

Tom's brief was to consider, first, how medieval commoners might have incorporated a pagan giant into their understanding of the world and the church's

CERNE GIANT LETTERS

Orion

As a local researcher-author of the ancient mysteries, I was most impressed by your special issue on the Cerne Giant Hill figure (DORSET 66). My own findings indicate that Cerne-Cernunnos is a version of Orion, the hunter-god constellation. A dog hill figure to the left of Cerne would relate directly to Sirius in astronomical terms.

I believe the above visual relationships between astronomical constellation, Cro-Magnon cave art, Dorset hill figures and our old alphabet-calendar are obvious.

British hill figures appear to relate to a once world-wide symbolism taken out from Cro-Magnon or Ice Age times from Asio-Euro-Africa.

The giants of old indeed teach us of a deeper heritage once the dogma, superstition and ignorance of modern mis-interpretation are removed. In this light I would like to congratulate you on a first class example of forthright and progressive journalism in your Cerne Giant special issue. As you point out, we should recognise and be proud of our real heritage.

Philip J. Grant
89 Paisley Road
Bournemouth

Mandrake

As Alton Pancras is near the Cerne Giant, and 'pancras' comes from words with a general sense of wrestling, I attempted decoding the name.

On the contrary, it reverted to occult matters and gave 'Mandrak'.

From many sources, including the Bible, we read of the mandrake as a powerful agent of fertility, also possessing fatal powers from its supposed likeness to a headless human body. The ancients saw the entwined gnarled roots of the plant as headless couples locked in sexual embraces.

Ghosts arose, correspondingly attuned to sexual matters of a decidedly odd order, and became an incubus gallow-bugger type of spook. Perhaps by reason of the Biblical mention, the mandrake cult was apparently sanctioned by the Christian church and we find Father J. Rahner of the Jesuits, in *Greek Myths and Christian Mysteries*, explaining by text and old illustrations how the headless mandragora was the bride in a mystic ceremony.

Whatever the full implications of these rites, it explains why the gross figure of the giant was allowed to remain well preserved, only a matter of yards from a Christian abbey.

S. W. J. Wood
31 Christchurch Road
Bournemouth

Navel

Yesterday I bought four copies of DORSET 66—the special Cerne Giant issue. Thank you for coming to his defence and for assembling in such a readable way all the

information.

I have been gathering all I can discover about him for some five years. Only a few weeks ago I came across a loose print, the drawing from the *Gentleman's Magazine* of 1764, in Dodge's shop at Sherborne and got them to frame it for me.

In your note to that drawing on page 7 of the special issue you write that "the navel has since grassed over".

As a matter of fact I don't think this is the case. I believe that the navel has been added to the penis—increasing the size of the Giant's erection!

Did this happen in 1887? This seems unlikely as Pitt-Rivers himself would have been aware of the navel from the *Gentleman's Magazine* and the version given by Hutchins. It looks to me like the drawing on the left has become that on the right . . .

I have not seen this suggested in print, and have cut out the illustrations by the *Gentleman's Magazine* and Flinders Petrie from the magazine, bringing them up to the same scale and am satisfied the navel has been incorporated into the penis, which in itself is a standing joke.

For all this I would not like Middleton to seek a re-shaping! Both the late Lord Digby and the late Lady Digby were against any covering up.

Gerald Pitman
Upgrene
Sherborne

Mr Pitman's comparison: the Gentleman's Magazine drawing of 1764 (left) with that of Sir Flinders Petrie (1926).

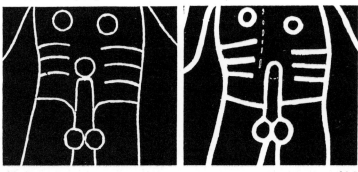

this became . . .   *this!*

Figure 45. Gerald Pitman wrote this short letter to the Dorset Magazine in 1978 (issue 70, page 27). Leslie Grinsell noted, in his article in Antiquity (1980, 54, page 32) that his own conclusion, that the navel had become added to the top of the penis, had also been reached and published by Pitman in 1978.

response, and, second, the more general question of how myths and legends evolve through time. In the following presentation Tom quite rightly notes that, whilst our brief is to discuss the changing significance of the Giant, we can only do this if we know how long he has been around. In particular our surmises about the relationship of the Giant, the Abbey, and the local population is based on the – tentative – assumption that the Giant was already in existence. Tom also addresses, in passing, the question of negative evidence. The fact that the Giant is not mentioned in church or survey documents may have more to do with the nature of the texts than with his presence or absence. And he demonstrates that memory can play strange tricks with history: local memory is short, local folklore endlessly inventive and traditional practices can rapidly attach themselves to non-traditional monuments.

* * * * * * * *

Memory, tradition, and the Giant

Tom Williamson

Looked at in one way, as a number of contributors to this volume have suggested, the age of the Cerne Giant matters little. As a focus for local beliefs and traditions, as an alien yet familiar presence looming above the town of Cerne, its simple existence is the crucial thing. It is a timeless feature of the landscape, without which Cerne would not be Cerne. The stories and traditions attached to the figure likewise seem timeless, weaving together community, landscape, and nature. Nineteenth-century antiquaries and folklorists recorded how local people believed that sitting, or perhaps copulating, on the grass within the Giant's phallus could cure barrenness in women (Harte 1986, 42–3). It was said, even as late as the 1940s, that women in fear of losing their partners would perambulate the Giant's frame, or talk with him at night. Folklore attempted to explain the figure's origins. A tradition, recorded as early as 1774, relates how it represents the outline of a giant who, having devoured a number of sheep in the nearby Vale of Blackmore, fell asleep on the hill side. According to some versions, 'A shepherd boy went up in the night and slew him, whereupon the people of Cerne carved round the outline of his body'; according to others, he was massacred by the assembled body of townsfolk (Harte 1986, 44–5). Various other stories credit the Giant with, among other things, participation in a bout of the traditional 'sport' (if that is the right word) of cudgel-playing.

Yet for certain purposes, the age of the Giant clearly does matter. Nothing in the landscape is timeless, and the significance of the great figure, and of its attached earthwork and associated folklore, are very materially effected by their age. An ancient Giant, as it were, tells us very different things about people, and about their relationship with the landscape, than a comparatively recent one. The figure's location a few hundred metres from the Benedictine Abbey of Cerne is crucial in this context. If the Giant is indeed a prehistoric or Romano-British feature, its survival here, in close proximity to a major religious house, must speak volumes about the relationship between orthodox Christianity and other beliefs in the Middle Ages.

The pace of conversion in Anglo-Saxon England, most historians now agree, was slow (Morris 1989, 90–2). Kings and tribal elites were evangelized early but the countryside was only slowly converted. As late as 1005 the 'Canons of Edgar' exhorted every priest to:

> Entirely extinguish every heathen practise; and forbid worship of wells, and necromancy, and auguries and incantations, and worship of trees and stones, and that devil's craft which is performed when children are drawn through the earth, and the nonsense which is performed on New Year's Day in various kinds of sorcery, and in heathen sanctuaries and at elder trees. (Whitelock *et al.* 1981, 320)

Indeed, according to some historians, large sections of the rural population remained effectively pagan for several centuries after this. Certainly, conversion was achieved through a series of compromises, involving both the adaptation of earlier festivals and the adoption of existing sacred sites. The best evidence for the latter comes from the oft-quoted letter said by Bede to have been sent by Pope Gregory to Mellitus in the initial stages of the Conversion:

> The idol temples of this race should by no means be destroyed, but only the idols in them. Take holy water and sprinkle it in these shrines, build altars and place relics in them. (Sherley-Price 1955, 81)

Nevertheless, archaeological evidence for continuity of this kind is far more tenuous than is sometimes suggested. Most churches were first established long after the initial conversion, as large minster territories fragmented into parishes during the later Saxon period, by which time most of their lordly founders would have come to embrace the faith (Blair 1988). Although some excavated churches have revealed evidence for earlier religious use on their sites, the majority have not done so (Williamson and Bellamy 1983, 81–2). Nor is it entirely clear how we should interpret cases like Rudston in Yorkshire or Knowlton in Dorset, where parish churches stand within or beside ritual structures of early prehistoric, rather than Anglo-Saxon, date: in the former case, a standing stone, in the latter, a henge (Williamson and Bellamy 1983, 77–8). While such relationships are clearly more than coincidental, they may have explanations more complex than those often suggested – that is, in terms of the Mellitus letter. These were already ancient places, perhaps long abandoned when churches were first built there: the Church may have been challenging the ghosts of dead religions, flexing (as it were) some spiritual muscle. Either way, we must note once again that although such examples are frequently quoted they are exceptions. It is easy to forget that no church stands on top of Silbury Hill, and that Salisbury Cathedral was not built within Stonehenge.

The location of the Cerne Giant some 250m from the abbey church thus falls into a wider, if problematic, pattern. The abbey may have been intentionally sited at a place of ancient sanctity, either to neutralize its power, or to use its attractions for its own benefit. But if the Giant's antiquity were confirmed it would add an important new twist to the old arguments. Unlike Rudston or Knowlton, the Giant could only have survived to the present if it had been at least sporadically maintained right through the Middle Ages. Scouring might have occurred only at long intervals – the feature is cut deeply into the hill side and, like the Long Man of Wilmington, might have become grassed over yet still have remained traceable even after a lapse of several years. But even so, the figure's survival proclaims that not only its existence but also its active maintenance were tolerated by the church, not only at the time of conversion but for long afterwards. The abbey community was either indifferent to such activities, or unable to stop them – or something in between.

The preservation of the Giant in this way, by a kind of parallel popular culture, quite separate from the orthodox structures of authority and organization within local society, might explain why the figure fails to be mentioned in the medieval and, in particular, in the copious post-medieval documents relating to the area (Bettey 1981; Grinsell 1980). It could be argued that the failure of the Giant to appear in the *Inquisitions Post Mortem* of the various abbots of Cerne; in the documents generated by the various post-Dissolution disputes in the town; or in the detailed survey made of the area by John Norden and his son in 1617; simply reflects the character and concerns of these sources. These were discourses concerned with values, rents, ownership, and boundaries. The Giant is on open downland and would not necessarily appear in topographic descriptions relating to parcels of property. Its maintenance by the local population, especially if this was on a sporadic, casual basis, would not necessarily figure in these or in any other documents produced by the landowning elite. If all this were true, then the Giant would stand as an expression of the autonomy of popular culture, its independence from the structures which have generated our main documentary sources. It would represent, as it were, the soul of the community, a community which was capable of some measure of collective action even in the late sixteenth and early seventeenth centuries, when the town was in decline, when it was without resident landowners of any consequence, and when even many of the principal tenants were non-resident (Bettey 1981, 119–20).

If the Giant is indeed an ancient feature, then the implications for our understanding of medieval and post-medieval society are considerable. But, as other contributors to this volume cogently argue, there are good grounds for believing that it is in fact of mid-seventeenth century origin: grounds other than the mere silence of these local sources. These arguments need not be rehearsed here: but once again, their implications can be. If the Giant was created as late as this then it seems, at first sight, extraordinary that within less than a century its true origins should have been forgotten. As early as 1754 Richard Pococke described 'a figure cut in lines' that was 'called the Giant and Hele, about 150 feet long' (Legg 1986, 12). Not long after this we have our first references to apparently archaic beliefs and traditions attached to the figure. Yet all this would again fit into a familiar pattern, although one which is never given sufficient prominence in books of the 'Mysterious Britain' variety. For it is remarkable how rapidly the origins of features in the landscape can be forgotten, and how rapidly apparently ancient traditions can become attached to them. Local memory is short, local folklore endlessly inventive. One example will suffice to make the point. In late and post-medieval times rabbits were often kept in groups of artificial cigar-shaped mounds – 'buries' or 'burrows' which archaeologists generally refer to as pillow mounds (Williamson and Loveday 1988). Their construction continued, in many parts of England, well into the second half of the nineteenth century. Yet by the 1920s, when they first aroused serious archaeological interest, their function had generally been forgotten and many had attracted a range of fanciful names: 'Druid's Grave', 'Giant's Grave', and the like. The group at Ravenstonedale in Cumbria, for example, formed the largest working warren in the county in 1800. The First Edition Ordnance Survey 25" map of the area, surveyed in 1860, labels the mounds as 'Giant's Graves' in the familiar gothic lettering reserved for antiquities. But perhaps modern historians and anthropologists take the stories and traditions attached to archaeological sites in general, and to the Giant in particular, a little too seriously. Some of them were clearly supposed to be humorous and primarily intended for the consumption of children.

In a similar way, 'traditional' practices can become attached to some very non-traditional monuments. Harte quotes the case of the funeral monument of Victor Noir, a radical journalist under Louis Napoleon, which stands in the Pere Lachaise cemetery in Paris. The pronounced bulge beneath the statue's trousers, like the Giant's more explicit endowment, came to be an object of pilgrimage for women anxious to conceive (Harte 1986, 44). The practice of embracing the seventeenth-century pillars of St Paul's Cathedral in London (recorded as late as 1923) is another example of the attraction of phallic objects to childless women (Bordes and Bordes 1978, 49).

The apparently ancient traditions and practices associated with the Giant are not, therefore, any firm guide to its antiquity. Like the Giant itself, they have a timeless air. They may be ancient, they may be not: and at one level this scarcely matters. But at another it does. The stories and beliefs attached to the Giant, like the figure's significant location so close to Cerne Abbey, cannot inform us of its age. But, once its age has been established, the Giant can tell us much about them: and in so doing, it can throw much light on the nature of popular culture and tradition, both in Cerne and elsewhere.

* * * * * * * *

BB: My third witness is Martin Brown who has worked for English Heritage on the Monument Protection Programme. He is now Assistant County Archaeologist for East Sussex.

Whilst Tom Williamson was dealing with oral traditions, Martin's brief was to consider the way in which, over the centuries, the Giant has been pulled into different written accounts, and how, from the rather rarefied antiquarian offerings of the eighteenth and nineteenth century addressed to a relatively small audience, they burgeoned into many different sorts of writing, including advertising and cartoons, and addressed a much wider audience and a much wider range of interests.

Martin has interpreted his brief generously. He felt that it might be useful to investigate the Old Man of Wilmington and to compare the accumulation of meanings woven around the Old Man and the Giant. His evidence links with that of Tom Williamson (above) and Hilary Jones (see below).

* * * * * * * *

The Long Man of Wilmington and the Cerne Giant: some points of comparison

Martin Brown

The origins and age of the Long Man of Wilmington are as mysterious as those of the Cerne Giant. Like the Giant, the Long Man has become a powerful symbol and has attracted a variety of researchers. An investigation of the Long Man and comparison of the two figures may shed some light on the monument under examination in this volume and offer some suggestions toward our response to it.

The Long Man lies on the north-facing scarp slope of Windover Hill, near Eastbourne in East Sussex (Figure 46). He stands holding a long staff in each hand. The length of the western staff is 72m and there is a distance of over 30m between the two staffs. Like the Cerne Giant the figure is outlined in white on the hillside, unlike the Giant there are no recognizable facial or anatomical features. Until 1873 the figure was reported as a faint indentation in the turf, visible in low sunlight or after light snow fall. In 1873–4 the outline was marked out in bricks. In 1969 these were replaced with pre-cast concrete blocks which still delineate the figure. At that time limited excavations attempted to answer questions about the original nature and date of the figure. Those excavations and their associated geophysical survey were inconclusive (Holden 1971).

Arguments over the origin of the figure have developed on similar lines to those surrounding the Cerne Giant. Although both figures have a comparatively recent proven origin, theories of varying plausibility for the creation of the figures have been proposed. The earliest known depiction of the Long Man is dated to 1704 (Farrant 1993) but stylistic comparisons have been drawn with Roman, Anglo-saxon, and Swedish Vendel artwork. These include late Roman coins which show a figure holding two military standards (*Labrara*) displaying the chi-rho (Heron-Allen 1939) and the Anglo-saxon Finglesham buckle which depicts a figure in a horned helmet wielding two spears (Hawkes 1965). Other interpretations have included the Norse god Baldur opening the doors of heaven to the Spring; the gods Woden, Thor, Apollo, and Mercury; a prehistoric surveyor; a Roman soldier or emperor; a haymaker or Green Man; even St Peter or, most bizarrely, the Prophet Mohammed. This last image was allegedly cut by Muslim prisoners brought to Sussex during the Crusades. Finally, the Long Man has been suggested as the site of a druidical wicker man. These various claims were discussed in the *Sussex County Magazine* (Sidgwick 1939) but no conclusion was reached; nor has

***Figure 46**. Aerial view of the Long Man of Wilmington, East Sussex. (Photography courtesy of Cambridge University Committee for Aerial Photography. SS–1. Crown copyright reserved. RAF Photographs)*

one been reached to this day. Nevertheless, new theories continue to be developed, including one which links the Cerne Giant and the Long Man and which suggests that the Giant is Richard I and that the ribs and nipples represent the face of a lion, symbol of the Lionheart king. The Wilmington Giant, meanwhile, is cast as his chancellor William Longchamps, hence the figure's name of Long Man (Whipp 1996).

In addition, there are a number of folkloric myths of the figure's origin which owe nothing to history or to archaeology. Most of these stories associate the Long Man, not surprisingly, with giants.

One thing is certain: the monument as it stands is a nineteenth century creation. Comparison with the eighteenth century illustrations shows that the modern figure itself is broadly similar in appearance to that depicted but it is by no means the same figure, since the turf cut Long Man was replaced in 1873 by one made of brick. We are now on Long Man number three, rebuilt in 1969. Indeed, it is unlikely that the figure ever was chalk-cut due to the angle of the hillside and the depth of the chalk and it appears that it survived until the nineteenth century as a turf figure.

It appears then that we are left with a figure of uncertain origin and recent date. What is the value of this figure? Archaeologically the Long Man is a feature in a landscape rich in archaeological features. He is part of the story of a developing landscape and stands as an obvious reminder that there is a significant time depth to human activity in the environment. The same can be said of the Cerne Giant. However, we must remember that the figures are much more than Scheduled Ancient Monuments. Given that the Man and the Giant are of unknown date and origin, one begins to wonder quite what is its archaeological value if archaeology is the study of human origin and development. Certainly the figures are a testament to the artistic expression, cultural life and unpredictability of our ancestors, but other datable monuments, such as Stonehenge or Fuller's eighteenth century follies in East Sussex, do that quite admirably, and they contribute to our understanding of periods of the past. What the figures do promote is a sense of wonder and mystery which is often denied us in the modern world: they are undeniably of some antiquity, but our lack of knowledge vests them with a magic which stimulates the academic, the artist and the alternative thinker in a way that most archaeological monuments did until the development of formal archaeology and the division of effort in the eighteenth and nineteenth centuries. Certainly our reaction to a particular period may be changed by discovery of a figure's origin, but perhaps, as they stand on the hill-sides, they challenge us to think and allow us to dream a little and maybe, by doing that, to approach a fuller understanding of our own time. This aspect of the monuments is as vital as their archaeological significance and message and it is to this which we now turn.

A folk tale of unknown date and origin tells how two giants lived on the Sussex Downs, one on Windover Hill, the other at Firle Beacon, a few miles to the west. The giants fell out and began to throw stones at one another until the

Wilmington Giant was struck and fell dead. He was buried in the long barrow on the hill-top. Some versions of the story record the Long Man as the outline of that figure. Others say that he is the outline of a giant killed, variously, by a heroic downland shepherd, by the people of Wilmington themselves, or by the monks from the priory in an allegory of the triumph of Christianity over paganism (Burne 1915). The tales may originally relate to the long barrow, which were often thought to be giants' graves in antiquity (Grinsell 1976), and may have inspired the cutters of the Long Man. Or the figure itself may be the source of the tale which developed after the cutting. How the various features on Windover hill relate one to another remains a mystery, but tale, barrow, figure and landscape are now all inextricably linked in the local imagination. Indeed, new stories continue to appear, such as the tale that the figure commemorates a prior of nearby Michelham Priory who used stilts to cross the marshes on his way to the town of Alfriston (Allen pers. comm.)

The tales demonstrate the place of the Long Man in folklore of some antiquity (Sidgwick 1939) but it is clear that the folklore of the figure and its symbolic value have continued even into the later twentieth century. A Long Man casts a long shadow.

As the Gulf crisis developed in 1990 the County Archaeologist for East Sussex was contacted by a wiccan priest who intended to perform rituals in opposition to the power of Saddam Hussein. These ceremonies would be carried out immediately above the Long Man, among the barrows on Windover Hill. This modern ritual use of the site demonstrates how the Long Man has a continued significance. Furthermore, on a number of occasions bunches of flowers and coins have been found left both on the surface of the ground and pushed between the blocks which form the outline. Moreover, it appears to be the place which is important. There are other Sussex Hills which have better barrows, causewayed enclosures and other well-preserved prehistoric sites on them and which do not attract the same ritual activity. One can only surmise that it is the Long Man which draws people to Windover Hill.

While the Long Man appears to be venerated it is also occasionally attacked. In recent years the outline has been painted red, a penis and breasts and a baseball cap have been added in paint and he has been outlined in orange flashing lights. These activities suggest that the figure has a place in the popular mind which occasionally inspires satire and small acts of defiance. These acts are very much in the spirit of Sussex's foremost traditional event: Bonfire, when, by turns, the Pope, Guy Fawkes and, on occasion, the Queen are burned in effigy, thus consigning both the traditional enemies of English freedoms and the defender of the faith and figurehead of England to the flames.

The figure is now also a much used symbol for a variety of local groups and commercial venture. He is easily visible and recognizable and can be reproduced with little effort. Furthermore he carries a suggestion of the unspoilt South Downs and a mysterious past. The image of the Long Man appears on a pub sign, at the entrance to a garden centre and on the label of a bottle of cider. He has also been

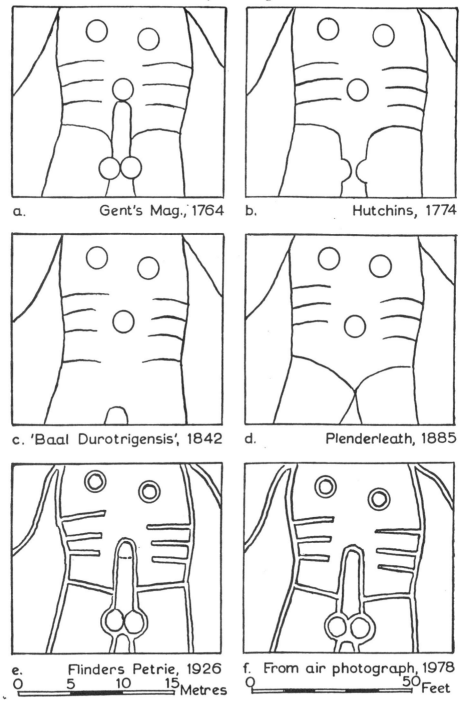

a.   Gent's Mag., 1764   b.   Hutchins, 1774

c. 'Baal Durotrigensis', 1842   d.   Plenderleath, 1885

e.   Flinders Petrie, 1926   f. From air photograph, 1978

Figure 47. The antiquarians get to work! Different versions of the Giant from 1764 onwards. (After Grinsell 1980, fig. 1; Reproduced courtesy of L V Grinsell and Antiquity Publications)

used as the badge for a Morris side who perform a dance called the 'Long Man', in which each man uses two sticks; for the A27 Action Group (formed to oppose the building of a trunk road); and for the Sussex Downs Ranger Service. He has even appeared as part of a tableau at the Lewes Bonfire celebrations. However, unlike the Cerne Giant, the Long Man has never achieved national celebrity. This is probably because he lacks the particular distinguishing features of his cousin in Dorset.

The figure's appearance in popular culture shows how long his shadow is. The Cerne Giant casts a similar shadow in popular culture and may appear in the most unusual places: my mother-in-law has never quite forgotten my gift to her of individually printed Cerne Giant cookies and it's not every archaeological monument which has been used to advertise beer, bicycles and condoms.

This adoption of the image into the popular consciousness may also be seen in more mainstream art. Lewes-based artist Carolyn Trant used the Long Man and his landscape in her series 'Rituals and Relics' which looked at the role of archaeology in the creation of a landscape. The Long Man also features in literature – *The Long Man of Wilmington looks naked towards the Shires* (Kipling cited in Marples 1949; Parish 1873) and song. Artists respond to the supposed antiquity of the figure, to the mystery of his origins and to his place within the wider landscape. A few years ago urban folk musician Billy Bragg presented a piece on the Cerne Giant on the Channel 4 archaeology programme 'Down to Earth'. He mused on the nature of the figure and how it might reflect part of our national character and history. So it appears that both monuments influence, inspire and provoke viewers to a wide range of responses.

The Long Man may originally be the work of ancient priests, bored monks, conquering Romans or Saxons or an eccentric squire. The Cerne Giant may have been cut by Durotrigians, Romans, monks or Holles's servants. I do not actually think that the figure's origins are of primary importance. Both archaeologists and members of the public do ask, 'When was it built?' 'What is it?' and will continue to do so, but the problem is probably more interesting than the answer. Indeed it may be that we need these prominent mysteries to prevent our getting over-mighty and filled with certainty about ourselves and the world.

Furthermore, I do not honestly believe that we really want to know. The mystery of each figure adds to his charm and his influence.

It is possible that there may be more chance of providing an accurate date for the Cerne Giant, but he exists in many more spheres than that of archaeology. We should be aware of and respect the many facets of the figure and, perhaps, respect his privacy.

The main thrust of my argument for this is concerned with the development of the image of the Cerne Giant, both in academic circles and in popular culture.

Antiquarianism develops in the later seventeenth century as part of the wider development of science, including the foundation of the Royal Society in 1660 and the foundation of the Society of Antiquaries in 1707. As the newly United Kingdom moved into a new century there was a definite search for a national history, of which what we would now term prehistory forms a part. This search for knowledge was given impetus by the rise of a leisured and wealthy middle class with money made from both the colonies and the growing English industrial base.

The Cerne Giant, like Avebury and Stonehenge, was an obvious monument for study and in 1742 the first antiquarian account appears (Wise 1742). The Giant makes regular appearances in antiquarian accounts over the next two centuries, but as times change so does his image. Many of the antiquarian accounts deal with the Giant as an artefact of pagans, druids and savages, rather reflecting the English gentleman's belief in Whig history and in the natural pre-eminence of western civilization. This is reflected in the references, or non-references to the phallus (Figure 47): for example, an article in the *Gentleman's Magazine* claimed the figure was 'the work of Papists' (Anon. 1764) of whom the Protestant Englishman expected no better than idolatry and corruption; similarly Sydenham uses the phallus as an excuse to expound on the corruptions of sun worship (Legg 1972). However, all too often descriptions of the figure are not accurate and society seems uncomfortable with the figure. A fact clearly demonstrated in 1868 when Lord Rivers cleans the figure in the face of objections from the local clergy who fear for the public's moral health.

The restoration of the figure by Pitt Rivers illustrates another strand in the story of the Giant and the countryside. By the mid-nineteenth century there were the stirrings of the modern conservation movement which developed from the eighteenth century study of 'the landscape' and particularly the Romantic aspects thereof. It was given real impetus by writers like Ruskin and Morris and may be seen as a reaction to industrialization and the commoditization of the land. There was a desire to get back to the land, but with mass tourism places perceived as beautiful and previously unspoilt are perceived to be threatened. Furthermore the care and management of the landscape begins to pass from the local population to those who believe that they know what is right. It is no real surprise that in 1919 the Giant becomes the 'property' of the National Trust. The Long Man passes to the Sussex Archaeological Society at a similar time.

At the end of the nineteenth century we also see the birth of archaeology as a science and another group of experts arrives to study, probe and manage the Giant. As a member of that group I am aware of the value of our work, but I recognize the need for sensitivity to our subject and to the villagers. That in turn brings us to the local voice.

The reaction to nineteenth century civilization produced a resurgence of regionalism which can be seen in areas such as folk song collection. The Giant began to emerge as a defiant symbol, suggestions that he was carved by the Dorset Clubmen, still a powerful symbol of independence today, emerged. This strand of the Giant's story has become increasingly important as he has been adopted by various New Agers, pagans and other members of the counter-culture (Figure 48). At the same time he has been used commercially by both the villagers and large companies including, amongst many others, Raleigh Cycles (Figure 49),

Figure 48. *Steve Bell's use of the Cerne Giant in political comment: The Guardian May 22nd 1996.*

Heineken, and Durex (Figure 50). Sometimes these uses of the figure are strenuously opposed by the villagers who regard it as an infringement on their own monument, perhaps even their own identity.

So, in the late twentieth century, we have a Giant (and a Long Man) who is multi-layered with a history like a morris dancer's coat of rags – a multi-coloured whole which clothes the figure and which is made up of many tatters of various sizes, some obscuring others, but all contributing to the total effect. A garment which can, and will be added to in days to come. By recognizing the changing stories of the Giant we do not diminish him, rather we add to his grandeur by recognizing the time, interest and emotion lavished on him over the centuries.

* * * * * * * *

THE ESSENTIAL OUTDOOR ACCESSORY

Knowing your equipment is up to the mark is essential for your enjoyment of the great outdoors.

The new Raleigh Pioneer Trail combines the go-anywhere qualities of a mountain bike with features like lightweight frame and "active suspension" saddle to take the effort out of discovering the hidden and not so hidden parts of Britain's countryside.

What's more, with its unique 15 year anti-corrosion warranty, you can be confident that you and your Pioneer will do more than stand up to the outdoor life.

Figure 49. The Giant and Raleigh's bikes.

Figure 50. *The Giant and Durex. (Photo: Steve Moss. Copyright reserved.)*

BB: My fourth witness is Hilary Jones, a member of the Stonehenge Campaign Group, Road Protester, and Animal Rights campaigner. Whilst Tom Williamson and Martin Jones have focused primarily on what people have said about the Giant, Hilary's brief was to consider people's activities – not just the scouring of the Giant, but the rituals and celebrations, past and present, that have taken place upon the hillside.

* * * * * * * *

Rituals and celebrations at the Giant

Hilary Jones

BB: We know that the Giant had to be cleaned, and surely, unlike the rather work-a-day approach of the National Trust, that must have involved a lot of celebration?

HJ: It's very difficult to give any hard evidence because this kind of social history is rarely written down and recorded, it merely continues and evolves as local custom. So we have no direct evidence relating to the Giant. There is however a certain amount of evidence of the scouring of other hill figures – most notably Thomas Hughes' *The Scouring of the White Horse* – which can help give a general idea of these kind of events.

Rodney Legg suggests that the Giant would have been scoured or re-cut a minimum of every thirty years. It is likely to have been more often than that – perhaps as often as every seven years. The task was not a small one and would have taken several days to complete (see Keithley *et al.* in Part I). For the villagers to be available, all normal work must have been suspended, and it's easy to see that the shared endeavour and the departure from the usual routine could turn this into a time of festival. Working hard together during daylight hours – would it not seem appropriate that when darkness stopped work a party atmosphere would prevail with revelry going on long into the night? Might there not also be celebrations when the task was completed? We know that the scourings of the Uffington Horse were followed by a two day fair consisting of booths, tents, side-shows, wrestling and tournaments. Wise (1742) writes of Uffington that objections were made to the fair on account of the disorder and debauchery which accompanied it. It is doubtful then that the villagers of Dorset saw the occasion as all work and no play!

BB: Might the scourings and celebrations have been linked to particular and important times of the year?

HJ: There's a strong case for the Giant to be linked to May Day observations. May Day was the time when the fertility of the earth was reaffirmed and celebrated.

Traditionally throughout Britain and Northern Europe young men and women would go into the woods and fields in the hours before dawn and would cut and bring back a tree to be used as the maypole. They would also gather May blossoms and greenery to decorate the pole and the village. They would arrive back at the village singing and dancing and announcing the arrival of Spring. May Day itself was spent in sports, eating, drinking and dancing at the foot of the maypole and was traditionally a boisterous festival.

May Day drew particular condemnation from the Puritans and in 1644 they succeeded in getting Parliament to ban May Day festivities. Orders were issued that all maypoles should be destroyed by constables or other local officials, with a fine of five shillings a week until the maypole was removed.

For annual maypole activities at the Giant we have only Childs, a former sexton, as our authority. He states that every year a fir tree was cut and taken up to the Frying Pan (the local name for the Trendle earth-work) and erected in the ring during the night. Next day it was decorated by the villagers who danced around it on May Day (March 1901). Others say that this is unlikely because there was a tree plantation in the Frying Pan. But actually this plantation was an abortive attempt which only dates to the early nineteenth century, and certainly we know that the Cerne Churchwardens wrote in 1635 that they paid 'Anthony Thorne and others 3s 10d for taking down ye maypole and making a town ladder of it.'

May Day is also known as Beltaine – the pagan Lunar Fire Festival. Earlier inhabitants may have lit bonfires on the hill above the Giant to mark the occasion. We do know that on May Day a sight-line taken vertically up the middle of the phallus would have pointed directly at the rising sun as it came over the downs (Figure 51). The line would also pass through the Frying Pan. Some have taken this as evidence that the Trendle was in fact some kind of temple with particular significance to Beltaine.

BB: Do you think there were times when the Giant fell into disuse? Antiquarians might have talked about him but there were no more village activities that centred around him?

HJ: The Giant does seem to have lapsed into disuse at certain times. The Victorians had very strong views on what was right and proper: and the Giant's sexual explicitness was neither. In 1868 the Dorset County Chronicle states, 'this ancient colossal figure has for some years presented a shabby appearance on account of the trenches being choked with weeds and rubbish and the outlines being otherwise defaced'. Lord Rivers gave orders for 'his Mightiness' to be cleaned and restored. The elongation of the Giant's phallus to include the navel, which Gerald Pitman mentions, may have been, in part, a protest against such Victorian sexual prudery.

There have been several attempts to cover his vital parts – which means that people were affected by him, even if only negatively! In 1956 a local vicar petitioned for his phallus to be removed or covered over, and as recently as the 1970s there was a campaign to allow the grass to grow over his face and phallus.

It was suggested that the National Trust should re-shape his feet so that he would look as though he was standing with his back to the Sherborne road!

Despite all this – or maybe it's cause-and-effect – the most enduring tradition is that the Giant can induce fertility in anyone who sleeps on his body. In 1922 Udal related that couples wanting to conceive actually had to have sex on the phallus of the Giant in order to receive his full affect (Udal 1922). This tradition continues right up to the present day. Gerald Pitman tells that very recently whilst walking on the Giant he found on the very tip of the phallus a large flint anchoring the photo of a young woman.

BB: Are there any other ways in which the Giant is used today?

HJ: The Giant is never left alone for long! He seems to capture even our modern imaginations and has been the site for everything from pranks to demonstrations.

In 1968 he was subjected to a sex change by judicious use of green emulsion and white distemper. During this molestation he was given long hair and breasts. In 1980 the artist Evans-Loude wanted to erect a twentieth century sex symbol as company for the Giant. He planned a Marilyn Monroe chalk figure on the opposite hill (*Daily Mirror*, 10th March 1980). In the new age of safe sex awareness the Giant has been the butt of two condom pranks: on April 1st 1988 he was given a plastic sheeting condom, and again in 1995 he was given a brown painted condom. In the late 1980s Durex also chose the Giant as the venue for the maiden flight of their hot air balloon!

Then there have been different campaigns that have used the Giant. He has seen a rally in 1993 of people campaigning for fertility treatments to be made available on the NHS, and in June 1996 he appeared on Hampstead Heath – minus a penis and plus a heart – as part of the Heart Research Campaign. In 1994, when local councils were being reorganized, Dorset County Council took the Giant as the symbol of its campaign to preserve its Authority. In 1995 some of the Twyford Down Road Protesters known as the Dongas Tribe camped near the Giant on their Freedom Trail. It was part of a campaign to highlight the destructiveness of the Road Building Programme. From tourist to pilgrim it seems that the people around him will invent and reinvent meaning and relevance for the Giant's existence.

BB: Last question! We all know that the Giant is fragile and must be preserved. Do you think that it's still possible to use him – incorporate him in activities?

HJ: We all of us must understand that monuments such as the Giant are fragile and, like the rest of our heritage, it is best to view them as 'on loan' for our lifetime. However it is all too easy to become carried away with the preservation of monuments to the point where they become merely ornaments. These places were built by communities to be used. They have long histories of ceremonies, festivals, rituals and traditional pastimes taking place within their boundaries. Some of us today view with terror the destruction being wreaked on our environment. For many of us these old places take on new meaning as we try to

Figure 51. *The Giant and the Trendle. It has been suggested that on May Day (Beltaine) a sight-line taken vertically up the middle of the phallus points directly to the rising sun as it comes over the downs. The line also passes through the Trendle which may have been a temple. (Aerial photography by Francesca Radcliffe. Copyright reserved)*

rediscover a way of working with nature, instead of against it. What better place to do that than at sites such as these that were built to mark the shifting heavens, the changing seasons and crop growth cycles.

Generations before have done the same and with proper management it should be possible for our and future generations to go on using these same sites whilst keeping wear and tear to a minimum. To preserve a monument but to disallow any social use of it is to preserve the body without the soul. When future generations research the history of these monuments and how they were used and viewed in the late twentieth century period, it would be a shame if they found that we used them merely as tools in our tourist industry.

* * * * * * * *

BB: So many different ways in which the Giant has been acknowledged. He has been celebrated, prayed to, credited with procreative powers, walked on, dug up, bowdlerized, satirized, talked about by learned people, woven into stories, drawn on mugs and tea-towels ... We would have liked to have asked local people to come forward as witnesses – new-comers, people who have lived at Cerne Abbas for generations, people who make a living from him, children ... But there was not time enough. So my last group of witnesses are outsiders, people talking about their feelings towards the Giant.

Sue Clifford is a Founder Director of Common Ground, an organization that emphasizes the value of our everyday surroundings and the positive investment people can make in their own localities. Common Ground tries to forge links between the arts and the conservation of nature and our cultural landscapes, offering ideas, inspiration, and information through publications, exhibitions and projects (for example Parish Maps, Apple Day, Local Distinctiveness). She has edited, with Angela King, *Local Distinctiveness* (Common Ground 1993).

* * * * * * * *

Staying power

Sue Clifford

For me the Cerne Giant attracts and emanates a cluster of meanings, only some of which I can articulate, all of which lead me to question upon question.

Presence, persistence, paradox and poetry: He is a giant, he diminishes all of us. He is a giant, a figure of the imagination. He is a giant, all over the world his stories are told again and again.

While we did not give him life, it is only through us that he lingers, if he had no meaning to us he would not be there. Yet all he is, is an absence of turf – and he is dynamic, active, vital.

Presence: Many giants populate our land, but rare it is that we can see them. Here above Cerne significance clings to a figure carved into the land.

Possibly here lies the sheep stealing giant slain by the locals, his outline then traced as though the CID had visited the scene of the crime. Or maybe this is an ancient sacred figure from which have grown tales of giants walking these hills and vales. Is he symbol of fertility, or of regeneration? There is something of the Green Man about him: is his club indicative of the Holly Knight, waiting to do battle with the Oak King, the seasonal round, the story of cyclical displacement and recurrence, time endlessly rolling rather than flying fast forward as we would have it. Or is this a fearsome frown on the brow of the hill to frighten Civil War soldiers from stealing the fields, signifying the superiority of the Club Risers (labourers and others who banded together to protect their crops in this part of the world). Or is this Hercules, a refugee from the Mediterranean sun? Perhaps simply what we have here is 'Billboard Willie' a great poster announcing cudgel games at Revels Farm, over the hill.

The richness for me is in all these possibilities and more, I want to engage with this character. I respect him as a store full of memories, facts to be discovered, a cue for legends to be retold, myths to be fathomed, old and new rituals to be performed. I do not need to know a definitive beginning – I fear it may mark his end, cut and dried, mystery desiccated and blown away on the wind.

Persistence: Our relationship with nature and the land is not so much about how things look or how old they are, but how we know them, how the place makes us feel. A place means something to us partly through the accumulation of stories. I wonder what local people know and feel? What presence does he exert in the everyday? Do you need definitive answers and if so why? Or if like me you are fed by compound cues, proud to pass on multiple speculations.

The thrill the Giant offers is surely in his very enigma, and his challenge is to demand we keep faith with the locality in passing on the intertwining tales – fantastical and academical. For, if all we see is him, I sense he will be disappointed. He is a figure in this landscape. He is tied to this soil, and, he particularizes this place. He also carries a weight of symbolisms in the wider world.

I can add a new sense of him for the next century – my eyes go both to the fine grain and to the backdrop against which all our lives are played. I can muse upon fertility – of the soil into which he is cut.

And I am drawn to paradox: the very fragility, the potentially ephemeral nature of his power, and yet the defiant persistence. He needs us for his continuity, if we want a rich landscape, significant to us, if we want fertility to be sustained, to be able to work with nature's generous regenerative capacities, then perhaps we have to take more care of the stories and work better to sustain the place.

While the Giant may carry memory, he is not a thing of the past, he is continuing history, he exists now, he belongs to us here, if he ceases to mean anything to us (if we don't remake his significance for ourselves) he will not endure.

So one important role is that of making me look at the land – he is, after all riveted to it, he is scored into chalk, he makes me stare at a hillside.

Within the expanse of land that he inhabits, there are remnants of hard work of many ages, ancient and modern field systems jostling with tracks and paths and roads and boundaries all tumbling together, and the map reveals an extraordinary cruciform confluence of valleys, in and above which layer upon layer of habitation, subsistence and existence has been drawn. Our forbears knew the land: the Giant's domain. His view is over an intimacy of valleys (collective noun), wonderfully complicated habitats, habitation and history, which his presence enhances, but without him there is power in this place.

Why is he here? Is there something about this place that we are missing because our attention is so focused upon the Giant himself?

In gleaning for possible answers, it becomes of interest to have an idea of when he appeared and through whose works – but to me it is of even greater importance to know why he has persisted. He must, like the Cheshire cat, have faded and brightened, but the secret of his perpetuation is not in his own magic, it is in the hands of the people of this place. His story, however long, could be recorded as a document of social decision making, he only exists because people here have wanted him to be here, and have worked to keep him.

This is a remarkable fact, and one which has poignant resonances for the National Trust. His life in whose hands? My hope is that his future will be part of the cultural common of this place, the National Trust may be the Lord of the Manor, capable of acting *in loco parentis* in times of trouble. But to keep the Giant in good heart, and perhaps the people and this place as well, it is my contention that they and the Giant should maintain their intimacy, they should know why they want him here .. now, and should make decisions and act together accordingly. This is what the twenty-first century could be about, decisions and actions locally accomplished, responsibility shared, democracy democratized, nature and culture constantly reworked to maintain local distinctiveness. We, strangers the Giant has the capacity to draw from beyond, need the integrity and authenticity which that reality would sustain.

Paradox and poetry: More precise than longitude and latitude, the co-ordinates here, are met in the Cerne Giant, he particularizes this place. This figure, like many other aspects of our landscape, is far from being merely figurative. The Land is our most elaborate storyboard. That we cannot precisely read it or translate the contradictions, leaves room for us all to join in the telling: layers of meaning, tangles of ambiguity, overlays of possibility, a great weaving of significance. Adding to the depth of knowledge must never narrow our imagination – it is this which created the Giant in the first place.

If we are to apprehend anything from the compression of history, it surely must be that facts and the quest for facts, can only get us so far, and that out of wisdom, not just knowledge, we have to learn again to confront paradox with poetry: a delicate Herculean task.

* * * * * * * *

BB: Sue Clifford suggests that we have to confront paradox with poetry, and so my final witnesses are three poets, members of the Devon River Poets: James Turner, Sandra Tappenden, and Jan Farquharson. They have recently published in their group anthology *Precise Angles of Light* (Clarkson and Tappenden 1998). Jan's poem is also available on cassette.[2]

Further to the Cerne Giant Mystery

We stood at the lay-by viewing point and viewed.
The scene of a hillside crime. Must be murder,
Look! the body outlined in chalk still clutching
a weapon in self-defence. Or suicide,
a day like this no doubt, east wind: he lay
on the hill and died of indecent exposure... Ancient god?
Elizabethan graffito? I took this photo
of Nessie sitting on his nose – she's eight –
and, standing on his shapeless chin, her mother
making notes. The ground is frozen hard.
And it's hard to think of him as threatening
with a club more like a balloon than knobbly wood –
or even as particularly old.
Middle thirties, I'd say. *I'd Swear he's friendly.*
I took this close-up of his cartoon testicles,
and another of his thirty-foot erection.
I've heard that if a barren woman sits
on his dick, or a couple make love there, she'll conceive.
No wonder it's longer every time they measure it.
But of course he's just a drawing on the surface,
nothing behind him but a Dorset hill,
and when we tried to read between his lines
we found no more than blades of frosted grass.
"Bye-bye Giant," said Nessie as we drove off.
The Giant's reply was lost in engine-noise.

James Turner, March 1996

The Giant Thinks Aloud in a Cartoon Bubble

Often I forget why I'm excited –
what it is I'm always ready for.
A good day is urgent cloud –
and grass nudging through
my strong, silent gaps.
If I knew how, I'd say
'tired', 'woman', or 'please'.

My head is filled
with the flight of birds –
the particular pitch of north east wind –
but underneath that
there are sighs hot as July
where a dream couple couple
and roll the length of my sex.
They laugh in the dark and
think the earth moves.
And it does.

All night I ache to drop this club
and relieve the virgin tension of myself.
If I could I'd turn tender and O –
slide my hard part deep into the soil –
let daybreak catch me just for once off-guard –
spent and soporific on the hill.

Sandra Tappenden, March 1996

Boys Will Be Cerne Giants

for Barbara

He reminds me of that older boy called Gus
    On the school bus.
'What makes it stand up straight like a ship's mast?'
    I said at last.
'Thoughts,' the boy said grinning, meaning just
    Straight up lust.
The simple matter made his forehead shine.
    He looked fine.
But now you seldom see another's straight
    Up excited state
In public and you weep – you wish the thing
    Would show like Spring!
You wonder why the sacred budding wood,
    The hymned tree, should
Be private. Rude. You wish you were this giant,
    Stiff but pliant,
Whose leonine and loose-looped legs and arms
    Like tracks through farms,
And little riding head and grippen toy,
    Are waved for joy.
I'd like to wave my hard-up member wide
    On the countryside
If I could show who rules, okay, on the hill,
    And stamp my will.
But no, I think this god points to the combe
    With his arm, a womb
Which lies along behind him in an arc
    Where stoat and lark
Conger, and grass and bush await in warm
    Magnetic form
And he can have the earth – I think he can –
    He as a man
With woman. Crest to combe and cheek to spur,
    Himself and her...
Surely she is that one, that breast of hill,
    Who makes him swell?
They've got the perfect place – all night, all day.
    She's his. She'll stay.
She's waiting now ... But – ah – he has to wait,
    At the combe's gate.

Jan Farquharson, March 1996

Summing up

BB: When you stand at the place on the road where you are told to stand to get the best view of the Giant, there are two National Trust placards. One has a picture of the Giant with his phallus nearly rubbed to oblivion – rather like the big toe of Saint James at Compostella. With the Saint you know that it is the loving hands or lips of pilgrims through the ages that have worn out his big toe. With the Giant you cannot be sure: curiosity, empathy, emblem of fertility, or something rude to be erased? The Giant has been touched and retouched through time, and the Giant never speaks to people with a single voice.

Next to the picture is the description of the Giant. It says, very certainly, that the Giant is Romano British. But here, today, we've discovered that such certainty is quite unwarranted. People – or rather 'we', a particular sort of people – find it hard to live with uncertainty . We want 'the facts', we want 'the truth'. Perhaps what we have begun to recognize today is that 'fact' and fiction are close bedfellows. And that if we had the 'facts', we would still not know. If there was a radiocarbon date, we would still not know what precisely it dated. And even if we knew, we still would not know much about 'why' or 'how', 'by whom', 'for whom', or 'what did it mean?' The birth-date of a person, or a Giant, is thin history. It tells us nothing about their lives.

I would like to suggest that what we might try to explore, when we talk about the past and the Giant, is not so much the birth – though of course it would be nice to know where to start the story – but the biography. The biography of the Giant. A biography that is intimately bound up with the biography of the landscape and of the community. A lot of our histories are rather inaccessible: they are in documents and archives. But landscape, and our Giant in the landscape, is not like that. Landscapes and monuments are history made visible and material. Landscapes and monuments are places that are worked and re-worked. They are there and they touch everyone, though some may pass by almost – although never quite – unheedingly.

We need to recognize that we make history (Marx put it well: 'we make history, but not under conditions of our own making'). We make history, we make the past, but the past also makes us. We need the past. Oliver Sachs wrote a book called *The man who mistook his wife for a hat* (Sachs 1985). It is quite a sad book. It is about what it is like to live when that part of the brain that stores up memories fails. How meaningless, fragmented, and utterly frustrating life becomes. Memories are a form of history. We have to have memories and histories in order to make sense of who we are, what life is about, what the future holds.

The Giant is pegged out on the hill, fenced in. We have tried for too long, through our particular writings of history, our particular ways of conserving and preserving the past, to restrain him. Sometimes we think that we have succeeded, we have got him, we 'know' about him. But like Gulliver when the Lilliputians pegged him down, he stirs and breaks the bonds. He refuses to be pegged down. He is a subversive old Giant, and, in conclusion, I would like to suggest that you, the reader, could also be subversive. You have been asked to decide whether the Giant is prehistoric, or whether he is post-medieval, or whether he is a living Giant – the Present Past. Be subversive: give two answers. With your first, decide when you think that he was born. And, with your second, give him a life, a biography. Admit that his continuing existence, his dependence on us and ours on him, is just as, if not more important, as knowing his birth-date.

Notes

1. In this section we have chosen to retain the form of the Cerne Abbas Enquiry. For readers who were not there, there was a judge and two assessors, and an audience who were also allowed to take a vote at the beginning and end of the day.
2. *DIGS – Archaeology into poetry* (Green Box Publications, Hooken, Branscombe, Seaton EX12 3DP).

Acknowledgements

I would like to thank Gerald Pitman for all his help and encouragement.

Bibliography

Allen, B, pers. comm. Bob developed this tale for a guided walk between Michelham Priory and its daughter church at Alfriston, near Wilmington.

Anon., 1764, Description of a gigantic Figure. *Gentleman's Magazine*, 34, 335–6

Bettey, J, 1981, The Cerne Abbas Giant: the documentary evidence. *Antiquity*, 55, 118–121

Blair, J, 1988, Minsters in the landscape. In D Hooke (ed), *Anglo-Saxon settlements*. Oxford. Blackwell. 35–58

Bordes, J, and Bordes, C, 1978, *The secret country*. London. Elek

Burne, C S, 1915, Scraps of folklore collected by John Philipps Emslie. *Folk-Lore*, 26, 153–70

Castleden, R, 1983, *The Wilmington Giant*. Wellingborough. Turnstone Press

Clarkson, J, and Tappenden, S (eds), 1998, *Pr*i*cise angles of light*. Exeter. White Box Publications

Curwen, E C, 1954, *The archaeology of Sussex*. London. Methuen

Farrant, J, 1993, The Long Man of Wilmington, East Sussex: the documentary evidence reviewed. *Sussex Archaeological Collections*, 131, 129–38

Grinsell, L V, 1980, The Cerne Abbas Giant: 1764–1980. *Antiquity*, 54, 29–33

Harte, J, 1986, *Cuckoo pounds and singing barrows: folklore of ancient sites in dorset*. Dorchester. Dorset Natural History and Archaeological Society

Hawkes, S C, Ellis Davidson, H R, and Hawkes, C, 1965, The Finglesham Man. *Antiquity*, 39, 17–32

Heron Allen, E, 1939, The Long Man of Wilmington and its Roman origin. *Sussex County Magazine*, 13, 655–60

Holden, E W. 1971, The Long Man of Wilmington. *Sussex Archaeological Collections*, 109, 37–54

Morris, R, 1989, *Churches in the landscape*. London. Dent

Legg, R, 1972, Cerne's strange figure on the hillside. *Dorset County Magazine*, 25, 28–29

Legg, R, 1989, *Cerne's Giant and village guide*. Milborne Port. Dorset Publishing Company

Lethbridge, T C, 1957, *Gogmagog*. London. Routledge and Kegan Paul

March, C H, 1901, The Giant and the maypole of Cerne, *Proceedings of the Dorset Natural History and Archaeological Society*, 22, 101–118

Marples, M, 1949, *White horses and other hill-figures*. London. Country Life Books. [Reprinted 1981. Gloucester. Alan Sutton]

Parish W D, 1873, *Wilmington – The Giant*. Unpublished MS in the library of the Sussex Archaeological Society

Rappaport, J, 1988, History and everyday life in the Columbian Andes. *Man* (New Series), 23, 718–39

Sachs, O, 1985, *The man who mistook his wife for a hat*. London. Duckworth

Sherley-Price, L (ed), 1995, *Bede's history of the English church and people*. Harmondsworth. Penguin

Sidgwick, J B, 1939, The mystery of the Long Man. *Sussex County Magazine*, 13, 408–420

Udal, J S, 1922, *Dorset folklore*. St Peter Port. Toucan Press

Whipp, C, *The Cerne Giant: the identity of the ancient rambler revealed*. Unpublished essay sent to the University of Bournemouth following the enquiry

Whitelock, D, Brett, M, and Brooke, C N L, 1981, *Councils and synods with other documents relating to the English church I, AD 871–1209*. Oxford. Oxford University Press

Williamson, T, and Bellamy, L, 1983, *Ley lines in question*. Kingswood. World's Work

Williamson, T, and Loveday, R, 1988, Rabbits or ritual? artificial warrens and the Neolithic long mound tradition. *Archaeological Journal*, 145, 290–313

Wise, F, 1742, *Further observations upon the White Horse and other antiquities in Berkshire*. Oxford. [Printed pamphlet]

PART V

Epilogue

The Giant on trial and the assessors' report

Katherine Barker and Timothy Darvill

The jury returns a view

Throughout the enquiry the audience were closely involved in the way arguments unfolded. After each case there was an opportunity for questions directed at the advocates or their witnesses. These discussions were lively and well-informed.

At the start of the day's proceedings the audience was invited to vote for one of the three cases as a measure of their pre-trial disposition towards the Giant. In all, 86 votes were cast, 61 for the Giant being prehistoric or Roman; 19 for him being seventeenth century or later; and 6 in favour of a date-neutral view. The breakdown was thus: 70% for Case 1, 22% for Case 2, and 8% for Case 3.

At the end of the day a second vote was held. This revealed an interesting shift of opinion. A similar number of votes were cast (83), of which 42 (50%) favoured Case 1; 29 (35%) Case 2; and 12 (15%) Case 3. This was an interesting result as it shows the power of debate and discussion in forming opinion.

The final vote was not, however, the end of the debate. Written submissions were subsequently received from a number of people who attended the trial, a number of further publications and projects have been undertaken, and a television programme was broadcast. In the following sections we draw attention to a selection of this follow-up.

Written submissions

More than half-a-dozen papers and notes were sent to the authors of this chapter in the weeks following the enquiry, some simply providing extra questions and views, other elaborating perspectives and providing further suggestions about points raised. It is not possible to reproduce everything, but some of the submissions are briefly summarized below.

Gordon le Pard of Dorset drew attention to a letter he had found from Heywood Sumner to the Surrey archaeologist Dr Eric Gardner. It was dated 30th July 1924. In it Sumner asks Gardner to accompany him on an 'expedition' to view the Giant in order to ascertain its condition. The reason for doing this seems to be some pressure from the editor of *Country Life* asking Sumner to comment on proposals for the care of the monument. It is possible that Sumner's visit lay behind the article on the Giant that appeared in the October 1924 issue of *Country Life* (Anon. 1924) in which the condition of the monument was held to be deplorable.

John Macpherson (based upon and with extracts from a document entitled 'The fifth province – the rise and fall of the Kingdom of Valentia' by Sion Gwyllt) suggests that while the second element of the place-name Cerne Abbas clearly derives from the presence of the abbey, the first part is less certain and deserves more research. The Giant is perhaps a territorial symbol, and perhaps faces west towards some ancestral homeland. The large club could be associated with the Celtic *dagda*, a member of the *Tuatha de Danaan*. Originally the club may have been a sword to judge by its carefully shaped handle and the rounded tip; the projections would be later additions in this argument. The head is interesting as there is much detail, but no indication of any hair; could there be some link with the *Moen* of Welsh folklore who is bald. Could there be some indication of deformity in the way the shoulders are depicted; could the person also have a hunch-back and hollow chest. There are possible connections with Irish traditions here, perhaps Conall Cernach a hero mentioned in the *Tain Bo Cualigne* and who guarded the southern border of Ulster. And what about the ribs? It would be rather odd to depict the ribs without some special reason. Could they actually be the representation of some kind of corset. Burials dating to the first millennium AD have been found to be wearing something similar at Llandough, Glamorgan.

Christine Whipp questioned whether the identification of the Giant's ribs, nipples and navel is correct, and whether they have been seen as anatomical when they should be considered as something else. Clothes are possible, but these elements might also be the face of a cat (eyes, nose and whiskers). Could the Giant's true identity be Richard Whittington (1194-1996)?

Recent projects and publications

The enquiry generated a lot of interest in the Giant, and numerous articles appeared in a wide range of newspapers, magazines and journals (e.g. Godfrey 1996; Legg 1996; Symington 1996a; 1996b). Andrew Selkirk reported the day in *Current Archaeology* (Selkirk 1996). All go to show that academic debate can potentially command considerable interest, although much recent work continues to escape the notice of some writers (e.g. Goodman 1998).

There has also been a change of treatment by the media, rather neatly reflected by a series of pieces in *The Independent*. The year before the trial we have Richard Maby in *The Independent on Sunday* (26th February 1995) announcing that 'The Cerne Abbas Giant ... for instance, was cut by the whole community in Celtic times and regularly "scoured" amidst great junketting ...' This may be compared with a recent piece in the *Independent Weekend Review* (25th July 1998) by Sophie Poklewski Koziell. Her caption for the aerial photograph that accompanies the recommended weekend walk around Cerne Abbas reads 'no one knows the age of Dorset's giant chalk man'. Her introductory paragraph then puts the reader into the picture: 'despite his Neolithic appearance there is some doubt as to how old he really is: some think he is Roman (AD 200-ish) some think he may be only about 200 years old ...'.

Figure 52. Aerial view of the Cerne Giant and accompanying Giantess, July 1997. (Photograph by Francesca Radcliffe. Copyright reserved)

Research has continued since the enquiry. Some of it has been introduced into the cases presented above as witnesses have re-written their contributions and prepared them for publication here. In addition, a new book on the Giant in press at the time of the enquiry has been published (Castleden 1996), and a new edition of Paul Newman's *Gods and graven images* has appeared with a new title and publisher (Newman 1997). Shorter contributions and reviews have appeared too (Castleden 1998; Copson 1998; Harte 1996; Legg 1998; Newman 1999).

Hill-figures are also now in cyber-space, with the establishment by Mark Hows of an internet site devoted to 'hill-figure' news. The address is: <http://www.homeusers.prestel.co.uk/hows/personal/hillfigs/>

The problem of how the Giant was set out was raised at the enquiry, but never satisfactorily resolved. There are many different ways of doing it, and to a certain extent the selection of an appropriate method will depend on when exactly it was done. As an experiment, however, staff and students from the Heritage Conservation course at Bournemouth University produced a temporary companion for the Giant using white polyethylene sheeting and meat skewers in July 1997. For this exercise the outline of a Giantess was set out on the grassy slope next to the Giant by using a drawing overlaid by a grid to plot the outline within a larger grid that was laid out on the ground (Figure 52; Barker 1997).

Beyond the village hall
During the day of the enquiry, and for several days before and after, a production team from BBC West filmed material to use in preparing a television programme based on the enquiry. This had the effect of taking the debate out to a much wider audience than could fit into the Cerne Abbas village hall. The programme was screened on BBC2 on 2nd May 1996, and in the following chapter Hamish Beeston explains how it was made.

Bibliography
Anon., 1924, The Giant of Cerne Abbas. *Country Life*, October 18th 1924
Barker, K, 1997, Brief encounter: the Cerne Abbas Giantess Project, Summer 1997. *Proceedings of the Dorset Natural History and Archaeological Society*, 119, 179-182
Castleden, R, 1996, *The Cerne Giant*. Wincanton. Dorset Publishing Company
Castleden, R, 1998, The Cerne Giant. *Current Archaeology*, 13.12 (number 156), 468-9
Copson, C, 1998, Giant conundrum. *Dorset Country Magazine*, 2 (June 1998), 13-15
Godfrey, A, 1996, Scientists vote on the member for Cerne. *The Wessex Journal*, 8, 7-11
Goodman, K, 1998, *Chalk figures of Wessex*. Salisbury. Wessex Books
Harte, J, 1996, The Cerne Giant: a long standing mystery. *3rd Stone*, 24, 5-9
Leake, J, 1996, Is the chalk Giant a great big joke? *The Sunday Times*, 3:3:1996, Section 1, 10
Legg, R, 1996, The Giant search. *Dorset*, 11 (July 1996), 12-19
Legg, R, 1998, Here be Giants. *Dorset Country Magazine*, 2 (June 1998), 8-11
Newman, P, 1997, *Lost Gods of Albion. The chalk hill-figures of Britain*. Stroud. Alan Sutton
Newman, P, 1999, Inexhaustible symbols cut into chalk. *British Archaeology*, 41, 6-7
Selkirk, A, 1996, The Cerne Abbas Giant. *Current Archaeology*, 13.4 (number 148), 143
Symington, M, 1996a, Legend of the Giant: fact or fallacy? *Country Living*, June 1996, 44-6
Symington, M, 1996b, When was the Giant conceived? *The Daily Telegraph*, 30:3:1996, Travel, 37

Making 'The Trial of the Cerne Abbas Giant'

Hamish Beeston

Getting an idea

The idea came from a Sunday newspaper, spotted by the Series Producer of Close-Up West, James Macalpine. He saw the potential interest of the debate and possible local opposition which could widen the story from an academic argument to a true documentary about how it affects people's lives. The clincher though, by far, was the nature of the Giant; big willies are bound to attract viewers!

First thing to do was make a couple of calls to establish what the story really was. One often finds that stories in newspapers (and other media) bare little relation to reality. The facts are distorted for the sake of a better angle. In this case, Ronald Hutton and Katherine Barker largely corroborated the article but stressed that the local people were hardly up in arms, as the newspaper has suggested. Still, the academics would say that, so I was quite confident that, even if there was no local outrage, there was likely to be a local sense that perhaps all this was a lot of fuss about nothing.

Filling in the background

With the story standing up (as it were), my boss formally commissioned the programme and the project was underway. Close-Up West is fundamentally a news and current affairs stand but each series of thirty tends to include several stories which lie outside the strict hard news agenda in order to provide some relief from the doom and gloom of closing down hospitals and planning rows. It is also not lost on the Series Producer (and I hope the BBC news barons) that the less newsy programmes also get the best audiences.

As a regional series, Close-Up West is broadcast to an area roughly comprising the counties of Gloucestershire, Somerset, Wiltshire and parts of North Dorset, depending on which way your aerial points. A recently erected booster aerial in Cerne Abbas meant fortuitously that the village would be able to get the programme whereas officially it is so far south that it falls into BBC Southampton or BBC Plymouth areas. Another consideration arising from being a regional series is that we have to try to reflect other similar stories in the patch. In this case my boss rather vaguely asked me to include something about the many white horse hill-figures which are so prominent in Wiltshire. I was initially unsure as to how they would fit into the Giant story but the order was there so white horses were in.

A search on the internet revealed the large number and relative youth (seventeenth century onwards) of the Wiltshire hill-figures. It also mentioned a plan to cut a new horse for the Millennium. No details were given of this story but I managed to track down the people involved with a few phone calls to the local museums and councils. Eventually the village in question was identified as Woodborough in the Pewsey Vale.

Getting the central story

The central story was to be that of the trial of the Cerne Abbas Giant. I know the official title for the day was a 'Commission of Enquiry' but this is television and the idea of a 'Trial' is frankly a lot sexier!

First thing was a *recce* (planning visit) to Cerne Abbas to see the Giant and to meet Katherine Barker and Vyvyan and Patricia Vale. The Vales retired to the village and now run the local history society. They helped to organize the trial and I thought their local but academic point of view could be another interesting element in the story to counter other less interested locals and the visiting academics. I also met Dave Fox, a local builder whose family have lived in the village for several centuries.

Two *recces* to Wiltshire were next to meet the villagers who were planning the millennial figure (their preferred design turned out to be sheep not a horse) and to visit all the surviving white horses, including the proven prehistoric Uffington White Horse in Oxfordshire. This lies just outside our region but is close enough, and relevant enough for the boundaries to be bent slightly. As with all *recces*, the aim was to find people with interesting stories who were likely to tell them well on camera and also find good locations to film in.

As the trial approached the treatment was still worryingly vague. The trial bit was straight forward enough but I had no idea how the white horse sub-plot was going to fit in or whether there would be any of the much hyped local opposition. For the sake of good television one rather incharitably hopes for argument and confrontation but the chance of the locals of Cerne Abbas picketing the Village Hall in protest of the assault on their beloved prehistoric Giant seemed rather remote. Even so, one of the leading players, Ronald Hutton, told me he was not quite sure how his seventeenth century case was going to be received.

Filming

The first day's filming was on the day before the trial. Rain scuppered my original plans to film outdoor sequences with some of the locals, so I had to think fast, particularly as I had a film crew costing well over £500 a day sitting around drinking tea. The new plan was to assemble Dave Fox and a few of his older mates who had lived in the village all or most of their lives, tempt them down to the pub with the offer of a few free pints and get them chatting about the Giant and the possible revelation of the trial that he is only a few hundred years old and not the couple of thousand they had always been led to believe. I managed to find four such characters and the beer began to flow.

The interview was long at 40 minutes but even when I knew no more than two or three minutes would make it into the final film, it was worth doing a lot more at this stage for two reasons. First, in all interviews you tend to cover the same ground several times as you listen for an answer you know can be used. Often people talk over each other or switch track mid sentence into something totally unrelated to the film. Second, in the particular case, as the trial had not taken place, I did not really know what topics would be raised and so I had to ask the group questions about practically everything that might come up to cover myself for all eventualities.

It also rained in the afternoon. This time I decided to interview the Vales about the local history society and their particular perspective on the Giant as relative newcomers to the village. I was not sure that, once the film came together in the edit suite, I would have enough time in only half an hour to get to this topic but their stories had been so interesting when I met them on the recce (and the crew needed something to film) that I did the interview, with wonderful results.

The day of the trial

The day of the trial came, and we turned up at Cerne Abbas village hall an hour or so before it began to set up (Figure 53). I had the rare luxury of two camera men for the day as I did not want to miss anything. Normally I would only take one camera to cover an event. The key section of a speech is filmed in close-up and then the camera man moves to pick up all the other shots – wides from the back of the hall, cutaways of the audience listening, exteriors etc. But in this case, I really had no idea when the best bits of the day would come or from whom. I therefore had one camera stay on whoever was the main speaker at the rostrum and film continuously throughout the day while the second camera moved about to get the other shots.

These extra pictures are very important, Firstly, they allow material from one speaker to be cut down to the bare essentials (crucial since I had to condense the six hour day down to at most twenty minutes of the final film) by cutting away to another picture to cover the joins in the speech. Secondly, other shots make the programme more interesting by giving an idea of the event and what else is going on in the hall, particularly people's reactions. Occasionally we were really lucky and the second camera was on the main speaker during a good bit, but from a different angle, say from up on the stage, which gave me the option to vary the shot for aesthetic effect, rather than out of necessity to cover an edit join.

Having one camera going all day and the other for most of it, meant that I was left with an awful lot of material. We shot 14 tapes on the day itself and a total of 30 for the whole programme. As each tape gives you about 35 minutes of filming, this meant that on average I would use less than a minute of material from each tape in the final programme! This sounds like an awful waste (and now I come to actually read it back to myself it sounds like a massive waste of time and money...) but such a shooting ratio is not that unusual. When filming one

Figure 53. *Filming the Enquiry. (Photograph by Katherine Barker. Copyright reserved)*

uses a lot of tape to get extra shots which could possibly fit into the programme and interviews always take longer than you expect. Some films, particularly short pieces for magazine programmes, are shot a lot more tightly, with a pre-filming script of carefully planned shots and points to come out but on longer projects like this one such an approach would be difficult, as until the trial actually took place I did not really know how the story would unfold or which of the main players would perform best. As a result I chose to film long, particularly at the trial itself, and then hack it mercilessly in the edit suite!

At the end of the trial I was aware that it had been a great day but having spent most of it rushing about the hall trying to sort out technical problems and direct the camera men to get in close for a particularly good bit, whilst always trying to stay out of shot, I had rather lost track of the various academic arguments. What was obvious though was that the case for the seventeenth century had gained a lot of credibility through the arguments and showmanship of Ronald Hutton. In the final vote, Tim Darvill's prehistoric case still won the day, but the large reduction of his majority since the morning's vote seemed crucial to me. This would be the central thrust of the film.

The trial in context

The trial over, I spent three of the other four days filming the white horse stories. By now it was obvious that the Uffington White Horse story would fit well into the framework of the trial as evidence of a prehistoric precedent for chalk hill-figures and the later Wiltshire horses showed that hill-figures were once again fashionable after the seventeenth century, thus adding weight to Ronald Hutton's case. I was still unsure where the Millennium White Sheep would go but it was such a great story that it had to go somewhere! It might have seemed difficult at first to incorporate the white horses story imposed by my boss, but it certainly had the odd perk, such as an hour spent whizzing over the Wiltshire landscape filming from a helicopter!

Back in Cerne Abbas on Easter Sunday I filmed Dave Fox up on the Giant talking about his memories of the figure over the years and his wonder at the need for a trial when, in his eyes, the age did not really matter; he was their beloved Giant whatever his age. I also wanted to capture some first impressions of the figure by interviewing tourists who had stopped on the road to view the Giant. Both these bits would illustrate Barbara Bender's case for the present-past by taking the story away from the academic debate on the date of construction. I also hoped the tourist *vox pops* would produce a few light giggly moments as people saw the Giant in all his glory for the first time!

Sorting the film

With most of the filming done, it was now time to try to get it all in some sort of order. Different producers do this in different ways. Some get an assistant to watch through the tapes, list the shots and transcribe the interviews and then work from paper. Others watch it all themselves and note the good bits. My preferred method is slightly different (and perhaps reflects my inexperience – this is only the seventh film I have made) in that I watch and transcribe all the tapes myself. It takes days to do but it gives me a complete catalogue of all my material and, more importantly, it allows me to judge which bits are actually going to work on television. A transcript done by someone else is a useful tool but only by looking at everything yourself can you actually pick out the good bits, the gems, that bring the programme to life.

At this stage, when faced with so much material, the way to start slimming it all down is to discard everything except the best bits which will form the basis of the first assembly. From the original 15 or 16 hours of material, there were about an hour's worth of gems; this probably says more about my directing ability than anything else. I noted where to find these gems on the tapes, tried to arrange them into a rough running order on paper which tells the story and began to edit. I always try to cover all the relevant topics with gems but if there are gaps in the narrative, less perfect clips can be found later or the point can be made in the script.

Editing

The edit is where the film come to life. It is two weeks crammed into a little dark room arguing with the editor and the occasional researcher who comes in to point out that the sequence you have agonized over for the last hour is boring, irrelevant, or more usually both.

When I had assembled the first one hour rough cut, I had just about worked out what all the various arguments were and which line the film would take. With apologies to all the players of the day, it was obvious that the hero of the film was going to be Ronald Hutton. He is made for television – the eccentric academic with long hair and antique clothes, thundering against the establishment view and smart blue suit of Tim Darvill. His flamboyant speech and sound bite delivery also gave him a disproportionate number of gems. I was a little concerned about putting too much of Hutton into the film but felt that as his was the new, less well-known argument, it could warrant a few extra minutes-and he was just so entertaining!

Given the need for simplicity, the main advocates could have easily carried the story on their own but I was keen to include some of the witnesses in the film. Again, who got in depended on who had the best gems and who presented a simple point in a clear manner. The fun and challenge of editing a film like this one is to balance out the information and entertainment. The academic arguments are fairly complicated and so the main points must emerge in a logical way in order for the viewer to follow the story. But a straight academic treatise could be boring for the lay viewer and so it is crucial to throw in a few funny bits to keep the audience entertained. In a programme about a naked hill-figure with a 30-foot long phallus, there was no shortage of gags to sprinkle throughout the programme. The challenge then became to keep the balance right and I had several 'taste and decency' viewings with my boss with heated discussions about the 'willy count'!

Once the three main cases, prehistoric, post-medieval, and present-past had been roughly assembled it became apparent that the story was too cluttered and complicated; there was so much good material that I was trying to tell too many stories. What I needed was a clear line to follow throughout the film and to hang the rest of the material off. My boss came up with this on his second viewing. He suggested that I should concentrate on the idea of the trial, to construct the film as a courtroom drama with clear prosecution and defence counsels, witnesses, a judge and jury, and to use the other stories (white horses, locals, tourists etc) as evidence for the main cases.

It was a good idea which he had mentioned when he commissioned the film but it had rather got lost in my mind in the subsequent weeks, buried under hours and hours of tape and esoteric historical debate.

Once the trial was foremost once more, however, it became easy to shake out the slack from the story. Unfortunately, this meant losing a lot of very good stuff and whole characters and sub-plots which did not fit into the rigid canon of the trial had to go. One of these was the Vales whom I had filmed early. Patricia Vale had assured me at the time that I would chop them out of the film. 'No, no, no!' I said, optimistically but they did end up on the proverbial cutting room floor and when I had to make the fateful call I felt very embarrassed.

Perhaps the most drastic loss was the whole of Barbara Bender's case for the present-past which was fascinating but had been looking rather out of place in the rough assemblies. I was sad to lose it all, particularly the hilarious poets, but felt that the wider issues around the Giant would be well served by the sequence filmed outside the trial.

Notable amongst these were the Millennium White Sheep (to show how some people today value chalk hill-figures so much that want to cut a new one) and the Helith Society. The latter is a group of around 70 people who each year dress up in evening wear and have a big party in the lay-by in front of the Giant. I had heard about this event at the trial but no one seemed to know who they were or where they came from. I was desperate to find and film them as, for all the talk in the village hall about how much the Giant meant to people throughout history, the Helith Society are the only people who still practice any kind of 'ceremony' on the Giant today, even if that ceremony involves getting tanked up on champagne and staggering up the hill to sit on his famous member!

Finding the Heliths

The hunt for the Heliths became a saga in itself, with myself and two researchers making phone call after phone call and chasing the story all around the country. Eventually, they were found to be based just up the road in Sherbourne, and were started by the man who makes the Giant shortbread which had been on sale at the trial, right under our noses! Some last minute filming got the Heliths in all their glory and their place in the film salved my conscience about ditching Barbara Bender.

Towards the end of the second week of the edit, the film was almost there and all that was left was the polishing. This is a very satisfying part of the process as for days you have been cutting and moving blocks of dialogue trying to make some sort of sense of the story and now, with the narrative pretty much there you can start putting in some pretty pictures to illustrate the points, cover edits, and create space for scripts. Script is vital in a film like this with a complicated story – a well crafted line can get you out of all sorts of filmic *non sequiturs*. It is also useful to cut down on time as whole sequences delivered by one of the film's characters can usually be summarized by a couple of pictures and a line of script.

The final cut

A final viewing from the boss gave us his approval, leaving only the introduction to shoot with the series presenter, Susan Osman, the day before the broadcast and the dub and VT sessions when all the other bits are added such as script, music, captions and credits. The programme is finished an hour or so before transmission and gives you one of the most nerve-wracking moments of the whole process, the technical review. The film must be exactly the right length, to the second, and however many times you have done your sums about how long the intro, film and credits are, it is always a relief to see the programme come in to time.

The film complete, the final task is to get a beer, switch the telly on, and watch the latest Close-Up West: something about giant willies tonight, I think...